Bands

January 1992

Popular Music in Britain

Series Editors:	*Dave Harker and Richard Middleton*
Peter Bailey (ed.):	*Music Hall: The Business of Pleasure*
J S Bratton (ed.):	*Music Hall: Performance and Style*
Dave Harker:	*Fakesong: The Manufacture of British 'Folksong' 1700 to the present day*
Dave Laing:	*One Chord Wonders: Power and Meaning in Punk Rock*
Paul Oliver (ed.):	*Black Music in Britain*
Michael Pickering and Tony Green (eds):	*Everyday Culture: Popular Song and the Vernacular Milieu*
Derek Scott:	*The Singing Bourgeois: Songs of the Victorian Drawing Room and Parlour*

Bands

The Brass Band Movement in the 19th and 20th Centuries

Edited by Trevor Herbert

Open University Press
Milton Keynes · Philadelphia

Open University Press
Celtic Court
22 Ballmoor
Buckingham
MK18 1XW

and
1900 Frost Road, Suite 101
Bristol, PA 19007, USA

First Published 1991

British Library Cataloguing in Publication Data

Bands: the brass band movement in the 19th and 20th
    centuries. – (Popular music in Britain).
    1. Great Britain. Music. Brass bands, history
    I. Herbert, Trevor   II. Series
    784.90941
    ISBN 0-335-09703-0
    ISBN 0-335-09702-2 pbk

Library of Congress Cataloging-in-Publication Data

Bands: the brass band movement in the 19th and 20th centuries /
    edited by Trevor Herbert.
        p.   cm. – (Popular music in Britain)
      Includes index.
    ISBN 0-335-09702-2 (Pb) : £10.99 (est.). – ISBN 0-335-09703-0
    (Hb) : £32.50 (est.)
      1. Brass bands – Great Britain.   I. Herbert, Trevor.   II. Series.
    ML1331.B26 1991
    784.9'0941'09034 – dc20   90-14152   CIP   MN

Typeset by Rowland Phototypesetting Ltd
Bury St Edmunds, Suffolk
Printed in Great Britain by St Edmundsbury Press Ltd
Bury St Edmunds, Suffolk

Contents

List of Illustrations

Editorial Preface

What *is* British popular music? Does such a thing exist? What makes certain music and songs popular? And who made the musical cultures of these islands? What did Scots, Welsh, Irish and North American people have to do with the process? What part did people in the English regions play – the Geordies, Cockneys, Midlanders and all the rest? Where did the Empire fit in? How did European 'high' culture affect what most people played and sang? And how did all these factors vary in significance over time? In the end, just how much do we know about the history of musical culture on these tiny patches of land? The truth is that we know very little, and this realization led to this series.

The history of British people and culture has been dominated by capitalism for centuries; and capitalism helped polarize people into classes not only economically, but culturally too. Music was never *simply* music: songs were never *simply* songs. Both were produced and used by particular people in particular historical periods for particular reasons, and we have recognized this in the way in which we have put this series together.

Every book in this series aims to exemplify and to foster inter-disciplinary research. Each volume studies not only 'texts' and performances, but institutions and technology as well, and the culture practices and sets of social relationships through which music and songs were produced, disseminated and consumed. Ideas, values, attitudes and what is generally referred to as ideology are taken into account, as are factors such as gender, age, geography and traditions. Nor is our series above the struggle. We do not pretend to have helped produce an objective record. We are, unrepentantly, on the side of the majority, and our main perspective is from 'below', even though the whole musical field needs to be in view. We hope that by clarifying the history of popular musical culture we can help clear the ground for a genuinely democratic musical culture of the future.

Dave Harker and Richard Middleton

Acknowledgements

Permission to use and reproduce material owned by libraries and private collectors is acknowledged in endnotes or in captions throughout this book. Contributors have, in some cases, made personal acknowledgement to individuals and institutions at the end of their chapters.

I feel that it is important for me, on behalf of all the contributors, to thank the many people in today's brass band movement who have generously given advice, support and access to material while this book was being prepared. I also wish to express gratitude to the series editors and the Open University Press for their co-operation. Julia Williams, secretary to the Arts Faculty of the Open University in Wales, co-ordinated and administered a number of matters concerning this book, often when I was not available to advise her, and did so with deft efficiency. The index was prepared by Annette Musker, T. J. Herbert gave invaluable assistance with the final proof reading.

My final and major debt of gratitude is to the contributors who co-operated with me in many ways and always showed willingness to accommodate my views. I have had the good fortune to have gathered a distinguished band of collaborators. If shortcomings still exist, I willingly accept total responsibility for them.

Trevor Herbert
The Open University in Wales

Notes on Contributors

Trevor Herbert is arts staff tutor and senior lecturer in music at the Open University in Wales. Before entering academic life he played trombone with several major British orchestras and chamber groups. Apart from publishing numerous musicological articles, he has co-edited six books on Welsh history.

Dave Russell is a senior lecturer in the School of Historical and Critical Studies at Lancashire Polytechnic. He is the author of *Popular Music in England, 1840–1914. A Social History* (Manchester, 1987), and a number of articles on Victorian and Edwardian popular culture.

Clifford Bevan is the author of the *The Tuba Family*, published in 1978. Since then he has contributed to the New Grove Dictionaries of *Music, Jazz* and *Musical Instruments*, including the article on 'Bands' in the latter.

Arnold Myers has been Honorary Curator of the Edinburgh University Collection of Historic Musical Instruments since 1980, and carried out much of the research and planning of the touring exhibition 'Brass Roots: 150 Years of Brass Bands' in 1989. He has played in brass bands in Bristol, Yorkshire and Scotland, and currently organizes the Early Victorian Brass Band, using period instruments.

Duncan Bythell teaches history at Durham University and conducts the Muker Silver Band in North Yorkshire. His previous publications include *The Handloom Weavers* (Cambridge, 1969) and *The Sweated Trades* (London, 1978). He is now working on comparative aspects of British and Australian history, and held Visiting Fellowships at the Australian National University in 1983 and 1987.

Vic Gammon studied history at the University of Sussex, where he completed a doctoral thesis on popular music in nineteenth-century rural society. He xii *Notes on Contributors*

performs traditional music, and composes mainly electronic music, particularly for drama. Having previously worked in higher education, he now teaches music in a comprehensive school at Hassocks in West Sussex.

Sheila Gammon has a long-standing interest in music and social history. Her previous work has included teaching and looking after an ancient monument.

Introduction

In December 1989, *The British Bandsman*, the longest established and principal organ of the brass band movement, devoted its entire front page to an editorial headed 'The Nineties – a crucial decade for bands'. It hinted at crisis and warned that demographic changes could lead to bands having 'more chairs than players'. The increased influence of sponsorship in 'band life', it lamented, 'has made the pound more important than the pleasure': 'Have we solved, or even addressed, problems which have restricted our effectiveness and caused us to remain somewhat isolated from the mainstream of British music making?'[1] It was a clear and salutary message to a movement which has often oscillated between self-criticism and sycophancy. The message also focused on and illustrated a recurrent problem that brass bands have in defining and articulating their cultural status and identity.

Brass bands occupy what one writer has recently described as 'a self-conscious "world" with its own specific and separate traditions'.[2] Because that 'world' is self-contained, with its own conventions, it is largely misunderstood by those outside it. Consequently, brass bands have become the victim of a caricature which usually stresses northern, masculine, working-class and hedonistic images. As with all caricature, the images have a thin strand of truth, but their distortion renders its subject a nonsense. Though brass bands have always been very strong in the North of England, they are not uniquely northern, nor have they ever been. Though they have been (in Britain, at least) a masculine domain, that is no longer the case. Though they are primarily a working-class movement, the membership of bands in the late twentieth century hardly supports the cloth-cap image. Even in the nineteenth century, when the membership of bands was overwhelmingly working class, the influence and involvement of the middle classes was always evident. The idea that hedonism is the motivating force in the brass band movement is also grotesquely wrong. Most brass bands, even the least accomplished ones, are intent on improvement. The best contesting bands chase technical excellence with unremitting diligence. There is also a seriousness of resolve that is seen in the organization of bands, a fastidious-ness and exactness that goes beyond musical matters, even to the discipline of deportment.

The music that bands play includes light music, music which displays solo or ensemble virtuosity, and music specially written for or suitable for performing in brass band contests as 'test pieces'. Test pieces have several features that make them something of a *genre*. The characteristics of this *genre* are determined by the rules and other pragmatisms of contesting. Test pieces last between ten and fifteen minutes and contain solo and ensemble passages. They usually exploit wide dynamic and tempo ranges. They usually tax a number of specific instru-mental techniques such as the various denominations of 'tonguing'[3] and a fairly wide pitch range. All of these features are within a musical idiom which is more or less common across all brass bands. The instrumental line-up of the contesting bands – cornets, flugel horn, tenor horns, euphoniums, baritones, trombones and basses – is more or less fixed (percussion is also used). The style of playing is different from that of orchestral brass players – the most noticeable characteristic is the continual presence in brass bands of vibrato; British orchestral brass players cultivate a 'straight' sound and apply vibrato only occasionally for lyrical effect. The best brass band players are easily comparable with average profes-sional orchestral brass players technically, but there are clear stylistic and idiomatic differences. Between the end of the Second World War and the early 1970s, many, probably most, professional trumpet, trombone and tuba players[4] in Britain were brass band players who had successfully crossed over this stylistic boundary.

Though the characteristics of the 'test piece' type of composition and the clarity of the idiom of brass bands may appear prescriptive, it would be entirely wrong to dismiss this type of repertory as merely functional and artistically arid. Composers as diverse, chronologically and stylistically, as Elgar and Holst, Birtwistle and Henze, have written for brass bands.[5] Many works have been adopted as test pieces rather than commissioned for that purpose. No 'great' composer has developed the medium by writing a series of works for it, but a number of twentieth-century composers such as Eric Ball, Gilbert Vinter and Edward Gregson have concentrated much of their efforts on bands.

Until the early twentieth century, the brass band repertoire primarily con-tained transcriptions of art music. The most popular source for transcription was the operatic repertory and, though original compositions for brass bands appeared from the last quarter of the nineteenth century, these were often imit-ative of the format, style and language of operatic selections. Transcriptions of art music still figure prominently in the repertoire. Original works are usually, but not always, programmatic and just as usually are written in a traditional tonal idiom.

Musical modernism, certainly its melodic and harmonic manifestations, has had little impact on brass bands, but brass band music is not always 'light' music. The style and conventions of the serious part of its repertory continue to be derivative of art music, if in more subtle ways. One is bound to ask, therefore, why and how the brass band movement feels distant, even disenfranchised, from the 'mainstream of British music making'; for whether the mainstream is 'art' or 'pop', brass bands do not reside easily in it.

Bands certainly have been kept at arm's length by the major British institutions. The BBC has used them on its 'serious' music channel, Radio 3, and on occasions since the 1970s in the Henry Wood Promenade Concerts, but those appearances have often served to highlight something of an 'Uncle Tom' quality about these events. Though one college[6] offers a degree in 'Band Musicianship', most other higher education institutions have subordinated them. Most bands raise money for their activities by subscriptions and fund raising – concerts, engagements, etc. They receive little in state grants, but many have commercial sponsorship.

The pop music world has had little to do with brass bands. In the mid-1970s the Brighouse and Rastrick Band succeeded in getting into the British 'hit parade' with an arrangement of the *Cornish Floral Dance*. The record's success was largely due to the endorsement of it by the BBC Radio 2 disc jockey, Terry Wogan, whose interest in it was largely one of caricature. The success of the record, paradoxically, tended to galvanize half-wise and half-baked attitudes outside the brass band movement about bands' supposed archaism.

A neat illustration of the ghetto-like existence of brass bands is found in their treatment by *The New Grove Dictionary of Music and Musicians*,[7] which acts as something of a catalyst for informed musical opinion and which by editorial admission 'reflects the tastes and preferences of the English-speaking world'.[8] The space it gives under the entry 'Brass Bands' is only marginally longer than the entry on the history of the triangle, and while personalities such as Johann Petzmayer, the nineteenth-century Austrian zither player, are duly acknowledged with an entry, Harry Mortimer, probably the most influential figure in twentieth-century brass banding, is not.

It would be easy to explain the ambiguity that surrounds the cultural status of the brass band by drawing attention to its essentially half-caste identity between art and popular music. In truth, the issues are more complex. Its deep roots within the working-class community have undoubtedly prevented many observers from acquiring the fullest appreciation of its achievements and potential. At the same time, contesting has a centrality to the brass band movement in excess of any other branch of amateur music making. Even choral singing in Wales, with its strong ties to the eisteddfodic tradition has not taken contesting as the primary *raison d'être*. Historically, contests are vitally important to the brass band movement. Indeed, the extent to which faith is placed in 'champion bands' and the notion that musical performance can be weighed up and scored, places banding apart from other forms of music making. Furthermore, the entire contesting ethos has given rise to sets of conventions which, while they bind bands nationally to a 'movement', have created a stifling and trapping orthodoxy. The brass band movement is, however, remarkable and unique. It has always been a genuinely popular movement and the extent to which the style and language of brass bands is determined by what the brass band movement is prepared to consume, as opposed to what is purveyed to it, is impressive.

I have several times referred to the brass band *movement*. It is not clear why brass banding is referred to as a movement, but it invariably has been since the nineteenth century.[9] The word carries with it resonances of progress, conversion, extension and perhaps fainter sounds of a crusade. It is this notion of the brass band 'movement' as a clearly defined activity which is symbolized by a coherent orthodoxy and which has a social as well as a musical significance that is the theme of this book. It is this theme that has conditioned the approaches of all the contributors.

Of the previously published literature on brass bands, two general books stand out: Russell and Elliot's *The Brass Band Movement* and Arthur Taylor's *Brass Bands* (1979),[10] both of which, with barely disguised enthusiasm, give a good broad history of the subject. There has been some British postgraduate research in which bands figure prominently[11] and a small number of general books on British social or music history that give the subject due attention.[12] This, though, to our knowledge, is the first time that an entire volume has been devoted to brass bands in what is primarily intended as an academic series.

The first two chapters, by myself and Dave Russell, deal with a number of themes and topics within two chronological periods – the nineteenth century and the twentieth century up to the 1960s. They take up a significant proportion of the book and, though they are intended as an overview, taken together, they are not intended as a comprehensive history of the brass band movement. Some of the more influential and important forces for change are illustrated and explained, as are certain underlying themes that have an importance on the central topic; these include notions of respectability and improvement, the influence of class and capitalism, the organization of bands and their relationship to other institutions.

The remainder of the book is given over to three topic chapters, a substantial technical appendix and two other appendices. Clifford Bevan's chapter on the development of brass band contests deals with a subject which is at the heart of the brass band movement. Though every other part of the book touches on the subject of contesting, it would have been impossible to deal adequately with it without giving it separate and exclusive attention. Notwithstanding what I have suggested may be negative factors, contesting has been the single most important force for 'standardizing' and 'nationalizing' brass bands. The title 'Brass Band Contests: Art or Sport?' may point fairly precisely to the cultural dilemma of brass bands. Appendices 2 and 3 contain calendars of contest regulations and results.

Chapters 4 and 5 create a more expansive context in which the British brass band movement should be seen. The idea of direct linear continuity in the history of brass bands is, at the very least, questionable. The 'plebeian' tradition of music making did not disappear when brass bands became established. The overlapping of the two activities, the longer-established amateur instrumental tradition and the brass band movement, serves to draw attention to some of the major features that characterized brass bands, such as the attention to musical exactness and uniformity in a comparatively tight text-based musical discipline. Vic and Sheila Gammon's chapter presents a new and importantly different context for the brass band movement and the values it espoused.

Chapter 5 is a case study of brass bands in Australia. By the end of the nineteenth century, bands of one sort or another were found throughout the United States and the British colonies. Brass bands not only formed the basis for working-class music culture in these countries, but also acted as a catalyst for all music culture as expatriate, garrisoned and protected communities strove to create oases of Britishness and 'civilization'. British brass band musicians occupied positions in the two most important nineteenth-century American military bands (those of John Philip Souza and Patrick Gilmour), formed bands in South Africa, and even in the distant corner of north-western Canada British missionaries formed bands among the Tsimshian Indians. It was in Australasia, though, that the British brass band movement was most clearly imitated. Dr Bythell, in dealing with Australian bands, offers an interesting comparison for this working-class cultural export and its counterparts in the 'old country'.

During the preparation of this book it became evident that not all of the important issues and topics concerning brass bands could be dealt with. I have, therefore, added a 'postscript' (Chapter 6) which suggests areas of future research.

Arnold Myer's technical appendix (Appendix 1) deals with the development of brass band instruments during the period covered by this book. The placing of it as an appendix, rather than as a chapter in the main body of the book, is brought about by the type of material that it contains and not because it is subordinate in importance to the preceding chapters. The brass band movement owes its existence to the invention and production in the nineteenth century of relatively cheap chromatic instruments. The development of the movement has taken place in parallel to refinements and changes in musical instrument technology. The story of these inventions and developments is obviously crucial to the history of the brass band movement.

Throughout these chapters themes occur and reoccur naturally. Issues concerning class, cultural theory and other aspects relevant to social history underlie most contributions. There are many questions and topics, though, that are not addressed to the extent that they deserve. The topic that most obviously deserves further attention is the repertoire and musical idiom of brass bands. These are not ignored but they deserve more careful scrutiny than it has been possible to afford them here.

While it has been my intention as editor to create some coherence, I have not been overly prescriptive upon the contributors. The central theme of the book is the brass band *movement*. The chapters are related but, as it were, free-standing. There has been little collaboration between contributors and, while I have taken steps to guard against major overlaps in the chapters, I have stopped short of subtracting material where such action would cause significant structural problems that may detract from the essentially self-contained nature of each contribution.

In common with other volumes in this series, our main intention has been to contribute to a wider understanding of issues in British popular music and in so doing to stimulate curiosity and future research into it.

6 Bands

Notes

1 *The British Bandsman*, 30 December 1989.
2 Ruth Finnegan, *The Hidden Musicians: Music Making in an English Town*, Cambridge, 1989, p. 47.
3 Brass players use three basic articulation techniques. In single tonguing, the player articulates 'tu, tu', etc.; in double tonguing, it is 'tuka, tuka', etc; in triple tonguing, 'tutuka, tutuka'. There are variants of this technique, but its principles have been well established since the sixteenth century.
4 French horns and trumpets are not used in brass bands. It is very common for cornet players to become trumpeters. It is much less common for brass band musicians to take up the French horn.
5 Gustav Holst, *A Moorside Suite* (1928); Edward Elgar, *Severn Suite* (1930); Harrison Birtwistle, *Grimethorpe Aria* (1973); Hans Werner Henze, *Ragtimes and Habaneras* (1975).
6 Salford College of Technology offers a BA degree in band musicianship validated by the Council for National Academic Awards.
7 Stanley Sadie (ed.), *The New Grove Dictionary of Music and Musicians* (20 vols), London, 1980.
8 Ibid., vol. 1, p. x.
9 A report in *The Times* (11 July 1860, p. 9) of the 1860 Crystal Palace contest referred to a 'brass band movement'; by the 1880s, the term was well established.
10 J. F. Russell and J. H. Elliot, *The Brass Band Movement*, London, 1936; A. Taylor, *Brass Bands*, St Albans, 1979.
11 J. Scott, 'The Evolution of the Brass Band and its Repertoire in Northern England', PhD thesis, University of Sheffield, 1970; David Russell, 'The Popular Musical Societies of the Yorkshire Textile District 1850–1914, DPhil thesis, University of York, 1979. See also M. J. Lomas, 'Amateur Brass and Wind Bands in Southern England between the late 18th century and *c.*1900', PhD thesis, Open University, 1990.
12 See particularly, Dave Russell, *Popular Music in England 1840–1914: A Social History*, Manchester, 1987.

1   *Nineteenth-Century Bands: The Making of a Movement*

TREVOR HERBERT

Most social historians and some musicologists believe that brass bands in Victorian Britain were an important part of working-class achievement. Few, though, have ventured beyond the more commonly available secondary sources to ask why a brass band *movement* existed at all, how it was different to the dozens of other leisure activities that sprung up at that time and why brass bands are important to Victorian cultural, social and music history. Whereas historians have noted that brass bands were a quintessential Victorian product with likely but often vaguely defined associations with paternalism, social control, and self-determinism, musicologists have confined the topic to a footnote of nineteenth-century British music history, and a short footnote at that.

The study of popular culture as a discrete, though widely encompassing, discipline is comparatively recent, and this goes some way to explain why music is still a relatively neglected source for social historians and why the type of granite-edged investigation that so many other topics of nineteenth-century popular activity has received has not been attracted to the musical sources of the period.

Few musicologists have been attracted to study nineteenth-century British music because the work of the mainstream Romantic composers of Europe has offered seductive, alternative challenges. As such, conventional musicology has lent tacit support to the idea of Britain being '*Das Land ohne Musick*'. Another reason why brass bands have attracted little scholarly interest from musicians is that they are categorized as 'popular music', an area which most musicologists have found unattractive. Indeed, the 'serious study of music' appears to be defined as the study of 'serious music'.

Brass bands could be regarded as one of the more important aspects of British art music as well as popular music in the nineteenth century. One of the achievements of the brass band movement is that it created the first mass involvement of working-class people in instrumental art music, not just in Britain, but possibly anywhere. But, even when this phenomenon was taking place, as early as the 1880s, there were sure signs of institutional attitudes to brass bands galvanizing to force them into the uneasy middle ground between art and popular culture. In the first edition of Grove's dictionary, J. A. Kappey, an army bandmaster and self-styled musicologist who, through various enterprises, had made no small profit from brass bands, declared that 'many bands had reached a high state of excellence', but, 'of course, looked upon as high art culture, brass bands are of no account'.[1] Given the status that *Grove* was to assume, Kappey's short article may have sown the seeds of a schism between bands and art culture which many in the movement would argue has existed ever since.

Musicologists and historians spend much of their time periodizing and much of the rest preaching of the pitfalls of periodization. It is difficult to resist the temptation to see the development of the brass band movement in the nineteenth century as falling into three, perhaps four, overlapping periods in which critical development stages are evident and in which such developments are explained by the presence of vitally important social, musical, cultural and economic trends. Certain phenomena and events also play a part, such as the technical invention that gave brass instruments fully chromatic facilities and the parallel careers of groups of individuals such as Distin, Sax and Jullien, or Swift, Gladney and Owen, names that figure prominently later in this chapter.

These periods condition the structure of this chapter. The first occupies the opening years of the century and ends at about the time when Victoria came to the throne. Although most writers have linked the wind bands of the early nineteenth century to the brass band movement,[2] I see these relationships, even though they are plentiful enough, as largely circumstantial. The second period is one in which a number of potent forces combine to provide the reason why brass bands, as opposed to any other types of amateur ensemble group, gained popular ascendancy. The third of my periods starts around the middle of the century. From this time the growth of the movement accelerates most strongly. The number of bands multiplies and their prominence in working-class life, as well as their function in the common territory *between* classes, is evident. In the last twenty or thirty years of the century, about half-way through this 'third period', it is possible to distinguish two subtle but major structural changes taking place. The first concerns what may be described as the 'standardization' of musical identity. While it is reasonable to regard this as one of the most important features of the period, it is worth exercising some caution, for, even though many vital musical identifiers which eventually defined the brass band idiom were consolidated at this time, the majority of bands still did not conform to the 'standard' line-up of instruments. The second change is in some ways more interesting. Whereas, previously, brass banding had been led either by commerce or by socially superior classes, from this time the working classes were vital participants in what was, at the very least, an equal partnership between organized working people and entrepreneurs. Also, brass bands became largely decoupled from patronage and paternalism, elements which were always confused.[3] It is in this period, interestingly enough, that brass band people start referring to themselves as a 'movement'.[4]

I

A point which has often been overlooked is that, prior to the nineteenth century, there had not been a widespread tradition of amateur brass playing in Britain. There were comparatively few professional brass players and these were based in London and the main provincial centres.

Only three types of brass instrument existed before the nineteenth century – trombones, trumpets and horns. The trombone is largely unchanged since its invention in the fifteenth century. The horn and trumpet were of relatively simple construction, giving their players the facility to produce a single harmonic series from each fixed tube length.

Trombones were introduced into England at the beginning of the Tudor dynasty. Indeed, their importation was part of the cultural expansion that was intended to assert that dynasty. The players were all foreign; the most important were Venetians, many of them clandestine Jews, who established a highly skilled dynasty of trombonists at the Tudor court.[5] From the early sixteenth century until the Commonwealth period the importance of trombonists in the Royal musical establishment was reflected in the consistency of their employment and the size of their fees. They were used to play gentle chamber music, dance music, probably (although none survives) declamatory processional music and, from the closing decades of the sixteenth century, to support sacred music, even the music of the liturgy itself.[6]

The main provincial employers of trombonists were the civic authorities who still employed waits. Waits, who had been part of civic foundations since the Middle Ages, performed at ceremonial functions and in earlier times were, it seems, employed to keep and sound the watch. Although the waits were regulated by local authorities and were required to conduct themselves under strict disciplinary regulations, evidence shows that they also worked independently of these authorities – either collectively or as individuals.[7]

The other main provincial employers were cathedrals, many of whom accommodated trombonists on their statutes. It is probable that in some cities the cathedral players were waits who were freelancing; it is certainly true that cathedrals without trombone players on their statutes made *ex gratia* payments to trombonists for special services.[8]

Trombonists before the last decades of the seventeenth century played with any combination of quiet and loud instruments. The only wind instrument with which they had more frequent ensemble grouping was the cornet (in Italian, *cornetto*; in German, *zink*). This is *not* the nineteenth-century cornet but an entirely different instrument made from wood and having a finger hole system similar to that of the recorder and with a cup-shaped mouthpiece similar to those used on brass instruments.

For the whole of this period the trumpet and horn had little special and individual significance in art music in Britain. Trumpets were militaristic, declamatory instruments; horns, too, were largely functional. Towards the end of the seventeenth century and through the eighteenth century fundamental changes took place in the musical role and status of brass instruments. These changes form an important context in which the development of brass bands should be seen.

By the end of the seventeenth century, the trombone, the only chromatic brass instrument, was obsolete in Britain. It began to fall out of fashion in the later years of the reign of Charles II. By the opening years of the eighteenth century, few in England knew what a trombone (or *sackbut*, its old English name) was. There are several reasons for this, but the primary one is that tastes then current in art music favoured homogeneous sonorities of the type produced by balanced string and wind groups. British tastes in art music have always been fairly uniform and centrally determined – for this reason the trend was national.

On the other hand, the trumpet had entered a period of ascendancy. A school of exceptional London-based trumpeters was contemporary with composers such as Purcell, Clarke and Blow, and there emanated from this coincidence a rich repertoire that, on the one hand, was virtuoso and, on the other, contained musical characteristics that were to define the idiom of the trumpet in Britain for more than a century. This musical idiom was strengthened and underlined by the endowment of a social status on trumpet playing (and to an extent horn playing, too – the horn had less musical individuality at this time). The most overt and potent device that acted in favour of making trumpet playing professional, centralized and in many other ways hierarchical, was the office of 'sergeant trumpeter', first instituted in the sixteenth century and to whom, in the seventeenth and eighteenth centuries, all trumpeters had to submit themselves to be licensed. This system of licensing may well have been in direct imitation of the Imperial Guild of Trumpeters and Kettledrummers, formed in 1623 and operated throughout the Holy Roman Empire under sanction of Ferdinand II.[9]

The regulatory systems for trumpeters became less clearly drawn in the later eighteenth century but it is possible that this thinly disguised freemasonry continued to condition some attitudes to professional trumpet playing – except, perhaps, the military which had its own set of regulations. The office of sergeant trumpeter continued to exist until the early twentieth century.

The trombone was reintroduced into Britain in 1784 for the celebrations at Westminster Abbey and the Pantheon in commemoration of the birth of Handel. All of the players at these performances were foreign, almost certainly Austrian or German. In the late eighteenth century, the trombone was effectively a new instrument as far as the British were concerned and there is not a shred of evidence to suggest that there was a single native-born trombone player working in Britain for more than a hundred years before the nineteenth century.

The waits were finally and formally made defunct in the early 1830s under the terms of the various municipal and parliamentary Reform Acts. The changing administrative infrastructure, together with the expediences caused by financial pressures that local and civic authorities faced, took away the last mechanism that supported them. Some writers have given this date and these events undue significance.[10] In fact, the waits had been an anachronism for more than half a century. The link between the waits and brass bands which some have erroneously drawn, and which Arthur Taylor,[11] for example, has treated with appropriate scepticism, is attributed to the fact that two members of the York waits (whatever they were in the 1830s) were subsequently members of a brass band. By the nineteenth century, the waits had no general characteristics which make it appropriate for them to be regarded as the stirring nucleus of the brass band movement.

II

The early nineteenth-century bands that have relevance to mid-nineteenth-century brass bands were those of the army, the auxiliary forces, village bands and church bands. Full-time military bands can be traced back to the seventeenth century, but most have their origins in the late eighteenth century. In the early nineteenth century most regimental bands were restricted to ten players and all were the private bands of the commanding officers concerned.[12] A standing order issued by letter in 1803 instructed that 'not more than *one* [*sic*] Private soldier of each troop or company shall be permitted to act as musicians'.[13] This order was largely ignored and 18 years later letters were still being dispatched instructing commanding officers to restrict the number of musicians in each troop or company.

Regular army bands were but one feature, however, of military music in Britain in the late eighteenth and nineteenth centuries. Many bands were associated with the militia which had been revived in 1757 and the volunteer corps which emerged in the 1790s. They were widely dispersed, and were funded primarily by subscriptions as well as (unwittingly) by government funding and by direct patronage of officers. They normally numbered between six and twelve players and were usually amateur, though many contained professional players. As well as percussion, the most common instruments in the bands were trumpets, clarinets, fifes and flutes on treble parts, with horns, bassoons, serpents and (much less usually) trombones on the lower parts.[14] Military bands played a mixed repertory. Concert programmes included titles of national and patriotic melodies as well as arrangements of popular art music. There was also a minor industry of publishing for military bands. Many bands had marches 'dedicated' to them by publishers which were issued in parts and score with a keyboard reduction. The music was not technically demanding but was functional and entertaining. As well as the published copies, manuscript sources survive. Probably the most eminent composer to write for the early military bands was Joseph Haydn, who, on his stay in London in the 1790s, wrote a *March for the Prince of Wales* and two *Marches for the Derbyshire Cavalry Regiment*.

Some of the players of the early military bands were to have an influence on brass bands later in the century. John Distin, for example, started his career as a bandboy in the South Devon Militia,[15] John Gladney was the son of the bandmaster of the 30th East Lancs Regiment,[16] and William Rimmer, one of the most eminent late-nineteenth-century conductors, was the son of a militia bandsman.[17] The Godfrey family, of which the composer Dan Godfrey was the most famous member, could trace its associations with the Coldstream Guards band back to the late eighteenth century.

The church bands of rural Britain, particularly England, also provided a tradition of amateur instrumental ensemble music making. Such bands were common throughout the country. The survival of a large written repertory of church band music indicates widespread musical literacy among players in these types of ensemble. It is doubtful, however, whether the repertory of such musicians was confined to that which is revealed in the surviving manuscript sources or to the music of the church or, indeed, to any written music. As Vic Gammon points out later in this book, there existed alongside the text-based practices of the church and village bands a vernacular, instrumental, 'plebeian tradition', which was well developed, improvised and 'popular'.[18]

Evidence of the extent of instrumental performance in English churches is abundant. McDermott[19] cites dozens in Sussex alone. Galpin[20] has drawn a similar picture in Dorset. William Millington, in his *Sketches of Local Musicians and Musical Societies*,[21] describes a network of bands in the North of England and even on the island of Anglesey in North Wales where the Anglican religion cohabited with the Welsh language, there are sources for church instrumental music.[22] One of the main functions of church bands was to double and support sung parts. It is undoubtedly true, however, that the bands acted as binding agents for church communities in a way similar to the manner in which Nonconformist music in the heartlands of Wales took on a deep social significance later in the century. The social function of bands may, in some cases, have been born of necessity because, though some parish priests encouraged church bands, others were absenteeist.[23] According to J. A. Latrobe, many left the choirs to 'regulate and inspirit [*sic*] the music of the church. In most places, the choir are left to their own fitful struggles, without any offer of clerical assistance.'[24]

Brass instruments did not figure prominently in church bands. Nicholas Temperley's summary of the instrumentation of church bands in the first thirty years of the nineteenth century cites no brass instruments,[25] but other sources occasionally do. McDermott's investigation of Sussex church bands revealed eight trombones, four serpents and a bass horn.[26] Unfortunately, McDermott's energy in research was not equalled by the rigour with which he detailed his findings and the dates when these instruments were found are not known. It is extremely doubtful if the trombones, for example, were in use very early in the century. The most common instrumentation for early nineteenth-century church bands was strings with woodwind. Bassoons and cellos were the most common bass instruments. Treble parts were generally played on violin, flute, clarinet or oboe.

The church bands were commonest between about 1780 and 1830;[27] the militia and volunteer bands were at their strongest somewhat earlier. It is important to stress that such ensembles did not die out. Church bands existed in some parts of the country at the end of the nineteenth century and the military bands, particularly those of the regular army, were a constant musical feature throughout the Victorian period.

From the second and third decades of the century, numerous accounts exist of functions such as fêtes, fairs, and other celebrations featuring a band. The bands are seldom named but they seem to have been ingrained into the tapestry of community life. Arthur Taylor has cited numerous examples of bands existing in the years previous to Victoria's reign[28] and there is evidence of similar bands being formed in Scotland[29] and southern England[30] in the same period.

Many examples can be drawn on to link early village, church or military bands to distinguished brass bands,[31] but while such examples may show how a particular band originated, they do not illustrate or explain the origins of the brass band *movement*. The zest with which some modern bands have adopted a strictly linear approach to history in order to establish a distant, unbroken pedigree has created some important distortions in this respect.

The early military, church and village bands did, however, provide an important legacy for the eventual development of the brass band movement. These early bands created, for the first time, a tradition of literate instrumental ensemble music making outside the professional, middle- and upper-class enclaves in which such activity had previously been centred. Their activities ordained an infrastructure that was to be sustained and developed through the century. That infrastructure is found in the presence of five critical conditions preceding the commercial, economic and social factors which fuelled the most rapid growth of bands that was to come: first, evidence of amateur instrumental performance; second, a performance convention that was primarily literate and text-based as opposed to aural and improvisatory; third, the witness of that activity by 'audiences' who were the peer groups of the performers; fourth, some evidence of supporting services for music (shops, instrument repairers, teachers and arrangers); and fifth, some evidence of cultural cross-over between art/ middle-class music and the lower orders. The evidence of the latter condition is found in the repertory that these bands played, primarily but not exclusively the repertory of the military bands.[32]

III

Though these early bands provide evidence of an 'infrastructure', the real and immediate prehistory of the brass band movement is found in the period between the late 1830s and the middle of the century. In this period, there was a sudden increase in the popularity of brass instruments. Though it was common for bands to describe themselves as amateur, 'brass band' playing was not exclusively amateur nor working class. Bands made up entirely of brass instruments existed from the 1830s.[33] In 1838, the Preston United Independent Harmonic Brass Band petitioned Mr Thomas Clifton, of Lytham Hall, Lancashire:

> Sir, By the desire of a Fue Respectable Friends of yours in Preston has caused hus to write to you with a Petition as a Solisitation for a job of Playing at your Dinnering Day as they told hus is taking place on Tuesday the 10th of March Inst. at Lytham which if you are having a Band of Music at Dinner we shall be very glad to be ingadged for you on that Day it is one of the first Bands in the country. Our Band consists of 10 in number it is a Brass Band and the Name of the Band is the United Independent Harmonic Brass Band Preston which our charge is not so much considering the Band the charge or Pay for hus for one Day is 8/6 each man for the number of 10 comes to £4–5–0 and Meat and Drink as soon as we get their and all the

time we stay their, if so hapen we have to come if you make up your Mind for hus to come to Play for dinner on that Day we shall please no doubt.

N.B. if writing for hus you must Direct to our leader Edwd. Kirby Leader of the United Independent Harmonic Brass Band at No. 31 Alfred Street, Preston.

We can come either in uniform or not according to the weather.

From your Humble Servants
The Band[34]

There is no other surviving information concerning Preston Harmonic Band; it was a *brass* band and this was deemed worthy of emphasis. The fee, by the standards of the time, was fairly substantial, certainly compatible with the players being professional or semi-professional. The day on which work was being sought was a Tuesday, suggesting that the players were earning a living either solely or partly from playing. If they were semi-professional, it follows that they were self-employed or had jobs in which they had control over their working hours.

Plate 1 Cyfarthfa Band, *c.*1855. One of the most successful mid-19th century bands, founded as a private band in 1838 by the master of the Cyfarthfa ironworks at Merthyr Tydfil, Robert Crawshay. The band in this photograph consisted of three keyed bugles, four cornets, two tenor horns, four trombones, one euphonium, one ophicleide, two bombardons, two other brass instruments and side and bass drums. (*Source: Cyfarthfa Castle Museum.*)

An example of a different type of origin for a band is illustrated by the story of the Cyfarthfa Band, founded in Merthyr Tydfil, South Wales, in 1838, by the industrialist Robert Thompson Crawshay.[35] (Plate 1 is the earliest picture of the band.) By the 1830s, Merthyr was by far the biggest Welsh industrial town and one of the greatest centres for iron smelting in the world. Immigration into the town was on an unprecedented scale. Crawshay started the band from scratch. He enlisted some local talent but appointed to critical positions players who were already established as professional players. These included a distinguished family of musicians from Bradford, London theatre players and travelling musicians such as those who visited the town with Wombwell's Circus and Menagerie.[36] Although the function and status of the band changed over the remaining years of the century it was founded as a private band. The players were given jobs in Crawshay's ironworks and probably some help with housing. Whether the players received payment for performing is difficult to establish but it is probable that fees for engagements were distributed among members.

Sources relating to the Crawshay band at Merthyr are the most extensive of this type, but the practice of a well-to-do landed gentleman supporting a brass band, primarily for his private use, was not unique to Cyfarthfa. There are, of course, many precedents for aristocratic patronage of musicians. In England, the strongest immediate precedent is found in the support earlier in the century of volunteer and militia bands by landed gentry who were the commanding officers of auxiliary force corps. There are, however, other examples. Thomas Lee, one of the earliest conductors of Besses o'th'Barn Band, was responsible for the formation of a private band for Lord Francis Edgerton at Worsley (Edgerton later became 1st Earl of Ellesmere). Lee was also associated with the Duke of Lancaster's Own Yeoman Cavalry Band, which was a brass band.[37] A private band was also formed in the 1840s by the son of the mill owner, W. L. Marriner, at Keighley in Yorkshire. Like the Cyfarthfa Band, Marriner's took part in early contests. It is also worth noting that Queen Victoria formed a private band in 1837 which consisted of seventeen players. Apart from a percussionist, all of them were brass or woodwind players and 'masters of more than one instrument'.[38] The private band eventually merged with the state band, by which time it was, in effect, a small orchestra, but in the middle of the century it was primarily a brass/wind band playing arrangements of works by Spohr, Meyerbeer, Weber and Beethoven, a repertory similar to that which was being performed by the Cyfarthfa Band.[39] This type of mid-century patronage of private bands may well have been a model for some of the industrial meritocracy a decade later, many of whom took great pride in having their works' band play at garden parties and other social gatherings for the well heeled.

IV

Many of the players in private bands were drawn from travelling show bands. Although Wombwell's was the most famous and perhaps the best, it was not the only itinerant troupe to have a distinguished band. Others included Batty's

Menagerie Band and Howe's Great London Circus. As early as 1833, the *Yorkshire Gazette* was praising the skills of four trombonists from Cooke's Equestrian Circus who had agreed to perform in the 24th Annual Yorkshire Amateur Musical Meeting. 'It is a pity', the paper lamented, 'they are not placed in a situation where their acquirements would be more conspicuously displayed'.[40]

Some of the brass players in these entertainment troupes did have conspicuous display. Around 1839, Tournaire's Circus featured 'Herr Popowitz', a musical clown who amazed audiences with masterly performances on brass instruments. His performances, according to the recollections of Enderby Jackson, included 'operatic solos, national melodies and airs with brilliant variations in a style unknown before his advent'.[41]

Other brass virtuosi gained national respect and fame among middle-class audiences. The most celebrated was the trumpeter, Thomas Harper. He was born in Worcester in 1786 and was sent to London to study with Eley, the Duke of York's military bandmaster. At the age of ten he played in Eley's East India Brigade Band and various London theatre orchestras. Both he and his son, Thomas John Harper, are known to have performed regularly in the provinces.[42]

Another great force for popularizing brass instruments was the popular (not to say populist) conductor, Louis Jullien. In his London concerts from 1840 and in the provincial tours he undertook every year, brass instruments were prominently featured. No individual players in Jullien's orchestra were afforded a higher profile than the cornettist, Koenig, whose *Post Horn Galop* became something of a classic, and the ophicleide player, Prospere. Many other great brass players were either permanently or temporarily associated with Jullien, including Thomas Harper.

It is easy to cast scorn on Jullien's unashamed extravagance and gaudiness and many have been reluctant to afford him his proper place in nineteenth-century British music history.[43] It cannot be denied, however, that his impact on audiences was immense. His brass players possessed genuine virtuosity and no matter how excessive it may seem to twentieth-century tastes, the sound of *Suona le Tromba* from Bellini's *I Puritani* played on twenty cornets, twenty trumpets, twenty trombones, twenty ophicleides and twenty serpents[44] must have been not just spectacular but also influential at a time when all brass bands were trying to gain a foothold in British musical life.

In December 1844, Jullien featured the Distin family in one of his London concerts. They played saxhorns which they had recently acquired from their inventor, Adolphe Sax, while on a visit to Paris.[45] The Distins already had a distinguished reputation as performers on brass instruments. They were playing as a family quintet in 1835[46] and gave performances throughout the country, but it was not until they converted to saxhorns and took out the British agency for the instruments that they had their most potent effect.[47] They toured widely, performing mostly in music and concert halls, and their main contribution to the development of brass bands (apart from the interest that they aroused through their own virtuosity) was that they popularized the Sax instruments. They were also involved from the early 1850s with a highly successful publishing enterprise which was responsible for a large number of widely distributed journals and score arrangements.

Jullien and the Distins had a great influence in the 1840s but it is doubtful how many of their concerts were attended by people, or indeed the class of people, who would be the members of brass bands in the decades that followed. Although it is impossible to be certain, it is likely that the audiences for the Distins' concerts and for Jullien's extravaganzas were primarily middle class. *Punch* provided a lucid description of those attending one of Jullien's concerts:

> Amid the merry, but decorous throng, we notice several families of professional gentlemen and tradesmen, as well as persons of higher rank; and many men, whom we personally knew, had brought their sisters . . . Many of the young men wore plain black suits and white ties, and though some of these youths, thanks to the early closing movement, may have been linen-drapers' assistants, a greater proportion evidently were of the aristocracy, and not a few, who abstained from actually dancing, had all the appearance of curates. A bishop occupied a private box among the spectators . . . The general tone of the assembly was that of perfect ease, and perfect propriety; the unrestrained and correct expression of amiability and animal spirits.[48]

V

The invention of the piston valve system and its application to brass instruments has properly been described as the principle reason why a large, working-class brass band movement came into existence. The various developments in brass instrument technology are detailed later in this book by Arnold Myers. However, it is worth mentioning at this point the fundamental advances that took place and the manner in which those advances affected mass working-class music culture. It is also worth emphasizing that, while these technical advances were fundamental to the brass band movement, they were also momentous in the entire field of instrumental music.

From the late eighteenth century, experiments were conducted in various parts of Europe aimed at the invention of a system which would enable brass players to play, on instruments of various pitches, the entire chromatic spectrum of the range of each of those instruments: in other words, every semitone between the lowest and highest note of the compass of each instrument. The telescopic, U-shaped, slide mechanism of the trombone gives that instrument complete chromaticism because every time the slide is extended or retrieved the tubing that the player is blowing through becomes (respectively) longer or shorter. This principle was successfully applied to a much shorter length of tubing than that used on trombones by the English inventor, John Hyde, in the late eighteenth century and was used by some professional players as a 'slide trumpet'. A more widely used invention was the keyed bugle. Keys (similar to those on clarinets) were applied to bugles and were widely manufactured. The most celebrated early English key system was that patented by Joseph Halliday in 1810.[49] It had similarities to eighteenth-century Austrian systems but no evidence exists to show a direct link between the inventors. Valve systems eventually superseded the other designs, but it is important to exercise some caution in attributing the development of brass playing in Britain in the nineteenth century exclusively to the invention and distribution of valved brass systems.

Perfectly serviceable valved instruments were invented by the end of the 1820s but the complete range of saxhorn instruments was not easily available in Britain until the mid-1840s. Before that time, valved instruments were no more common in brass bands than keyed instruments. The early development of bands was primarily the development of keyed instrument combinations. The publications of brass music were aimed as much at keyed brass players as valve instrumentalists. Thomas Harper published his *Airs* for keyed bugle in about 1825, and Tully's *Tutor for Keyed Bugle* was published in 1831 as part of Robert Cocks & Company's *Series of Modern Tutors*. Cocks also published McFarlane's *Eight Popular Airs for Brass Band* in 1836 which is regarded as the first British publication specifically for brass bands. MacFarlane's instrumentation calls for three keyed bugles on the *primo* treble parts as opposed to cornopeans (the early name for the cornet), but of course the same music could be played on either instrument.[50] In 1836, Blackman and Pace published *The Cornopean Companion of Scales* . . . and it is evident from publications and surviving records of the instrumentation of bands that cornopeans were used throughout the country, but it is equally obvious that early valve systems did not usurp the popularity of keyed instruments. The London firm of Pace was advertising cornopeans in the late 1830s and, according to Enderby Jackson, the Distins possessed Pace piston instruments before their famous Paris encounter with Adolphe Sax in 1844. However, the Distin family had made their reputation using slide trumpet, French horns, keyed bugles and trombone, and it was keyed instruments that Robert Crawshay bought from Pace in 1840.[51] The fact should not be overlooked that most of the best British brass players of the first forty years of the nineteenth century played keyed instruments or slide instruments; valve skills were not widespread until the 1840s.

The other proof of the survival of older, key-based technology is the dogged survival of the ophicleide until quite late in the century. The ophicleide was eventually replaced by the euphonium – manufacturers encouraged the change by offering euphoniums as prizes for the best ophicleide players at contests – but mid-century reports of the death of the ophicleide were greatly exaggerated. Sam Hughes, who, with the possible exception of Prospere, was the greatest ophicleide player of the nineteenth century, never, as far as is known, played a valved instrument. It was as a specialist on the ophicleide that he was appointed to a professorship at Kneller Hall in 1859 and at the Guildhall School of Music in 1880. Indeed, Kneller Hall appointed Alfred Phasey as euphonium professor at the same time as it appointed Hughes. A more extreme example of the way in which the older technology overlapped with the new was the persistent faith of Thomas Harper in the future of the slide trumpet. He played the slide trumpet all his life and his *Instructions for the Trumpet*[52] is almost entirely devoted to the slide trumpet. His son, though a brilliant valve instrument player, continued to teach the slide trumpet at the Royal Academy of Music and, while he was the author of *Harper's School for the Cornet-à-pistons* (undated), he also published in the mid-1870s *Harper's School for the* [Slide] *Trumpet*.[53] Even at the very end of the century, trumpet players at the Royal Opera House were wrestling with the demands of the Italian opera repertory on slide instruments. One of their players, W. Wyatt, invented a double-slide instrument in 1890.

A related point here concerns the idea that technical progress goes hand-in-hand with musical, cultural or artistic improvement, and it is worth rebutting the absurd notion that virtuosity on brass instruments was exclusively related to valved instruments. Since the 1970s a number of professional trumpet players have learned the techniques of keyed brass instruments and demonstrated a technical facility on these instruments of the same order as they do on valve instruments. Primary sources, in the form of manuscript music sources for keyed instruments, bear out the same point.

The Distins gave the Sax designs a powerful endorsement. This endorsement encouraged more instrument manufacturers, music publishers and others to recognize that a market had come into being which had not existed previously. That market was easily identified as the inhabitants of the comparatively new industrial communities and especially the more 'affluent' members of the working class. Valved instruments possessed qualities that rendered them particularly suitable to be produced and marketed in large quantities. The musical virtues of the newly designed instruments were self-evident. When a valve was depressed it instantly changed the length of tubing that the player was blowing through. The instruments were, therefore, fully chromatic, were reasonably in tune across their entire range and the valve principle could be applied to *any* voice of instrument from the highest cornet to the lowest bass or bombardon. This was a critical advantage of valve over key system instruments, for in the latter only bugles and ophicleides were successful enough to have common usage.

Valved brass instruments also had pragmatic features that were equally important. Their production required a less exacting process of manufacture than key system instruments. After the initial 'tooling' was completed, they could, at least in part, be manufactured by mass production methods. The older designs and other instruments such as keyed woodwind and string instruments continued to rely on traditional craft skills. Each valve instrument was played with just the three most dextrous fingers of the right hand. To a right-handed player the initial experience of holding a brass instrument is comfortable and natural; this is much less the case with a violin or flute, for instance. Consequently, brass instruments could be learned easily and a common fingering technique could be applied to each voice of instrument. The instruments were durable, they used easily available raw materials, and the manufacturing process employed variants of many other processes of metal fashioning that were in use for a plethora of domestic and commercial machines and utensils. Though Arnold Myers argues in Appendix I of this book that the widespread adoption of brass instrumentation can be attributed merely to taste – 'a preference for the sound of concerted brass instruments' – it is my view that economic, pedagogical and other pragmatic factors were critically important to the birth of the brass band movement.

From the middle of the century, the number of manufacturers and retailers of brass instruments increased dramatically. Some concerns were just importing foreign instruments, but many started manufacturing their own models. The

Plate 2   Shopfront of the firm of Joseph Higham at 127 Strangeways, Manchester, in 1892, showing the proprietor, Mr Peter Robinson, with most of his seventy-strong staff. (*Source: Howard Higham Robinson Esq., Bradford.*)

Manchester firm of Joseph Higham (see Plate 2), formed in 1842, was advertising itself as 'Makers to the Army' by 1852. Distins set up a manufacturing business in the early 1850s and some of the longer-established firms eventually diversified into brass instrument manufacture. Scott[54] has cited 86 British patents relative to brass instruments that were registered at the London Patent Office between 1853 and the end of the century, and between 1845 and 1862 twenty-nine specifications for improvements to brass instruments were registered under the terms of the 1843 Design Act.[55] Interest in the newest designs of brass instrument was intensified by the appearance of many at the 1851 Great Exhibition. The most successful exhibitor was Sax, who won a 'Council Medal', but two British designers won 'Prize Medals' – George MacFarlane for his 'Improved cornet-à-piston' and John Köhler for his 'Slide Trombone, and for the application of his patent valves to other metal wind instruments'.[56]

The widespread adoption of valve instruments, mainly the Sax designs, occurred at a time when entrepreneurialism had its fastest impact on the music industry and ran parallel to what Cyril Ehrlich has called 'the flood' of activity that occurred in the musical profession in mid-nineteenth-century Britain.[57] Between 1841 and 1851 the number of professional musicians and music teachers active in England and Wales rose from 6,600 to 11,200. In the next decade the numbers were to rise again to 15,000[58], and though there was a steady increase over the remainder of the century (38,600 in 1891), it was the 1840s and 1850s that were the real springboard for musical activity in the late Victorian period. The growth of the musical profession in Britain is important to the development of bands because it corresponded to an increase in the entire range of services and activities that supported music, and this phenomenon was not confined to London and a few provincial centres. Concert-going became a more common activity and, perhaps more important as far as the story of brass bands is concerned, the franchise for listening to 'serious' music widened beyond the middle classes. This was not the first time this had happened but from the middle of the century it was on an altogether different scale. One wonders, indeed, how prominent the middle classes were in concert audiences. A report in the *Sheffield Independent* in 1858[59] noted that 'with the exception of the gallery' (which was, presumably, occupied by the less well-off), 'the house was not more than half filled'.

Another important development at this time, occasioned by growth in the professional sector, was the increase of musical education at all levels. Many private teachers of music – most, apparently, with a lust for the acquisition of diplomas and certificates – set up shop as 'Professors of Music'. These teachers were of critical importance to the development of brass bands. Conductors listed for the 1860 and 1861 Crystal Palace contests included the evocatively named Thomas Tallis Trimnel, Professor of Music, who conducted the 6th Chesterfield Volunteer Band; James Melling, Professor of Music (Stalybridge Old Band); Isaac Dewhurst, Professor of Music (4th West York RF Halifax); W. Frogitt, Professor of Cornet (Deptford Pier Saxhorn Band); and A. Scoll, Professor of Music (Scoll's Operatic). Many more bands throughout the country were trained by men who knew little or nothing about brass instruments, but considered themselves qualified to teach virtually anything musical.

VI

Another factor which was helpful to the development of banding was the attitude, widely prevalent in the Victorian period, which held music and, in particular, art music to be a force for moral and positive good among working people. The performance and, indeed, the reception of music was a 'rational recreation', a panacea for the many ills to which the working class were believed to be susceptible. Evidence of these views abounds in the nineteenth century and varies from the bizarre postulating of the Reverend H. R. Haweis, whose *Music and Morals*[60] cheerfully proclaimed that certain types of melody could induce moral virtue and was reprinted twenty-one times between 1871 and 1906, to the equally enthusiastic, but more measured, testimonies of people like George Hogarth. In 1846, Hogarth had written in his short-lived weekly newspaper *The Musical Herald*:

> The tendency of music is to soften and purify the mind . . . the cultivation of a
> musical taste furnishes for the rich a refined and intellectual pursuit . . . a relaxation
> from toil more attractive than the haunts of intemperance [and in] densely populated

manufacturing districts of Yorkshire, Lancashire and Derbyshire, music is cultivated among the working classes to an extent unparalleled in any other part of the kingdom . . .[61]

but it was when he teamed up with W. H. Wills to write 'Music in Humble Life' in Dickens's journal *Household Words* that Hogarth caught the spirit of current attitudes exactly:

Another set of harmonious blacksmiths awaken the echoes of the remotest Welsh mountains. The correspondent of a London paper, while visiting Merthyr, was exceedingly puzzled by hearing boys in the Cyfarthfa works whistling airs rarely heard except in the fashionable ball-room, opera-house, or drawing room. He afterwards discovered that the proprietor of the works, Mr Robert Crawshay, had established among his men a brass band which practises once a week throughout the year. They have the good fortune to be led by a man (one of the 'roll-turners') who must have had somewhere a superior musical education. I had the pleasure of hearing them play, and was astonished at their proficiency. They number sixteen instruments. I heard them perform the Overtures to *Zampa*, *The Caliph of Bagdad*, and *Fra Diavolo*, *Vivi tu*, some concerted music from *Roberto*, *Don Giovanni*, and *Lucia*, with a quantity of Waltzes, Polkas, and dance music. The bandmaster had them under excellent control; he everywhere took the time well, and the instruments preserved it, each taking up his lead with spirit and accuracy; in short, I have seldom heard a regimental band more perfect than this handful of workmen, located (far from any place where they might command the benefit of hearing other bands) in the mountains of Wales. The great body of men at these works are extremely proud of their musical performances, and like to boast of them. I have been told it cost Mr Crawshay great pains and expense to bring this band to its present excellent condition. If so, he now has his reward. Besides this, he has shown what the intellectual capacity of the workman is equal to, and, above all, he has provided a rational and refined amusement for classes whose leisure time would have been less creditably spent than in learning or listening to music.

The habits and manners of these men appear to have been decidedly improved by these softening influences . . .[62]

There are a number of views as to how and why music was perceived to be operating in this way. Mackerness has argued that any act of collective endeavour, such as banding, which required by definition co-operation among working people, was seen as being good.[63] Another explanation concerns the 'goodness' that many believed was inherent in high art music. Association with it through performance was, therefore, association with virtue. A less complex but equally compelling reason as to why playing in a brass band was regarded as a 'rational recreation' was that many working-class men quickly acquired and lucidly demonstrated deft skills as instrumentalists. These skills could be immediately recognized and appreciated by their social superiors, because they could be easily assessed in a long-established scale of middle-class values. There was another related reason as to why, initially at least, the impetus for the formation of working-class brass bands in the valve era was encouraged by a socially superior sector of society. The higher classes, witnessing the growth of a self-conscious working-class identity, perceived it to be a potential problem. Whether that problem was real or imagined is of little consequence to us here. The important point is that the more enlightened members of the middle classes sought to engage working-class people in a cultural middle ground where certain activities, pastimes and pursuits were common across classes.[64] Ultimately, the parameters of that middle ground and, indeed, its internal identity were determined from above rather than below but the factor, the substance, that unambiguously characterized the point of contact was the repertory that bands played, because the repertory was primarily art and middle-class light music.

VII

The availability of relatively cheap instruments that were comparatively easy to play, the existence of a network of educated music 'professors' of one sort or another, the new social environment in which working people found themselves and the commonly held belief among the most influential in society that music was a path to rectitude provided the context that nurtured the mid-century development of brass banding. It is impossible to measure this increase with any accuracy. At the end of the century, brass band magazines tried to calculate the number of bands in existence; their estimates were almost certainly exaggerated. For the period between the 1840s and 1880s one can only draw on impressions as to the number of bands that were active in Britain; these impressions have to be gained from those that merited press attention or are mentioned in concert advertisements. Several sources mention the proliferation of bands. Enderby Jackson reflected that in the middle of the century and following the wide availability of valve instruments 'almost every village and group of mills in the north of England had its own band. It mattered not to them how the bands were constituted, or of what classification of instruments was in use'.[65]

The 1850s were a particularly important period of growth for banding. It was in that decade that many of the most important developments took place which generated a brass band movement that was widely based and primarily involved working-class people.

There was no standard pattern for the origins (or transformation) and sustenance of brass bands, but from the middle of the century there appear to be three major types of band. First, there were bands which were linked to a single workplace or who were the beneficiaries of some form of paternalism or direct and sustained patronage from a single, wealthy, benevolent source. The second type were subscription bands which relied for their origins and development on support from a wider community, perhaps through other institutions such as mechanics' institutes or temperance societies. These two categories are often difficult to distinguish from each other because works bands were often subscription bands. The fact that a band carried the name of a mill or factory did not necessarily mean that it owed its origins to the owner of that mill or factory. Indeed, as I discuss below, the sort of patronage commonly presumed about Victorian brass bands – that is, direct benevolent patronage by a mill or factory or mine owner – probably accounted for only a small percentage of the bands that were formed. The wealthy industrial middle classes were important, however, because it is equally true that subscription bands, while taking money from anywhere they could get it, relied heavily in their early days on such people as major subscribers. The third category were those bands which originated with or were adopted by the 1859 volunteer movement. Some volunteer bands received subscription money, others middle-class patronage. The funding of volunteer bands is sufficiently complex and important to warrant special attention.

Direct industrial patronage did exist from at least the 1840s. The cotton manufacturers, George and Joseph Strutt of Belper, formed a musical society and 'whatever time [that was] consumed in their musical studies [was] recovered in their working hours'. They were often heard to be 'blasting on the ophicleide and trombone'.[66] Another industrialist, Titus Salt, was sufficiently ambitious for his Saltaire Band that he promised it a bonus of £50 if it won the 1860 Crystal Palace contest.[67]

Of the bands that were formed by direct industrial patronage in the 1850s, none is more famous than the one formed in the village of Queensbury in the West Riding of Yorkshire. There had been a band of sorts associated with the village since 1816; it appears to have been run by a local publican called Peter Wharton. The village grew rapidly in the first half of the century due to the successful enterprise of John Foster. Foster was the son of a yeoman farmer. He was initially involved in coalmining but later he established a cotton mill on a piece of land known as 'Black Dike' [sic]. Queensbury, or 'Queenshead' as it was at that time known, was a typical example of a small community which existed around a single employing institution. In 1855, Foster, who is reported to have been an amateur French horn player earlier in the century, created a brass band, apparently from the barely smouldering embers of the old village band. The *Huddersfield Observer* noted that Foster had provided each of the principal requisites – (valved) instruments, a room in which to practice, a band teacher and uniforms.[68] The essential price for Foster's altruism was that the band should henceforth be known as the Black Dyke Mills Band; it is doubtful whether he anticipated that, despite the high quality of his textiles, the mill would become more famous for its band.

The story of the Black Dyke Mills Band is exceptional because the band's achievements are so exceptional, but it offers a neat illustration of several features that were common to bands of its type. It was formed in a small community rather than a large conurbation. It was to Foster an act calculated to 'improve' his workpeople. Many more of the Foster family's gestures in the nineteenth century were aimed at expanding the cultural base of the community: the building of an Albert Memorial outside the mill gates within eighteen months of the consort's death, the provision of a school, a library, a modestly ornate 'Victoria Hall'. Indeed, the adoption of the name Queensbury instead of Queenshead (the name of one of the local public houses) was a part of the same process. It also provides a good example of the acuteness of change between brass bands and their immediate predecessors which make theories of continuity in small town music making through the nineteenth century seem questionable. Though Wharton's band is known to have existed in 1816 and though there was some sort of musical activity in the village in the years immediately prior to 1855, there is little evidence of continuous musical activity through the first half of the century. Within a few years of its formation, the Black Dyke Mills Band was playing transcriptions of Italian opera in major contests. To draw a causal relationship between the old village band and the 1855 band is analogous to claiming that the motor car was the direct descendant of the bicycle.

Subscription bands, which became more and more numerous as the century progressed, were often started from scratch. Notices were posted in the village of Lynn in Norfolk in November 1853 which announced 'a public meeting' at the Town Hall 'precisely to take into consideration the propriety of forming a sax-horn band, when the attendance of all persons favourably disposed towards such an object amongst the working class of society is respectfully invited'.[69] By 1855, the Lynn Working Men's Band was firmly in existence, playing quadrilles in the town's 'commodious room' to collect money for 'coals for the poor'. In August 1853, a 'Grand Musical Fête' was held at the Pomona Gardens, Cornbrook, for the benefit of the City Royal Brass Band.[70] The Accrington Band was a subscription band which, as early as 1842, was successful in getting enough money from local gentry to buy instruments.[71] Most bands eventually became subscription bands because as the century progressed they relied less on direct patronage and more on homespun entrepreneurship.

VIII

The relationship between the volunteer movement and the brass band movement is complex and intriguing. Contest reports testify to the number of bands that, from as early as 1860, carry the names of volunteer corps. Many of these bands existed under different names before the formation of volunteer corps, but others, probably a minority, had their origins in the volunteer movement.

By the 1850s, the perceived threat of invasion by a foreign force had grown to proportions that could not be ignored – this period has been termed 'the second scare'. Two factors sharpened concern. The first was the strength of the French armed forces. Franco-British tensions seldom subsided during the century and were heightened by the foreign policy of Napoleon III. The second cause of concern was that, though the British armed forces were large, well equipped and trained, a significant proportion of them were, at any one time, abroad defending and enlarging the Empire. The militia were re-established by the Militia Act of 1852, but seven years later steps were taken to constitute a widely dispersed home volunteer force. On 12 May 1859, Jonathan Peel, Secretary of State for War, sent a circular letter to the Lord Lieutenants of all counties instructing them to form a force of volunteers. The 'principal and most important provisions' were that volunteers would 'be liable to be called out in case of actual invasion' and that while under arms they 'would be bound by military law'.[72] Thirteen days later, Peel circulated a second letter, softer in approach and more sensible of the pragmatisms of recruitment:

> The conditions of service should be such, while securing and enforcing the above necessary discipline, to induce those classes to come forward for service as volunteers who do not . . . enter into the regular army or militia . . . Drill and instruction for bodies of volunteers should not be such as to render the service unnecessarily irksome.[73]

There was no necessity for an Act of Parliament to establish the 1859 volunteers. The terms of the 1804 Yeomanry and Volunteers Consolidation Act were invoked. Volunteers were exempted from the militia ballot but were required to receive military training and attend twenty-four drills a year.

From the beginning, bands were seen as a desirable and, to many, an essential part of the volunteer movement. They had a practical use at drills and they afforded a sense of occasion to special events such as 'annual reviews'. In many respects they authenticated or at least gave an air of authenticity to the activities of the volunteers as they strove for a serious military image with all of the necessary resonances of imperialism and patriotism. They were also valuable in promoting good relations between volunteer corps and communities. No provision was made for the funding of bands by the government through the War Office. It is obvious, however, that moneys paid in the 'capitation grant', the official mechanism for government funding, were being secreted to pay for bands and soon the issue of volunteer banding became controversial. Within a year of the foundation of the first corps, a correspondent to *The Times* criticized the extravagance of the movement which, he feared, would be 'the rock on which it is likely to split':

> The expenses of some corps are enormous 400 l or 500 l; being expended on their bands . . . Now, bands ought to be viewed as luxuries, and paid for, as is done in some cases, not out of the funds of corps, but by a special subscription.[74]

Many bands were formed by the volunteers from scratch and, of these, most were probably funded in the proper way by private subscription. A popular way of raising money was to impose on officers an annual subscription over and above the normal corps subscription (as a rule, about 10 guineas a year), specifically for the band fund.[75] Concerts were also held to raise funds. A graphic account of how bands were formed within the spirit of the standing orders was given by Charles E. Murray, Captain commanding the 16th Middlesex Rifles, in a response to *The Times* letter quoted above. 'Marching out without a band', he said, 'would become a dismal business':

> Out of some 30 applicants . . . I have formed a band of 17 performers . . . from a separate subscription I have furnished them with instruments and clothes and given them paid instruction.
>   The terms on which they serve are
>
> 1 They are attested members of the corps.
> 2 On leaving, they are bound to resign their instruments, etc.
> 3 They agree (beside meetings for practice) to play once a week at 6pm at HQ.
> 4 If wanted for a whole day, for instance for the great review, then and only then to be paid for loss of time.[76]

Warren —

herewith my book
on bands we mentioned
a couple of times.
No rush on it.   L.

How's Walter? I'd
like to send him best
wishes but not sure
of the best way. Phone this home?
                        Write a note?

Murray emphasized that the men were 'respectable' and, he added: 'As to position in life they are of the tradesmen and respectable artisan class'. He hoped that 'unpaid bands may become as general as they are possible'. However, many bands were paid and directly engaged by corps to perform the duties of volunteer bands. In 1874, the Penrith Volunteer Band was costing its corps £52 a year and the Whitehaven Band £74 a year.[77] In the 1880s, the Dobcross Band was demanding £60 a year to wear the mantle of 'Band of the 34th West Yorkshire Volunteers'.[78]

In 1861 at least ten of the entrants to the Crystal Palace contest carried the name of a Rifle Volunteers Corps. The well-established band of W. L. Marriner from Keighley openly referred to themselves as 'W. L. Marriner's Band, also the Band of the 35th Rifle Volunteer Corps'. A year later they were again calling themselves 'W. L. Marriner's Private Brass Band'. The 1st West Yorkshire Volunteer Fire Brigade Guards was the same band which a year earlier had entered as the Flush Mills Band from Heckmondwike.[79]

The patriotic element of volunteering afforded it the status of a rational recreation; but the discipline of volunteer corps was variable. There was sustained and stout defence of volunteering in the establishment press, but there was much to defend, not only the behaviour but also the incompetence of some corps. In 1861, volunteers at Exeter 'by some strange oversight . . . forgot to keep their sponge wet' and were 'horribly disfigured' by the resulting explosion.[80] There were regular reports of volunteers being accidentally killed when 'on the march' and the *Volunteer Gazette*, in one of its regular reports of such incidents, mentioned the 'unfortunate occurrence' of a young boy being shot while the 3rd Cheshire Rifles were practising.[81]

Men who carried arms and attended a specified number of drills were termed 'effectives'. Bandsmen were not classed as effectives unless they had satisfied the relevant requirements. Some bands contained no effectives, because of the camouflage of their funding, particularly where they were no more than civilian bands which were contracted in. Despite the desirable qualities that these bands had, they were a mixed blessing, as it was often impossible to impose military discipline on them. A correspondent to the *Volunteer Service Gazette* in 1868 who signed himself 'a commissioned officer of the volunteers', described bands as 'one of the main causes of the disgrace which has recently fallen on the volunteer force'. He had found at camp a volunteer band marching along with 'a train of boys and girls kicking up a dust' and had later found the same men in a railway train where they were using 'disgraceful language and were too drunk to stand'. Some had challenged a fellow passenger to a fight. He added:

> I think that this incident shows that it is from the bandsmen of some corps that the volunteers get into disrepute. They are notorious for straggling away from their corps and feeling themselves under no sort of constraint and acknowledging no authority whatsoever.[82]

Volunteer bands were not always impartial in radical and political activities. In August 1868, the Band of the 2nd Cambridgeshire RVC allegedly escorted the Liberal candidate at Wisbech and in July 1873, the Band of the 5th Fife Artillery Volunteers illegally participated in a trade union demonstration. The 1st

Worcestershire AV Band gave a concert in aid of the Conservative Working Men's Association at Newport, and in August 1883 a volunteer band at Renfrew allegedly took part in a procession of the Orange Grand Black Chapter in Glasgow.[83] A worse incident took place in the outskirts of Liverpool in September 1883 when two volunteer units fought each other; the fight was apparently caused by a volunteer band deliberately playing a tune which inflamed an Irish mob.[84]

An 1862 Royal Commission on the volunteers[85] concluded that there was too much emphasis on the social activities which seemed to be the real reason why many joined the corps. The social side of the volunteers can be, at least in part, traced back to the second of Peel's 1859 circular letters to Lord Lieutenants of counties which strongly inferred that volunteer duties should be enjoyable and, in the best sense, recreational. While the volunteer movement was regarded as serious and important – reports of volunteer activities were regularly featured in *The Times* and usually stressed the formal functions of the movement – it is evident that the recreational aspect persisted. This ambiguity surrounding the image of the volunteer movement continued in the 1860s and 1870s and the bands often acted as a focus for these controversies.

The relationship of the volunteer corps to the brass band movement in the nineteenth century is probably more important than is generally realized. Some proof of this is revealed in the 1878 Departmental Committee Report on the Volunteer Force of Great Britain, chaired by Lord Bury.[86] For the Bury Report, all volunteer corps in the country were circulated with a questionnaire that asked them to detail under a number of separate headings the average expenditure over the five-year period from 1873 to 1877. Of the 278 returned questionnaires, all but a handful admitted that they supported bands. It was in the interests of the various corps to understate band expenditure and it is certain that the estimates under this heading were lower than actual spending. However, many returns show that the support of a band was a major financial item. Some officers who were called to give evidence to the Commission admitted to spending a large part of the capitation grant on bands. Lieutenant Colonel J. A. Thompson of the 1st Fifeshire Light Horse VC was challenged:

> Your band cost you 10*s.* a man: that is a heavy item to come out of the capitation grant: it was £62 last year for 119 men – that takes up the whole equipment fund . . . it runs away with your capitation money.[87]

To which the officer replied: 'Yes, it does'. Captain and Adjutant Ball of the 1st Middlesex Engineer Volunteer Corps admitted to an average annual expenditure of £280 on the band. When asked for particulars of that expenditure, he replied:

> we pay a bandmaster. That expenditure will be lower in the future. We have a new system. We give the bandmaster £12 a year and he provides instruments, clothing and everything for the band. We enrol any men that he likes and we give him the capitation grant for those men. If he has 30 men he can draw the capitation allowance.[88]

Major Sloan of the 4th Lancashire RVC declared an expenditure of £105 and further pleaded that the band 'should be exempt from firing as the buglers are.

Their attendance as bandsmen qualifies them for efficiency as far as drill is concerned'. He suggested no substitute of duties: 'We have as good a band as we can get . . . but they look upon firing as a heavy task . . . to keep up a good band is one of our difficulties and a good band is necessary in order to get recruits.'[89]

The need for corps to have good bands was not disputed but issues concerning their discipline and funding remained a major subject of contention. Ralph H. Knox, deputy accountant general at the War Office, who was also a lieutenant in the 2nd Middlesex RVC, cited bands as one of the three principle causes for excess expenditure on volunteer corps (the other two were extra pay to permanent staff and county associations). J. R. A. MacDonnal, editor of the *Volunteer Service Gazette*, suggested that the cost of bands should be exclusively borne by commanding officers. Bury concluded: 'No allowance for bands is made in the disembodied period for any branch of the auxiliary forces, any expense under this head being defrayed by private subscription. The Committee cannot advocate any allowance under this head.'[90] In 1887, the Harris Departmental Committee, being sympathetic to the problems of recruiting officers because of the costs required of them for 'balls, bands, refreshments and so on', and noting the recent changes in the funding of regular army bands, recommended that 7.5 per cent of the capitation grant be made for the funding of bands.[91] However, this recommendation was not acted on until the end of the century.

The repertory of volunteer bands was not strikingly different from that of civilian, contesting bands. The type of music they were required to play at drills, primarily marches, was a standard feature of the non-volunteer band repertory and there is sufficient evidence of volunteers playing at band contests and concerts to conclude that when volunteer bands were brass bands, and many of them probably were, their musical identity was barely distinguishable from that of their non-volunteer counterparts.

Notwithstanding the controversies that surrounded the behaviour and discipline of a proportion of bands, others probably benefited from the patriotic and respectable associations of volunteering. The material results of such associations manifested themselves most potently in the band funds. It was in the economics of banding in the nineteenth century that the volunteer force had its impact. It provided a ready source of financing for instruments and bandmasters; drill halls very often doubled as bandrooms and the provision of uniforms was an additional bonus.

Apart from those bands which owed their foundations to the volunteer movement, many were either saved or revived by it. The Bacup Band, after disintegration and amalgamation, were reconstituted to great effect in 1859 as the 4th Lancashire Rifle Volunteers (see Plate 3).[92] The Oldham Band, formed in 1865, became Oldham Rifles in 1871 and was enormously successful under Alexander Owen. The volunteers were also responsible for stimulating interest in banding in areas of the country distant from the industrial North. In Sussex, for example, the Arundel Band were maintained for years as the 2nd Administrative Battalion Royal Sussex Rifle Volunteer Regiment and there were similar stories at Rudgwick, East Grinstead and Crawley.[93]

Plate 3 : Band of the 4th Lancashire Rifle Volunteers (later Bacup Old Band) in October 1865. This was the pre-eminent brass band in the period 1862–71. Its instrumentation was typical for this period, though the use of an alto trombone was old-fashioned. (*Source: Mr Thomas Lord, Bacup.*)

IX

The volunteer movement created and saved many brass bands in the second half of the nineteenth century. This was a time when their number multiplied further, when public interest in them was at its height and when brass band contests were important not just to the movement but to the entire fabric of popular music culture. The period has appropriately been called the 'Golden Age'. It was also a period when the commercial pressures of the brass instrument and sheet music industry were at their most impressive. The pressures exerted by the forces of commerce were adequately matched by brass bands with organized, lucid and entirely rational strategies for self-determination and economic independence.

From the late 1850s the costs of musical instruments fell. This was due partly to the removal of protective import tariffs such as the 1860 Cobden–Chevalier treaty and partly to increased trade volume and a higher level of competition among domestic manufacturers and retailers. Cyril Ehrlich has illustrated the way in which the prices of woodwind and string instruments decreased in the second half of the nineteenth century;[94] a similar picture emerges for brass instruments. In 1839 D'Almaine was advertising cornopeans at prices between £5.12s.6d. and £8.8s.0d.; in 1840 Charles Pace was charging £8 and £10 for cornopeans. In about 1873, Boosey & Co., trading as Distin, were offering a 'new model cornet in B♭' for £3.3s.0d. Even in 1889, Joseph Higham was able to advertise new cornets at £3.3s.0d.[95] It is true that these prices were for the cheapest models, but even the more luxurious versions were not beyond the means of a reasonably successful, enterprising band. It is often difficult to determine the actual price of brass instruments in this period. All purchasers seem to have benefited from a Byzantine system of discounting. Cash, cheques, deferred payments and any other means of payment were discounted. There must also have been a huge market for second-hand instruments, for while many bands started up and flourished in the second half of the century, many folded up after a few years.

There was no precedent for the quantity of instruments that were available. By 1895, Bessons employed 131 men in their London factory making 100 brass instruments a week. Between 1862 and 1895 they produced 52,000 brass instruments. Joseph Higham employed 90 men who produced 60,000 instruments between 1842 and 1893.[96]

From the middle of the century, hire-purchase schemes were available. In 1855, the Bradford Brass Band was engaged in a hire-purchase agreement,[97] and as the century progressed many others entered into similar agreements. At the end of the century, Algernon Rose observed that 'the credit system has become the very basis of the brass band'.[98] Brass instrument manufacturers used several ploys to persuade people to buy brass instruments or exchange their current ones for newer 'improved' models. The award of new instruments as contest prizes for 'the best soloists of the day' was a calculated effort in this direction. Instruments were often advertised not just as new models but as entirely different systems and designs. New and improved valve systems were being introduced, each one claiming to be better than the others. As Arnold Myers explains later in this book, there was a genuine problem with the way some valve designs affected intonation, especially on larger instruments. Manufacturers frequently claimed to have produced a definitive solution to the problem and turned their endeavours to searching for suitable superlatives to explain its excellence. The advertising explosion was not confined to Britain. In the USA Ernst Albert Couturier, a cornet virtuoso who had made a name for himself with Gilmour, employed autobiographical sketches to endorse instruments:

> One night before I was to play solos with *le Garde Republicaine* in Paris, I did five miles at a dog trot in driving rain. I had been practising for five hours daily on my European tour. The next night, as I stood before the audience, waiting for the conductor's nod, a question assailed me. 'Why is it', I thought, 'that, train as we may for breath control, and practice as we will for technical perfection, we brass players must remain at the mercy of an imperfect instrument?'[99]

Some manufacturers offered cash incentives to those who won contest prizes using their instruments. In the 1890s, Silvani and Smith were offering the first band to win a first prize at the Belle Vue Contest, Manchester, using 'a complete set of their instruments', a reward of £50 in cash. Manufacturers also placed great store on the endorsement of leading army bands, and on the awards of prizes at international inventions exhibitions. Besson's proud boast in 1888 was that it had won 42 highest honours from international exhibitions and 39 medals of honour awarded to 'the Besson prototype band instruments', including one award which was 'the ONLY medal ever awarded for TONE quality. Another proof of the incontestable superiority of the prototype instruments'.[100] Attempts were also made late in the century to seduce bands to the latest fashions. An example of this was the persuasion by manufacturers on bands to convert from a brass to a 'silver' band. This meant nothing more than that the brass instruments were subjected to a process of electro-silver plating. This process added considerably to the cost of instruments and in 1892 the Pendleton Brass Band paid the high price of £339.14s. for a set of 24 ESP instruments from Besson.[101]

There were a variety of ways by which bands met the costs of buying instruments and otherwise sustaining themselves. In his *Talks with Bandsmen*, Algernon Rose advocated a procedure by which aspiring bandsmen could approach their employer for his support by supplying them with a model letter:

> Dear Sirs,
>   We, the undersigned, being desirous of employing our leisure time in practising music, request your permission to form a brass band in connection with this factory. We shall feel honoured if [you] will consent to become President of the Band. Unfortunately, we are unable at the beginning to defray the entire cost of the purchase of instruments. Messrs. [Bessons] are prepared to sell us the brass instruments required, provided that the firm, whose name we should like to take, will act as surety for the deferred payments.
>   We are, dear sir, yours respectfully[102]

Rose was probably describing a practice that was well established and it is interesting that his advice was to procure guarantees, not sponsorship. As I have said earlier, a number of bands were the recipients of direct patronage by industrial entrepreneurs, but it is doubtful if this type of practice was extensive. R. T. Crawshay, as far as we know, was only loaning instruments and facilities to the members of his band. His cash books contain indications of regular payments *to* Crawshay from the bandsmen 'for instruments', suggesting that they were repaying loans.[103] It was much more usual, particularly towards the end of the century, for bands to rely on entrepreneurial income and subscriptions. Subscriptions came from the members of the bands themselves; for example, W. L. Marriner's Band at Keighley, Yorkshire, as early as 1842, was imposing monthly subscriptions on its members.[104] Special expenditures, such as the purchase of new instruments, caused bands to issue appeals for general subscriptions. In 1866, the Llanelly Band purchased a set of fifteen instruments at 'the lowest trade price of £75.16.3'. This amount was raised as follows:

Subscriptions at the start of the band	£36. 2. 6
Concert, November 1885	£ 7. 3. 2
Athletic Sports, June 1886	£13.16.11
Balance	£ 1.13. 7 [*sic*][105]

The Band also carried a balance of £14 made up from subscriptions from the members for 'current expenses'. Events like concerts were enormously important in the economics of nineteenth-century banding. The St George's Works Brass Band, Lancaster, in 1885, operated on a monthly balance of about £4. This amount included total contributions of about 4s. to 7s. a week from members. But the collection or fee for a single concert would raise almost £4 in one evening.[106] Seaside bands at major resorts were often professional. They operated on much larger balances, up to about £500, but their funding was based on the same principles. The Llandudno Promenade Band, for example, on Saturdays in August 1874 was collecting amounts between £25 and £27 a day.[107] Apart from the costs of upkeep of instruments and uniforms and necessities such as heating, lighting and sometimes hiring rehearsal rooms, the other regular items of expenditure were the fees to conductors. These often came to about 5s. a week. The cost of journal music was another regular expense. Journals varied in price but bands spent between 1s. and 2s. per issue per month. In the 1880s, *Wright & Round's Journal* cost between 19s. and £1.9s.6d. a year.

A substantial source of income for the major bands was prize money from contests. The more successful of them such as Besses o' th' Barn and Black Dyke measured their winnings in pounds, shillings and pence. In the first thirty years of its contesting career, Besses o' th' Barn had won prizes to the total value of £3,359.17s.[108] Prize money varied according to the status of the contest. Small contests, like the ones at Clitheroe, Middleton and Rochdale, were worth between £5 and £7; larger ones were worth a lot more. Belle Vue paid about £35 plus benefits to the winners in the 1870s. For winning the 1887 contest, Kingston Mills Band received a cash prize of £30, a euphonium valued at £30 [*sic*] and each member of the band won gold medals to a total value of £78.15s.[109] Many bandsmen received direct payments for playing in concerts and contests. Even the smaller bands in the South-East of England charged 2s. or 3s. per player plus a free dinner for their services.[110] It is likely that the unsavoury scenes that followed disputed results at contests in the latter part of the century were caused as much by the injuries that the bandsmen felt to their wallets as to their pride.

X

Mid- and late-Victorian bands were able to exercise strict and successful control of their finances because most were constituted on fairly democratic lines and adhered to lucidly expressed sets of rules and regulations. Most of the surviving band constitutions exhibit prominent concern for the proper handling of money. Subscription rates were fixed and outgoings carefully policed. One senses a certain pride in the authorship of such documents; they are often self-consciously detailed, little is left to doubt or chance. Many bands engaged solicitors to draw up their deeds and constitutions. Even small enterprises such as the Maelor Brass Band League near Wrexham, whose sole purpose seems to have been to run an annual contest with a cup as a prize and which would be entirely constituted if two bands entered, went to the trouble of engaging a leading local solicitor to draw up a lengthy trust deed which was attested by all of the proper deed and stamp duties.[111]

The most remarkably forward-looking and entrepreneurial band of the nineteenth century was the Besses o' th' Barn Band from Whitefield, Lancashire, which in 1887, with all the necessary legal proprieties, formed itself into a limited company. It is generally assumed that the band had started as Clegg's Reed Band in or by 1818. John Clegg was a local cotton manufacturer and keyed bugle player. Privately owned documents relating to Besses o' th' Barn include a set of 'Articles' of the 'Stand Band', dated 1828. The leader is named as Thomas Lee, who is known from other sources to be associated with the early years of the Besses o' th' Barn band. The instrumentation of the Stand Band is not revealed in the Articles, but James Melling is named as a committee member – possibly the same man who wrote *Orynthia* (see p. 42). The remarkable thing about the Articles is their detail and rigour, matching most documents of this type composed later in the century. Assuming that Stand Band was Besses under an earlier name, it indicates a long history of self-government, discipline and careful administration. The Band had been extremely successful and 1887, the year of Victoria's jubilee, brought a flood of engagements and contest successes which gave it sufficient faith in its musical and entrepreneurial abilities to engage the Manchester solicitors, Alfred Grundy and Son, to draw up and prove the necessary documentation. The company was called the 'Besses o' th' Barn Old Band Union Limited'. It had already bought a 'club' building which was the registered office. The object of the company was 'to establish and maintain a brass band . . . and to sell, improve, manage, develop and maintain the property of the band . . . to invest the monies of the band . . . and do what else was required to further the objects'. The fourth article of the company concerned the income from contests and concerts:

> To enter and play at Brass Band Contests in Great Britain and Ireland; to acquire money by playing for remuneration in any other manner and to get up, conduct, and carry out any concert or other entertainment, or to join any other company, society, or person in carrying out the aforesaid objects.[112]

Because bands were fastidious over record-keeping, the sources that have survived and are available show that the practice of paying players was common. Band account books often record the distributions between members of takings from contests and engagements. The records of Marriner's Band, Keighley, leave little doubt that players were being paid at a time when they were taking part in contests (contests usually outlawed professionalism) and a written agreement drawn up between the Idle and Thackley Band in 1898 and Willie Hawker is entirely explicit:

> Willie Hawker does herby [*sic*] agree to give the whole of his services as solo Trombonist to the above band for 12 Calendar months at a sum of £5.0.0. And that he receives all engagement moneys when other members do . . .[113]

It is important to stress that band rulebooks show evidence of wider concerns than financial ones. They are laced with safeguards for the democratic processes, but most delegate musical authority to the bandmaster or conductor. St George's Works Band delegated 'All power . . . to the bandmaster during practice'[114] and the Idle and Thackley Band allowed 'the Bandmaster for the time being . . . [to] have full control over all the members of the band and if any member or members disobey him, or otherwise misbehave himself shall be fined'.[115] Musical and social indiscipline were guarded against. Idle and Thackley Band would 'expel any member for misconduct or for not being musically gifted enough to become a good player in the band'. Bands also legislated to promote the ethos of social harmony and co-operation that many of the rational recreationalists held in such high regard. The rules of W. L. Marriner's Caminando Band, perhaps not surprisingly, provide a good example of this:

> As this brass band is formed for mutual amusement and instruction in music, and, as peace and harmony are essential to its welfare, it is highly requisite that no dispute or angry feeling should arise among its members, therefore for the prevention of any such occurance [*sic*], the following rules and regulations have been adopted.[116]

This sentiment was enforced by Rule 7 of the Band's regulations which threatened to impose upon its members 'for every oath or angry expression, a penalty of 3/-'.

The primary reason why nineteenth-century bands were so well organized is that they had to be in order to survive. From the moment a band entered into a hire-purchase agreement it was bound to a debt that could only be repaid if it was organizationally and musically successful. Such pressures were intensified if the guarantor of the loan was the employer of most or all of the band's members. Working men's associations, mechanics institutes and the friendly societies provided experience in and models for the organization of bands.

Another factor which encouraged the formality of the business organization of bands were the rules and regulations that surrounded contests (see, for example, Plate 4). The earliest entrepreneurial contests were primarily aimed at entertainment. As the movement gathered pace the seriousness and fervour of contestants had to be accommodated by careful legislation. Such legislation was further supported by the formation, later in the century, of band associations. Controversies concerning musical matters were sometimes eclipsed by financial arguments and there was tension between those who wished to develop genuine amateurism and the well-established contesting bands whose members had grown used to having their incomes supplemented by share-outs of contest prizes. In 1893, Thomas Valentine, representing Besses o' th' Barn, Wyke Temperance and Kingston Mills, three bands who had a lot to lose from the imposition of pure amateurism, wrote to *The Cornet* in response to 'The Proposed National Amateur Brass Band Association':

> It has been mentioned to me that several Contests are intended to be held next year on still stricter rules than at the recent Blackpool contest – that is to say, no paid players of any kind to compete, and as this affects more or less every band of note I HEREBY CALL A MEETING . . . [to take steps] to protect such bands.[117]

In 1903, the issue of payment to contesting bandsmen was still prominent. The organizers of a new contest at Huddersfield felt that it was a matter that had to be settled before any progress could be made. The contest secretary frankly admitted:

> We cannot get a really big entry with the present system of shut playing bands (and their conductors) look upon it as an engagement & so it is, without any pay [*sic*]. They don't like the principle of it, this is what they kick against. I believe if we only gave 6*d*. to each bandsman we should have a bigger entry.[118]

PEEL PARK, BRADFORD.

Grand Double Brass Band Contest.

The Committee respectfully announce that a DOUBLE CONTEST, open to all First Class and Amateur Bands in England, will take place in the above Park

On SATURDAY, SEPTEMBER THE 1st, 1860.

SIXTY POUNDS WILL BE GIVEN IN PRIZES:

FIRST CONTEST.

(Open to all Amateur Bands who have not gained a Prize of £10 or upwards.)

FIRST PRIZE	...	...	...	£12
SECOND Do.	...	...	...	8
THIRD Do.	...	...	...	5
FOURTH Do.	...	...	...	3
FIFTH Do	...	...	...	2

REGULATIONS.

1. Each Band intending to compete shall pay an entrance fee of ten shillings and sixpence on or before WEDNESDAY, the 22nd August, and shall forward to the Secretary the name and address of their Leader, and also the number of Performers.
2. No person shall play with more than one Band during the Contest, and no man shall be allowed to play in a Band who has not been a Member at least three months.
3. No Professional Musician allowed to play with or conduct any Band, and no Clarionets allowed.
4. The number of performers in each Band shall be not less than thirteen, or more than eighteen.
5. No Professional or Military Bands allowed.
6. Each Band shall play from the town to the Park, and be in the Park punctually at Two o'clock. The Leaders shall then proceed to draw lots to decide the order in which the respective Bands shall play. The Contest to commence at Three o'clock.
7. Each Band shall play one piece of their own selection, the name of which, together with the name of the composer, shall be sent along with the entry.
8. The whole of the Bands performing in this Contest shall play "Rule Britannia," at the close; and all Bands performing in both Contests shall, unitedly, at the close of second Contest, play the "National Anthem," previous to the award of the Judges being made known.
9. Two Judges and an Umpire shall be appointed none of them to be resident within forty miles of Bradford. In case of dispute between the Judges or the Bands, the Umpires decision to be final. Their names shall not be published until after their decision has been given.
10. The Judges shall decide on a *first hearing*, and no repetition of pieces be allowed except in cases of unavoidable accident.
11. The Prizes shall be paid to the respective Leaders, according to the decision of the Judges, before leaving the ground.
12. Any Band neglecting any of the above Regulations, or making false representations, shall forfeit their entrance fee, and lose all right to play in the Contest.

The Bands gaining the First and Second Prize in this Contest shall be at the service of the Committee until Nine o'clock; and all the Bands engaged in the Contest will be under the superintendence and direction of Mr. Thomas Davy, both in the Town and Park.

N.B. The enclosed form to be filled up by the Bands and addressed to Mr. Fred. Tuke, 12, Queensgate, Bradford.

Plate 4 Bradford Brass Band Contest Regulations, 1860. Contest regulations varied but not very much. The rules for this contest are similar to many that are found in the same period. (*Source: West Yorkshire Archive Service.*)

Contests offered material rewards and acted as forums for the entire brass band movement. This was particularly important before the advent of specialist magazines which, when they were introduced from the 1880s, served to intensify the interest in contests and underline their importance. It would be grotesquely unfair, though, to characterize the significance of contests as uniquely or even primarily financial. The most important aspects of contesting were musical and these matters are discussed below. Contests at a more general level engendered feelings of pride, not just among the members of bands but among the people of the communities in which they resided. The most enduring image of contesting bands in the late nineteenth century emanates from their earnestness and seriousness of resolve. The hackneyed image of a red-faced bandsman contentedly puffing at a Bb bass in the upstairs room of a public house while a pint of beer waits under his chair is a hopeless misrepresentation of the truth. Contesting bands were single-mindedly and determinedly in pursuit of excellence.

XI

There are three types of source that cast light upon brass band repertory in the nineteenth century: the printed sources, the surviving manuscript part books, and miscellaneous documentary sources such as concert programmes. Examples of each of these types of sources survive in archives and private collections throughout Britain. The printed repertory, includes solos, quartets, brass and military band journals and the printed so-called 'standard instrumentation' repertory which appeared later in the century. These are important because they represented examples of the relationship between publishers and a wide social audience. The bands were no more than executants of this type of repertory. Published music for early brass bands started to appear in the 1830s. Mac-Farlane's *Eight Popular Airs for Brass Band* was released in 1836. In 1837 D'Almaine published *The Brass Band*, a set of popular pieces arranged by J. Parry, a former militia bandmaster and music critic of the *Morning Post*.[119] Parry's *Brass Band* was the mainstay of the W. L. Marriner's Band in the early 1840s. From about 1840 publishers started producing brass band journals. The first regular subscription journal for brass band is probably the one published by Wessel & Co.[120] Brass band journals were musical publications; they contained no text other than musical text. Bands subscribed to them and received up to twelve publications each year. The instrumentation was flexible; alternative parts were provided for different instruments. Wessel's journals in the 1840s were for solo cornet-à-pistons, 1st and 2nd cornet-à-pistons, two horns, three trombones and ophicleide with *ad libitum* parts for Db cornet-à-pistons or bugle, two horns, three trumpets and kettle drums. The arrangements were workmanlike and functional. They contained a mixture of light pieces and arrangements of art music. Military band journals were published independently of brass band journals. Several other publishers published band journals. Smith's *Champion Brass Band Journal* was published in Hull from 1857; Chappell, Distin, Jullien and Boosey published journals. Distin's journal which was published by Boosey from 1869 was

FOR A BAND OF TEN. – 1st Cornet in B flat; 2nd ditto; 1st Cornet in E flat; 1st and 2nd Tenors in E flat; Euphonion; Bombardon; Side and Bass Drums. The Euphonion and Bombardon parts may be had in either the Treble or Bass Clef.

Subscription: Ten shillings and Sixpence per Annum for Ten Performers (Postage Free in the United Kingdom), payable in advance. Price to Non-Subscribers: One Shilling each Number.

This Journal is arranged to suit a Band of any size, and extra Parts may be had for the following Instruments: Repiano Cornet in B flat; Cornets, 3rd and 4th, in B flat; Solo Tenor in E flat; 2nd Baritone in B flat; 1st and 2nd Trombones in B flat (either in the Treble or Bass Clef); Bass Trombone; and Contra-Bass in B flat. Price of extra or duplicate Parts Twopence each, or to Subscribers Three Halfpence.

There was also a considerable trade in the publication of solo and smaller ensemble pieces. In the mid-1840s, Boosey started publishing its *Repertory for Cornet and Piano*. These were mainly arrangements of operatic arias; they cost 3*s.* each. In 1847, Distin published a *Selection of the most Favourite Swedish melodies as sung by Md. Jenny Lind* for cornet-à-pistons, saxhorn or tuba with pianoforte accompaniment *ad lib.* Koenig's *Journal for Cornet-à-piston and Piano*, which was published by Chappell, eventually contained 140 items. Wessel also published *The Amateurs' Brass Band Quartets* (1852) for three cornet-à-pistons and ophicleide or valve trombone, and from about 1860 Robert Cock & Co. started publishing their *Brass Band Magazine*, costing 2*s.* per arrangement and apparently aimed at smaller bands of modest means and ability. By the early 1860s journals were mainly devoted to arrangements of Italian opera. In 1875, Thomas Wright and Henry Round started publishing a brass band journal in Liverpool. Later publications by this firm were to be very influential.

The surviving manuscript part books are crucially important to understanding the musical identity of bands. Whereas printed music indicates what a publisher saw fit to purvey, manuscript part books indicate what bands were actually playing. Though some 'Professors of Music' were advertising their services as arrangers of music for bands, most of the surviving sources are known to be in the hands of the resident bandmasters. These sources have a 'bespoke' quality. They indicate not just the titles in a band's repertory, but to a large extent, the technical ability of its players. Bandmasters would not have arranged music so that it was beyond the capabilities of their players, but they would have done their best to exhibit the outer limits of their techniques. The known surviving manuscript books are scattered; many sources of this type have yet to be traced and analysed. Among the major sources are the Goose Eye Band Books at Keighley in Yorkshire, the Black Dyke Mills Band Books at Queensbury in Yorkshire and, by far the most comprehensive and earliest complete run, the set at the Cyfarthfa Castle Museum in Merthyr Tydfil, South Wales. The Black Dyke Band Books are incomplete – only eight books survive, dating from not long after the Band was formed in 1855. They contain forty-three pieces, a mixture of dances (quadrilles, polkas and waltzes) and a number of Italian opera transcriptions. The Goose Eye Band music, dating from 1852, contains more than thirty pieces. The repertory here is of an entirely different order. Overwhelmingly, the emphasis is on light music – dances, song arrangements with a few arias, or chorus arrangements of art music. Five of the pieces – *Morning Star Polka, Bonnets of Blue, Rock Villa Polka, Lily Bell* and *The Light Horseman* – are attributed to the Hull composer, arranger and publisher, Richard Smith.[121]

Six sets of the Cyfarthfa Band Books survive in a total of 105 part books: each set is cumulative. Even this large collection is only part of the repertory. The music played in the 1840s, when the Band was in its early years, is lost. The pieces that survive can be dated no earlier than the mid-1850s. The collection is exceptional because it provides the largest coherent sample of surviving Victorian brass band music.[122] The pieces in the books can be categorized into three groups – dance music (quadrilles, polkas and waltzes are the most popular), transcriptions of art music (the most popular source is Italian opera), and miscellaneous religious and secular pieces that were of local interest (Welsh airs and so on).

Manuscript band parts, dating from later in the century, survive in band libraries and private collections. For example, the Besses o' th' Barn band library contains some of the operatic transcriptions by Alexander Owen and John Gladney. These sources, like many of the Cyfarthfa pieces, are particularly interesting because they contain the original interpretive annotations.

Although there are clear differences between, for example, the repertory at Keighley and that at Merthyr, there are similarities in the repertory of major bands. Most collections contain art music, popular pieces and what can be loosely described as functional tunes such as national anthems, Christmas carols and works which are idiosyncratic to particular localities. Original compositions for brass bands constitute a tiny proportion of the repertory. One is bound to ask what forces were at work to create these concordances. This question is best answered by looking not just at the manuscript music and printed parts but also at the original sources from which arrangements were made. I have already pointed to the increased availability of published music of all types available from the middle of the nineteenth century. Art music, particularly foreign art music in its pot-pourri form, was popular among the middle classes. Choral music, such as oratorio and major orchestral works, was also available at comparatively modest prices. Novello's publications, for example, were widely distributed. There was also a market for quadrilles, polkas, and waltzes in short score form produced for domestic pianists. Another type of music aimed, initially at least, at the middle-class market were piano arrangements of Italian opera extracts. British publishers lost no time in making Italian opera extracts available to the public. Verdi's *Il Trovatore* was first performed in Rome on 13 January 1853. In February 1853, *The Music Publishers' Circular No. 2* carried a 'Musical Announcement' from Boosey & Sons:

> Verdi's new opera *Il Trovatore*. This opera has just been produced in Rome, with the most extraordinary success, the composer having been called before the curtain fifteen times before the curtain during the performance – seven pieces now ready. The remainder of the opera is now in press.

It was probably from sources such as these that bandmasters and journal editors made their arrangements. James Smyth's brass band arrangement of the overture to *La Forza del Destino*[123] was in circulation within a few months of the opera's first performance at St Petersburg in 1862.

Brass band journals, which also emphasized operatic transcriptions, were, perversely enough, the source for further arrangements and transcriptions. It is known that some bands had copies of journals and also had manuscript arrangements of the pieces contained in those journals.[124] So it is likely, for example, that a band arrangement found in Merthyr Tydfil in the 1860s was fourth-hand via the composer's original, the short score, the journal arrangement and then the rearrangement by the bandmaster.

Although there is a great deal of similarity between the brass band repertory and middle-class musical tastes that ran parallel to it – art music, quadrilles, waltzes, certain 'coon' songs, and so on – there are certain types of popular Victorian music that seldom appear as arrangements for brass band. Few arrangements of music hall songs are found in brass band sources, but perhaps this is not surprising given the quest for respectability which underpins the brass band movement for most of the nineteenth century. Also, one seldom sees arrangements of domestic 'parlour song' even though this was hugely popular and was as widely available as the operatic repertory.

There are obvious reasons why contests contributed to the standardization of the repertory. The cross-fertilization of ideas brought about by the congregation of many brass bands had other effects. Such occasions provided opportunities for the creation of a common understanding of the musical idiom of the brass band and of the individual instruments in it. Many of the works that survive from the nineteenth century make enormous demands on players, not just in that they required players to show technical agility and wide dynamic and pitch ranges, but also considerable stamina. The players in the Cyfarthfa Band were required to play complete symphonies (all four movements) by Beethoven, Mozart and Haydn. Besses o' th' Barn Band, under Alexander Owen, were tested with selections from Italian opera which lasted for 35 or 40 minutes at a time.

In the last two decades of the century, the instrumentation that is still used by publishers of brass band music today – a mixture of cornets, saxhorn-type tenor and bass instruments and trombones – was formulated. Publishers, perhaps most influentially the Liverpool-based Wright and Round, following the practices of some of the major northern bands, moved towards and then established a common system of instrumentation. Confirmation of the widespread acceptance by contesting bands of this standard ensemble is found in theoretical publications later in the century such as Lodge's *The Brass Band at a Glance*, which not only lists the instruments used but also its clefs (treble for all instruments except trombones), transpositions and ranges.[125]

It would be wholly misleading, however, to gain the impression that brass bands became comprehensively uniform at this time. Ord Hume wrote in 1900 of 'the remote village band which is generally composed of an unlimited number, from ten upwards'. Such bands probably outnumbered the contesting bands with 'standard instrumentation'. 'Contesting', said Ord Hume, 'is in my opinion, the only way in which to raise the standard of moderate bands'. But many, even most, of these bands may never have competed. Their instrumentation varied as players left or joined. These bands were still playing from 'their favourite journals' and had enough of them to 'paper the walls of their band rooms with music'.[126] The Cyfarthfa Band was still playing and adding to its manuscript band books in 1908, although it was no longer a regular contest prizewinner. The music it added was as demanding as much of the rest of the repertory, showing that, in some cases at least, contest success was not the only indicator of technical ability.

The mediators of musical tastes among brass band people by the late 1840s were the middle classes. The repertoire played by the Distins and by Jullien's soloists usually, but not always, centred on dance music – particularly quadrilles, waltzes and polkas, which were the most popular dances of the period. Pieces such as these were turned out in vast numbers by various composers. Hundreds of middle-class institutions and topical events, were honoured by having a polka or quadrille named after them. Another popular practice was to base dance music on operatic themes. Thus titles like *Lucrezia Quadrille* (based on a theme from *Lucrezia Borgia*) and *Lucia Polka* (based on a theme from *Lucia di Lammermoor*) abound. Dance music found in brass band repertories can be taken as having two distinct meanings, both of which reflect their origins in middle-class tastes. First, the music was quite literally danced to. In Merthyr in the mid-nineteenth century the wagon sheds of Crawshay's ironworks were regularly transformed into sumptuous ballrooms[127] by decorating them with flowers, where the local dignitaries danced to the most popular music of the day played by the Cyfarthfa Band. It is likely that many of the very early 'brass' bands were, in effect, dance bands dedicated to this sort of function. However, quadrilles and more particularly polkas also formed the basis for instrumental virtuoso solos. In the same way that dance music was metamorphosed into the first independent 'absolute' instrumental music in the sixteenth century by being subjected to decoration, embellishment, division and other (initially) extemporized conventions, so polkas formed one of the first vehicles for cornet virtuosity through the application of the long-established but spectacular brass techniques of double and triple tonguing. It was to middle-class audiences and anyone else lucky enough to be in earshot that Koenig and the Distins performed such pieces and, though they set a standard that amateur players could not at first match, they imposed an impression of what virtuosity on brass instruments was and what type of music was associated with it. It is probably a coincidence that the polka was introduced into London in 1844, the same year as Adolphe Sax's instruments, but it is less likely that the involvement of Jullien in the popularity of both the instrument and the dance had much to do with chance.

From the 1850s, when, as has been seen, bands became much more prolific, the repertory and musical tastes tended to be shaped by three main forces: the bandmasters; the music publishers; and, to a lesser extent, the organizers of contests. Because the only people who bought brass band music were the bands, there is little direct evidence for the popularity of particular pieces or types of music among audiences. Music which was fun to play may not have been such fun to listen to. However, the frequency with which certain types of music – Italian opera, for example, and particular works such as selections from *Lucrezia*

Borgia – occur in printed and manuscript sources makes it difficult to draw any other conclusion than that such pieces were well received by the people who heard them. Contest promoters influenced the music and even the techniques of brass bands because they were the organizers of the events that gave bands their most conspicuous exposure. The music played at contests had to entertain and exhibit a particular *type* of virtuosity. Any brass player knows that one of the most difficult types of music to play is that which requires very slow movement across wide pitch intervals at a very quiet dynamic, but this type of virtuosity does not draw gasps of admiration. Spectacular runs over scalic passages does, however, have the desired effect.

From the time that brass bands were a common and widespread movement, their membership was largely made up of people of the skilled working classes. From about the same time, these same classes very quickly produced their own musical leaders. Conductors at the Crystal Palace contest of 1860 had to indicate their occupation on the contest forms. They included thirteen who describe themselves as 'professors', bandmasters, conductors, musicians, etc., but also there were three cloth-weavers, two overlookers and others who entered their occupation as innkeeper, lead-ore smelter, warp dresser, heald knitter, woollen spinner, publican, manufacturer, tailor, schoolmaster, mechanic, miner, cloth percher, blacksmith, carpet department [worker], joiner, cloth operative, and spade finisher.[128]

A number of highly distinguished and very influential brass band conductors emerged. Of the earlier conductors, James Melling, a Manchester-based 'music professor', enjoyed some prominence. He worked closely with the contest pro-moter, Enderby Jackson, on a number of projects. Melling was conductor of Stalybridge Old Band. He was reputed to be one of the main suppliers of manuscript music to Yorkshire bands in the 1840s and 1850s.[129] He was also a composer; his *Orynthia* was the test piece for the 1855 Belle Vue contest. This was the first time that a common test piece was set, although no copy of it is known to have survived.

Other conductors who were composers and arrangers came from the lower classes in the second half of the century. Enderby Jackson is best remembered as a promoter, but he was also a composer whose *Yorkshire Waltzes* (see Plate 5), *Bristol Waltzes*, *Venetian Waltzes* and *Volunteer Quadrilles* were specifically aimed at brass bands. A composer called J. Perry wrote marches for many Scottish contests in the nineteenth century, and in the Yorkshire textile district there were a number of prolific working-class composers of brass band music. These included Edward Newton, a textile worker who wrote and published over 300 marches; George Wadsworth, a monumental mason whose works made up a large part of the catalogue of the Rochdale publisher J. Frost & Son; and William Hesling, a weaver.[130]

Richard Smith, the publisher of *The Champion Brass Band Journal*, was a noted conductor. He was engaged by Titus Salt to train his Saltaire Band. By 1861 Smith was enough of a celebrity to earn a major profile in the *Illustrated News of the World*.[131] Another conductor who seems to have been particularly respected was George Ellis, who was associated with a number of bands but particularly

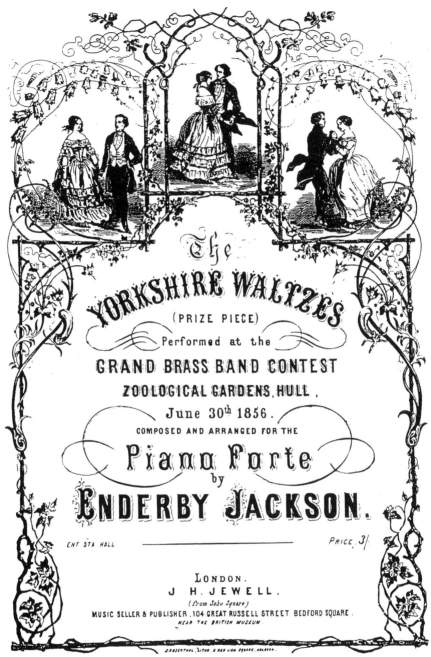

Plate 5 Enderby Jackson's *Yorkshire Waltzes*, 1856. The *Yorkshire Waltzes* was a brass band test piece, but the only surviving printed source is a piano arrangement. It is likely that Jackson's involvement finished with the completion of the piano part and local bandmasters arranged the music for their bands. (*Source: British Library.*)

with Bacup Band between 1869 and 1871, when it won thirteen consecutive contests.[132]

The three most important northern brass band conductors in the last quarter of the century were Alexander Owen, Edwin Swift and John Gladney; between them they dominated contests for decades. Gladney was the only one of the three who came from a musical family. He was born in 1839, the son of the bandmaster of the 30th East Lancashire Regiment. He started playing the flute at eight, the violin at nine, saw a great deal of service abroad and travelled with opera companies as a clarinet player. For some time he was the clarinet player and conductor of the Scarborough Spa Band.[133] He played the clarinet with the Hallé Orchestra in Manchester and this was his professional base until the end of the century. He was associated with many of the top bands.

The other two men had more humble origins. Alexander Owen was brought up in an orphanage in Swinton and was taught to play the cornet at an early age by a military bandmaster.[134] Edwin Swift was born in Linthwaite in 1843. He left school at the age of nine to become a shuttler, and he continued to work in mills until he was thirty-two years old. His first musical experience was in a drum and fife band; he then learned the cornet. He played for the Linthwaite Band and was principal cornet and bandmaster at the age of 14. He led Linthwaite to victory over Gladney's Meltham Mills Band in 1874.[135]

Gladney, Swift and Owen conducted and trained several bands. Other conductors spent their entire careers with just one. George Livesey, for example, conducted no band other than Cyfarthfa in the 50 years following his first association with it. Throughout the country there were distinguished musicians of working-class origins who exercised great influence on the musical life of the communities in which they worked.

XII

Although local band trainers and conductors contributed significantly to the fashioning of the brass band movement, there were other influences which were less direct but equally potent. In the second half of the nineteenth century, the music publishers exercised a considerable influence on musical taste; most were based in London. London was also the centre for almost all brass instrument manufacture. There were firms in the North of England but the most successful made London attachments. Richard Smith, whose Hull-based *Champion Journal* was so successful, was himself resident in London from 1878,[136] and Joseph Higham, who had traded since the 1840s from Victoria Bridge, Manchester, eventually had a London address. The most important exception to the metropolitan stranglehold on banding was the Liverpool firm of Wright and Round.

It has been argued that brass instrument manufacturing was based in London because London was the port of entry for raw materials. This argument is not entirely convincing. Several manufacturing industries in the North of England relied on raw materials that had to be transported across country from distant ports of entry. An alternative explanation as to why so much of the production of music and instruments for brass bands was based in London when so many of the bands were in the North and West is simply that the established London firms were successful in holding the market. A great deal of that success can be attributed to the close and not entirely ethical relationship between the publishing and manufacturing companies and the bandmasters of the regular army. Almost all of the regular army bandmasters had connections with the commercial side of brass banding. The army bandmasters were themselves involved in an uneasy relationship with the military. This unease emanated from two factors. First, there was concern over the number of foreign musicians who controlled army bands. Second, there was significant disquiet about the extent to which the civilian bandmasters were using their military associations in order to earn commissions from instrument manufacturers.

The initiators of this corruption were the instrument manufacturers who influenced the army appointment mechanisms by acting as agents between regiments and foreign bandmasters. *The Musical Times* was advertising Boosey's 'Register of Bandmasters' in 1854. Charles Boosey was prominent in these dealings. His position was made perfectly plain to a prospective bandmaster:

> We have but one stipulation to make with you if you accept a situation through our influence. We do not ask for any remuneration but we do expect you to support our Firm exclusively, that is to say you will send us all orders for any instruments etc. that you require, for we need not remind you that Bandmasters have considerable influence with officers.[137]

It was eventually clear to the office of HRH, the Commander in Chief, that the high cost of maintaining bands was due to commanding officers leaving 'their dealings with the instrument makers chiefly in the hands of bandmasters', and a letter from the Adjutant General to Commanding Officers dated 24 February 1858 recommended that in future any bandmaster who under any pretence whatever received discount fee remuneration or reward should be subject to instant dismissal. The same letter suggested that instead of using instrument manufacturers as their agents for the hiring of bandmasters, 'they would do better by advertising in the public papers'.[138]

The foundation of what eventually became the Royal Military School of Music at Kneller Hall was stimulated by this need to train more native-born bandmasters but these, too, were active and influential in the movement. From its first issue in 1887, *The British Bandsman* pointed to army bands as the standard to which amateur bands should aspire. Many of the full-time army band conductors were also the principal conductors of volunteer bands, for which they received significant rewards. Others adjudicated at band contests or arranged music for brass band test pieces. Regular army men had intimate links with publishers. The majority of the London-based band publications were edited by them. Chappell's journal was arranged by W. Winterbottom of the Royal Marines; Fred Godfrey of the Coldstream Guards was also involved with Chappell's; Wessell's had J. R. Tutton of the Royal Horse Guards on its staff; D'Almaine used J. G. Jones of the 16th Lancers; James Smyth of the Royal Marine Artillery also put out arrangements. The Godfrey family were particularly prodigious. Charles Godfrey of the Royal Horse Guards Band was responsible for arranging the test pieces for the Belle Vue contests every year for more than twenty years. Bandmasters occupied musical and social positions which were considerably higher than those occupied by musicians in the North of England and in other parts of the country distant from London. They were familiar with styles, repertoires and tastes that were fashionable in London and that were recently imported from abroad. Throughout the second half of the century these men occupied a pivotal position in musical life in Britain.

XIII

Many bands owe their origins to religious and moral movements whose ideals found easy accord with those of the rational recreationalists. Playing in a brass band was an improving activity that supposedly kept its members away from public houses and other centres of corruption. While abstinence movements promoted brass bands, the relationship between Sabbatarians and bands was tense because bands were often called upon to play in the open air on Sundays. Sunday was the one day of the week when most people of all classes had free time. The conflict was brought sharply into focus as early as the 1850s. In 1856, Parliament voted overwhelmingly to oppose the opening of the British Museum and National Gallery 'to promote the moral and intellectual improvement of the working classes' following morning service on Sundays. This injected new zeal into the Sabbatarians, who tried to extend prohibition to the performance of bands in London's pleasure gardens. At the vanguard of this movement was Edward Baines, a long-time and passionate advocate of Sabbatarianism. His *On the Performance of Military Bands in Parks on Sundays* was a lengthy and widely distributed tract which enjoined all people including the sovereign to ban Sunday open air music because:

> if it was right for bands to be performing in London, it cannot be wrong in any town or village in the kingdom . . . Such performances would cause admonishment, grief and indignation to fill the breasts of millions of Christians . . . the strains of martial music cause the pulse to bound and fire the imagination . . . crowds are sure to follow them and among these crowds arrayed in their Sunday finery thousands of young girls and young men with no more than the average amount of vanity and weakness will be brought into circumstances of extreme peril . . . Is there any Christian father or mother who would be willing to let their children or servants attend such scenes?[139]

Baines's attitudes were not broadly shared and many bands, brass and military, performed regularly on Sundays. In 1891 *The Orchestral Times and Bandsmen* noted that the Sunday performances of the Cyfarthfa Band in Merthyr Tydfil were 'a musical sermon'.[140]

Some bands had formal or loose attachments to Anglican churches and Nonconformist churches and chapels. The presence in the repertoire of Welsh bands such as the Cyfarthfa Band, for example, of sacred music may well be linked to the growth from the middle of the century of *Gymanfa Ganu*, the festivals of Welsh hymn-singing held at Whitsun and Easter in Welsh Nonconformist chapels.

Temperance and Rechabite movements were also prominent in banding and several bands can trace their origins directly to such organizations. Bramley Band, whose members pledged total abstinence in 1836, is credited as being the first temperance band.[141] They were one of two temperance bands which entered the first (1853) Belle Vue contest; the other was Mossley Temperance Saxhorn Band. Such bands were established throughout the country. In the Rhondda Valley, the band which became the Cory Workmen's Band was formed as the Ton Pentre Temperance Band. Further west, the Llanelly Band was formed from an abortive attempt to start up a Rechabite band. In Wyke, Yorkshire, the temperance band which became one of the most distinguished of the century was in direct opposition to the non-temperance 'old' band and suffered violence, threats and abuse to property from the latter's supporters.[142] Not all temperance bands were true to the ideals of the temperance movement. As bands became more efficient and successful, the major priority was the sustenance of musical standards and one can only contemplate the dilemma facing an ambitious temperance bandmaster confronted with a brilliant player who was smelling of drink.

The Salvation Army was the only religious denomination that absorbed brass bands to such an extent that they became one of the features that characterized it. The first Salvation Army band was formed in Salisbury by Charles Fry, a builder and Wesleyan who became a Salvationist. With his three sons he made up a brass quartet that played at a 'musical service' on 7 August 1878.[143] The idea quickly caught on. In 1879, a band was formed in Consett, followed in 1880 by others in Northwich, Nottingham, Hull and Whitechapel. The following year another fourteen towns in England, as far north as Carlisle and as far south as Exeter, had Salvation bands. By 1883, the *Salvation War* was claiming:

> the formation of hundreds of brass or other bands with over 5,000 instruments during this year is an event which must needs leave its influence on the future musical history of the country. The playing of these bands has been made a great ground of complaint against us everywhere but so far from there being any sign of them being objectionable, this is one of the surest evidences of their virtues.[144]

The author added hopefully: 'the simple truth is that the band empties the public houses far and near'. General Booth, who had long since espoused support for secular music in Salvationism, was supportive of bands. It was one thing, however, to have brass bands in the cause of Salvationism; it was quite another simply to have brass bands in the Salvation Army. The growth of independent, semi-professional brass bands, the controversies that had surrounded the relationship between bands and the volunteer forces and, perhaps, the independence of temperance bands from their original purpose, caused Booth to take steps that ensured that Salvationist bands would be discrete from the brass band movement for more than a hundred years. Early in 1881, little more than two years after the formation of the first Salvation band, he published ten directives to bands in the *War Cry*. These directives included instructions that:

> no-one will be admitted or retained a member of any band who is not a member of the Army . . . in no case are instruments to be used to play anything but Salvationist music . . . in no case will any committee be allowed in association with any band . . .

in cases where a treasurer or secretary is required by a band the treasurer or secretary of the corps to which it is attached shall act in that capacity.[145]

The separation of Salvationist banding from the brass band movement was consolidated in 1883 when Booth set up the Salvation Army Music Department. The original members of staff were Fred Fry (one of Charles Fry's sons), Richard Slater, a London-based violinist, and Henry Hill, a Hull police sergeant.[146] This led to the establishment of a publishing enterprise and within a year the first issue of *The Salvation Army Brass Band Journal* appeared.[147] In 1885, Bramwell Booth, the Chief of Staff, issued general orders respecting brass bands: 'from this date no band will be allowed to play from any music other than the Salvation Army General Band Book'.[148] In 1889, the enterprise widened to include the manufacture, repair and sale of musical instruments.[149]

There was no standard line-up in Salvationist bands and many retained clarinets until quite late in the century, but Salvationist bands were primarily brass bands (see Table 1).

The steps taken to separate Salvationist brass bands from the brass band

Table 1   There was no standard instrumental line-up for Salvationist bands. *The Musical Salvationist* (vol. 10, 1896, p. 47) published this table showing the instrumentation of 22 of its bands late in the nineteenth century.

	1	2	3	4	5	6	7	8	9	10	11	12	13	14	15	16	17	18	19	20	21	22
Soprano	—	—	—	—	—	—	—	—	—	—	—	2	—	—	—	1	1	—	—	—	—	—
1st Cornet	7	4	6	6	6	6	5	5	6	7	6	5	7	5	5	5	6	5	5	5	4	5
2nd Cornet	4	4	4	4	2	2	4	4	2	2	3	3	2	4	2	4	4	3	3	2	2	2
1st Tenor Horn	3	3	2	3	2	2	3	2	2	2	2	2	2	1	1	2	1	2	2	1	1	2
2nd Tenor Horn	3	2	3	1	2	2	—	3	2	2	1	1	1	2	2	1	1	2	1	2	2	2
1st Baritone	3	3	1	2	2	2	2	1	2	2	2	2	2	1	2	1	—	1	1	2	1	1
2nd Baritone	2	2	1	1	2	2	1	1	2	1	1	1	—	2	1	2	2	1	2	1	1	2
1st Trombone	2	1	1	2	1	1	3	1	2	1	2	1	1	2	1	1	2	1	1	—	1	1
2nd Trombone	2	1	2	1	1	1	1	1	1	1	1	2	1	1	2	1	—	2	1	1	1	1
Bass Trombone	1	—	1	1	1	—	1	—	1	1	1	1	1	1	1	1	—	—	—	—	1	—
Solo Euphonium	3	4	2	3	4	3	3	2	2	4	2	2	1	2	2	2	2	3	2	1	2	—
B♭ Bass	2	4	1	4	1	4	4	4	2	3	4	2	3	2	2	3	3	2	2	4	1	2
E♭ Bombardon	3	3	3	3	3	2	2	3	1	2	3	2	2	3	3	2	2	2	2	2	2	1
B♭ Clarionet	—	5	5	1	2	4	—	1	3	—	—	1	—	—	—	—	—	—	—	—	1	—
E♭ Clarionet	—	—	2	1	2	—	—	1	—	—	—	—	1	—	—	—	—	—	—	—	1	—
Cymbals	1	—	—	—	1	—	1	—	1	—	—	—	1	—	—	—	—	1	1	—	—	—
Side Drum	1	1	1	—	1	1	1	1	1	1	1	1	2	1	2	—	2	1	—	1	1	—
Bass Drum	1	1	1	1	1	1	1	1	1	1	1	1	1	1	1	1	1	1	1	1	1	1
Totals	38	38	36	31	34	33	32	31	31	30	30	29	28	28	27	27	27	26	24	23	23	20

1 Clapton, Congress Hall
2 Nunhead
3 Bristol I
4 Barrow I
5 Portsmouth I
6 I HQ
7 Penge
8 Northwich
9 Boscombe
10 ITHQ
11 Oldham I
12 Exeter
13 Regent Hall
14 Hull II
15 S. Shields
16 Luton II
17 New Brompton
18 Ramsgate
19 Worthing
20 Luton I
21 Northampton
22 Doncaster

movement were remarkably successful. However, from the late nineteenth century there was considerable involvement of individual Salvationist players in contesting bands. In one important respect, Salvation Army bands provided an opportunity which hardly existed at all in the brass band movement – the opportunity for women to play brass instruments. In 1880 an order was issued: 'we do here express our desire that as many of our officers and soldiers generally, male and female, who have the ability for so doing shall learn to play on some suitable instrument'.[150] In the years that followed the Salvationists gave encouragement to women musicians and though many did play, it was still felt, at the end of the century, that more encouragement was needed. *The Officer* noted:

> Cannot some of our enterprising D.O.s and F.O.s introduce the innovation of our Swedish comrades? A D.O. of that country assures us that there is not half the trouble in managing such mixed bands as with those where the men have everything their own way. For one thing, it is almost impossible for seceders to carry off the whole band in case of trouble. The women can usually be reckoned upon to stick to their guns, even if the men quit their post. Knowing this, the men seldom desert, in fact they are ashamed to show the white feather.[151]

XIV

Throughout this chapter I have highlighted what I see as critically important influences on the brass band movement. Many of these influences originated with or were inspired by the middle classes. It is difficult to imagine how brass bands could have existed at all without the essentially capitalist-inspired motives of inventors, instrument manufacturers and publishers. It is equally true that the music that was played by brass bands in Victorian Britain to a large extent mirrored middle-class tastes. Even the relationship between bands and the volunteer movement, a brief but important phase in band history, was primarily inspired by the middle class.

It would be entirely wrong, though, to gain the impression that the working classes were mere pawns in this story or that individual and community working-class culture was impotent. Indeed, one of the features of the brass band movement in Victorian Britain that makes it similar to other working-class leisure activities was the extent to which it received this 'downward flow' of cultural products and made them its own, investing them with a new and lasting identity.

It is worth recalling that the brass band movement stimulated the first mass involvement by the working classes as performers of instrumental art music. This achievement (at least to this extent) was probably unequalled in any country where Western art culture had a stronghold. They had inspired the composition of no 'great' original works but the fact that they played art music in transcription should not detract from, or devalue, this extraordinary accomplishment. One wonders, anyway, how 'authentic' were the Victorian performances of Handel, Haydn and Mozart that were attended by middle-class audiences.

In open-air concerts and contests, tens of thousands of working-class people had their first experience of 'serious' instrumental music through brass bands.

The estimates given by newspapers for the number of people attending such contests need cautious treatment, but *The Times* estimated admissions of more than 22,000 for the second day of the 1860 Crystal Palace contest.[152] The 1864 Belle Vue contest is reported to have drawn an audience of 25,000.[153] The prices for such events were relatively low, certainly in the range common for other forms of popular mass entertainment.[154] Overwhelmingly, the repertoire at these events was arrangements of classical music. Audiences, irrespective of their individual wealth, sex or literacy, had unequivocal access to high art music in this way.

There were additional and more subtle relationships between brass bands and their audiences. Virtuoso performers were of the same social class, and often the same community, as their audiences. There emerged from the players in brass bands a number who possessed a special virtuosity. These players became musical heroes; they were often the focus of community pride and exemplified working-class achievement and potential. From the 1880s, the band press started devoting space to profiles of such players who, thus, gained national reputations. In due course, brass band players would enter and eventually monopolize the principal positions in the leading professional orchestras of Britain though they carried with them the musical idiom and style of the brass band, they were technically comparable to the best professional players.

By the late nineteenth century brass bands had become a popular music tradition that, to a very large extent, was based on the performance of high art music. One is bound to ask whether any part of the legacy of the nineteenth century contributed to their decline and permanent residence in a more or less self-contained cultural ghetto in the twentieth century. A large part of this phenomenon can be attributed to the centrality of contesting in banding. Contests were the principal forum for brass bands. They raised standards of playing and contributed to the establishment of commonly held ideas about musical idioms and conventions. They also were primarily responsible for defining the purpose of bands as the pursuit of musical and technical excellence.

There were, however, negative products which were hinted at as early as 1859 in Charles Dickens's thinly veiled satire on brass band contests, 'A Musical Prize Fight'.[155] Contests, while encouraging virtuosity, encouraged virtuosity of a particular type that soon became a stereotype. They fashioned a strict and lasting orthodoxy – musical and social – which may well have contributed to the comparative reluctance of the major composers to develop the genre. Also the notion of contesting as a *raison d'être* for brass bands, implying as it does a set of criteria that can be weighed up, measured and scored, is an anathema to basic principles of high art.

An even darker side to band contesting was the frequent outbreaks of violence that accompanied the announcement of contest results. Such scenes caused anguish to many who genuinely and accurately recognized that they would undermine what was seen by the late nineteenth century as a musical and organizational achievement of the working classes. Sam Cope, founder of *The British Bandsman*, a ubiquitous self-made musician who advocated forward-looking benevolent and educational schemes for bandsmen and who saw 'No reason why Tom, who plays the cornet, should be in a lower social or musical grade than Dick, who plays a violin',[156] lamented the 'jealous rivalry' of contests and published numerous articles castigating the gratuitous indiscipline that often marked their conclusion.

While contests may have been a self-inflicted restraint on the movement's wider development, there were other changes taking place at the end of the century which had broader class and cultural relevances. These changes were encouraged by the complex array of signals that emerged which enabled certain types of activity to be seen as 'popular' and others as 'art'. These denominators were often synonymous with definitions of 'working class' and 'middle class'. This process of redefining the cultural status of certain activities owes much to what Eric Hobsbawm and others have called 'the invention of traditions'[157] that occurred from the 1870s. In this process brass bands became aligned to events such as May Day, trade union demonstrations and miners' galas, which epitomized working-class identity and behaviour. The process was further galvanized by the establishment of class-based musical developments such as subscription concerts and a tendency of some musical institutions, the universities and conservatories for example, to keep brass bands at arm's length. This, in turn, gave orchestral playing a higher level of respectability than playing in a brass band. Consequently, by the turn of the century playing in and listening to brass bands was one of the leisure pursuits that had, in a comparatively short space of time, developed an identity sufficiently clear for it to be recognized as one of the features that characterized the behaviour of the British working class.

Acknowledgements

I am grateful to the librarians and archivists who have assisted me during my research for this chapter, and to Dave Russell, Richard Middleton, Mike Lomas and Arnold Myers for reading the earliest draft and making valuable suggestions; also to William Boag; to Alma Sanders for material relating to the Besses o' th' Barn Band; to the custodians of the Black Dyke Mills Band library; to the Curator and staff of the Cyfarthfa Castle Museum; and, finally, to Julia Williams, who typed the manuscript and provided a great deal of assistance in the preparation of this chapter.

Notes

1 G. Grove (ed.), *A Dictionary of Music and Musicians*, London, 1879–89, s.v. 'Wind-band'.

2 See, for example, D. H. Van Ess, 'Band Music' in N. Temperley (ed.), *Music in Britain. The Romantic Age 1800–1914*, London, 1981, p. 138.

3 P. Joyce, *Work, Society and Politics. The Culture of the Factory in Later Victorian England*, London, 1982, has argued that processes such as this reflect the changing nature of business and the shift to limited liability companies.

4 By the end of the century it seems to have been usual to refer to 'the brass band movement'. It is impossible to say when this first occurred but a report in *The Times* of 11 July 1860, on the Crystal Palace Contest, mentions the term.

5 R. Prior, 'Jewish Musicians at the Tudor Court', *Musical Quarterly*, vol. LXIX, no. 2 (1983), pp. 253–65.

6 See T. Herbert, 'The Trombone in Britain before 1800', PhD thesis, Open University, 1984, pp. 361–76.

7 Ibid., pp. 377ff. and pp. 427ff. The first record of a trombonist being employed as a wait is found in the Repertory of the Court of Aldermen for the City of London in 1526 (Guildhall Library, London, R7.f.137).

8 Canterbury Cathedral included trombonists on its statutes in the sixteenth century. See ibid., p. 83.

9 S. Sadie (ed.), *The New Grove Dictionary of Music and Musicians*, London, 1980, s.v. 'Trumpet I'.

10 This link is mentioned in ibid. (s.v. 'Brass Bands'); it is also given some emphasis in J. F. Russell and J. H. Elliot, *The Brass Band Movement*, London, 1936, Chapter 1.

11 A. Taylor, *Brass Bands*, St Albans, 1979, p. 23.

12 See H. G. Farmer, *The Rise and Development of Military Music*, London, 1912 (revised edn 1970).

13 University of Glasgow Library, Farmer MS.115 (Letter dated 5 August 1803 from Harry Calvert, Adjutant General of the Forces.)

14 See E. Croft-Murray, 'The Wind Band in England' in *Music and Civilization* (British Museum Yearbook 4), London, 1980, pp. 135–163. See also, M. J. Lomas, 'Militia and Volunteer Wind Bands in Southern England in the Late Eighteenth and Early Nineteenth Centuries', *Journal of the Society for Army Historical Research*, vol. LXVII, no. 271 (autumn 1989), pp. 154–66.

15 J. L Scott, 'The Evolution of the Brass Band and its Repertoire in Northern England', PhD thesis, University of Sheffield, 1970, p. 441.

16 R. A. Marr, *Music for the People*, Edinburgh and Glasgow, 1889, p. 120.

17 Southport Public Library, Sp.920.RIM (William Rimmer Documents).

18 See also V. Gammon, 'Babylonian Performances: the Rise and Suppression of Popular Church Music, 1660–1870' in E. Yeo and S. Yeo (eds), *Popular Culture and Class Conflict 1590–1914*, Brighton, 1981, pp. 62–88.

19 K. H. McDermott, *Sussex Church Music in the Past*, Chichester, 1923.

20 F. W. Galpin, 'Notes on the Old Church Bands and Village Choirs of the Past Century', *The Antiquary*, vol. XLII (1906), pp. 101–6.

21 W. Millington, *Sketches of Local Musicians and Musical Societies*, Pendlebury, 1884.

22 A clarinet and syrinx from this period survive at the Old Church of Llaneilian, Anglesey. I am grateful to H. E. Griffiths, Rector of Amlwch, for providing me with this information.

23 See Gammon, 'Babylonian Performances', pp. 71ff.

24 J. A. Latrobe, *The Music of the Church Considered . . .* , London, 1831, p. 72.

25 N. Temperley, *The Music of the English Parish Church*, Cambridge, 1979, p. 197.

26 Ibid., p. 198.

27 Ibid., p. 197.

28 Taylor, *Brass Bands*, pp. 17–21.

29 See 'The History of the Brass Band Movement', University of Glasgow, Farmer Manuscripts 99/2, a two-page typescript article by H. G. Farmer referring to the researches of Mr George Thompson of Airdrie and listing a number of early Scottish wind bands.

30 W. Alberry, 'Old Sussex Amateur Bands', *Sussex County Magazine*, vol. XVIII, no. 12 (1944), pp. 314–20.

31 For example, see Taylor, *Brass Bands*, Chapters 1 and 2, *passim*.

32 For example, Millington, (*Sketches*, pp. 11ff.) writes of parish instrumentalists and choirs meeting 'for the practice of vocal and instrumental music, principally oratorios of Handel, Haydn and other eminent composers'. See also R. Elbourne,

Music and Tradition in Early Industrial Lancashire 1780–1840, Woodbridge, 1980, pp. 115–33.
33 There are several claims as to what was the first all brass band (See Taylor, *Brass Bands*, Chapter 1).
34 Lancashire County Records Office, DDC1 1187/18 (Clifton of Lytham Muniments).
35 See T. Herbert, 'The Virtuosi of Merthry', *Llafur. The Journal of Welsh Labour History*, vol. 5, no. 1 (1988), pp. 60–7.
36 Wombwell's was in Merthyr in 1846 (*Cardiff and Merthyr Guardian*, 1 August 1846); it is probable that it made annual visits to the town.
37 B. Rogerson, 'A Touch of Local Brass' in *Eccles and District History Society Lectures*, 1977–78, pp. 4.1–4.4.
38 J. Harley, 'Music at the English Court in the Eighteenth and Nineteenth Centuries', *Music and Letters*, vol. 50 (1969), pp. 334–6.
39 See T. Herbert, 'The Repertory of a Victorian Provincial Brass Band', *Popular Music*, vol. 9/1 (1990), pp. 117–31.
40 *Yorkshire Gazette*, 5 January 1883.
41 E. Jackson, 'Origin and Promotion of Brass Band Contests' in *Musical Opinion and Music Trades Review*, 1896 (serialized).
42 Sadie, *New Grove*, s.v. 'Harper, Thomas'. See also S. Sorenson and J. Webb, 'The Harpers and the Trumpet', *The Galpin Society Journal*, vol. XXXIX, (September 1986), pp. 35–57.
43 See, for example, R. Nettel, 'The Influence of the Industrial Revolution on English Music', *Proceedings of the Royal Musical Association*, vol. 77 (1946), p. 33.
44 A. Carse, *The Life of Jullien*, Cambridge, 1951, pp. 53–4.
45 Ibid., p. 52. See also W. Harwood, *Adolfe Sax 1814–1894 – His Life and Legacy*, Baldock, 1980, Chapter IV, *passim*. The instruments were not announced as saxhorns at Jullien's concert. According to Distin, the organizers had refused to give this title to them because their launch a few weeks earlier had been a failure.
46 See *The Scotsman*, 11 July 1835 and 13 April 1836.
47 The Distins performed primarily on horns, slide trumpet and trombone before the famous meeting with Sax. However, Enderby Jackson, 'Origin', states that they were playing valve instruments made by the London firm, Pace, before 1844.
48 *Punch*, vol. XXVII (1854), p. 255, quoted in Carse, *Life of Jullien*, pp. 49–50. Some impressionistic evidence loosely links working-class audiences with Jullien's concerts. Manuscripts relating to Marriner's Band at Keighley refer to some members of the Band walking from Keighley to Bradford to see Jullien; it is not known, though, what social status these players had. Also, Enderby Jackson, 'Origin', somewhat floridly describes 'foundries and workshops . . . [being] crowded with disputants on the musical marvels Jullien brought to their district'.
49 A. Baines, *Brass Instruments: Their History and Development*, London, 1976, pp. 194–5.
50 See Scott, 'Evolution of the Brass Band', pp. 124–9 and 194–6. D'Almaine published a collection under the title *The Brass Band* in 1837; the arrangements were by J. Parry, formerly bandmaster of the Denbigh Militia.
51 National Library of Wales, Cyfarthfa Paper, Box XIV (Invoice from Pace to Crawshay 21/3/1840).
52 T. Harper, *Instructions for the Trumpet*, London, c.1835.
53 Sadie, *New Grove*, s.v. 'Harper, Thomas'. See also Sorenson and Webb, 'The Harpers'.
54 Scott, 'Evolution of the Brass Band', pp. 424–30.
55 J. Webb, 'Designs for Brass in the Public Records Office, *Galpin Society Journal*, vol. XXXVIII (April 1985), pp. 48–54.
56 P. Mactaggart and A. Mactaggart, *Musical Instruments in the 1851 Exhibition*, Welwyn, 1986, pp. 104–6.

57 C. Ehrlich, *The Music Profession in Britain since the Eighteenth Century: A Social History*, Oxford, 1988, Chapter V.

58 Ibid., p. 236.

59 *The Sheffield Independent*, 22 May 1858.

60 H. R. Haweis, *Music and Morals*, London, 1871.

61 *Music Herald*, 4 July 1846, p. 24. This article contains material from Hogarth's *Musical History. Biography and Criticism*, London, 1836.

62 'Music in Humble Life', *Household Words*, 11 May 1850, pp. 161–4. The authorship of the article is identified in A. Lohrli, *Household Words: A Weekly Journal 1850–1859*, Princeton, NJ, 1973, p. 60.

63 E. D. Mackerness, *A Social History of Music*, London, 1964, p. 164.

64 H. Cunningham, 'Class and Leisure in Mid-Victorian Britain' in B. Waites, T. Bennet and G. Martin, *Popular Culture Past and Present*, London, 1982, pp. 69–70.

65 Jackson, 'Origin'.

66 *Musical Herald*, 28 August 1846, p. 40.

67 Taylor, *Brass Bands*, p. 54.

68 *Halifax Courier*, 15 September 1855, p. 1.

69 Lynn Museum, Norfolk.

70 *Manchester Guardian*, 20 August 1853.

71 Taylor, *Brass Bands*, p. 25.

72 C. S. Montefiore, *A History of the Volunteer Force: From Earliest Times to the Year 1860*, London, 1908, p. 403.

73 Ibid.

74 *The Times*, 15 August 1860, p. 5.

75 I. F. W. Beckett, *Rifleman Form: A Study of the Rifle Volunteer Movement 1859–1908*, Aldershot, 1982, p. 41.

76 *The Times*, 22 August 1860, p. 5.

77 Beckett, *Rifleman Form*, p. 116.

78 H. Livings, *That the Medals and the Baton be Put on View*, Newton Abbot, 1975, p. 15.

79 Private collection of Mr Raymond Ainscoe of Kirby Lonsdale, kindly conveyed by Arnold Myers.

80 *The Rifleman*, 23 May 1861.

81 *The Volunteer Service Gazette*, 20 June 1861, p. 406.

82 *The Volunteer Service Gazette*, 25 July 1868, p. 531.

83 Beckett, *Rifleman Form*, p. 145.

84 Ibid., p. 273.

85 PP 1862 [c.3053] XXVII 89, *Report of the Royal Commission on the Condition of the Volunteer Force*. See also A. Tucker, 'The Army in the 19th Century' in R. Higham (ed.), *A Guide to the Sources of British Military History*, London, 1972.

86 PP 1878/79 [c.2235] XV 181, *Report of the Bury Departmental Committee*.

87 Ibid., pp. 1216ff.

88 Ibid., p. 2213.

89 Ibid., p. 2550.

90 Ibid., p. xviii.

91 PP 1887 [c.4951] XVI 271, *Report of the Volunteer Capitation Committee*.

92 Taylor, *Brass Bands*, p. 50.

93 Alberry, 'Old Sussex Amateur Bands', pp. 318–19.

94 Ehrlich, *The Music Profession*, pp. 100ff., gives an excellent succinct account of the economics of the music industry at this time.

95 Price lists for most of the companies quoted here are reproduced later in this book.

96 Scott, 'Evolution of the Brass Band', p. 103.

97 D. C. Russell, 'The Popular Music Societies of the Yorkshire Textile District 1850–1914', DPhil thesis, University of York, 1979, p. 38. See also pp. 138–45.

98 A. Rose, *Talks with Bandsmen: A Popular Handbook for Brass Instrumentalists*, London, 1895, p. 305.
99 Quoted in G. D. Bridges, *Pioneers in Brass*, Detroit, 1972, p. 38.
100 *The British Bandsman*, December 1888.
101 *Wright & Round's Brass Band Journal*, 1 January 1892.
102 Rose, *Talks*, pp. 303–4.
103 See Herbert, 'Virtuosi of Merthyr'.
104 University of Leeds Brotherton Library, W.L. Marriners Caminando Minute Book.
105 *Llanelly and County Guardian*, 28 October 1886. I am grateful to Dr David Evans of the University College of Wales, Aberystwyth, for sources relating to the Llanelly Band.
106 'The Treasurer's Book for Members of the St George's Works' Brass Band, Lancaster 1885–1886', Morecambe Library, Lancashire.
107 Gwynedd Archive Service XM/3121/791 (private papers of Thomas Hughes).
108 J. N. Hampson, *Besses o' th' Barn Band: its Origin, History and Achievements*, Northampton, *c.*1893, p. 70.
109 Ibid., pp. 72ff.
110 See Alberry, 'Old Sussex Amateur Bands'.
111 Clwyd Archive Service DD/WL/251.
112 Hampson, *Besses o' th' Barn Band*, pp. 42–3.
113 Bradford District Archives 54D80/1/6.
114 Morecambe Library, 'Treasurer's Book'.
115 Bradford District Archives 54D80/1/5, p. 2.
116 University of Leeds Brotherton Library, W. L. Marriners Caminando Band Minute Book.
117 *The Cornet*, 15 November 1893.
118 Huddersfield Public Library S/HT.1 (Brass Band Minute Book, Huddersfield Band of Hope Union).
119 Scott, 'Evolution of the Brass Band', p. 194.
120 There is some doubt as to when Wessell's Brass Band Journal was first published. Scott has dated it 1837. The British Library dates books 10–14 1845. This suggests that the first issue was in the early 1840s.
121 See Scott, 'Evolution of the Brass Band', p. 215.
122 T. Herbert, 'The Repertory of a Victorian Provincial Brass Band', *Popular Music*, vol. 9/1 (1990), gives a preliminary checklist of the titles in the repertory.
123 Ainscoe Collection, shown at the 1989–90 'Brass Roots: 150 Years of Brass Bands' exhibition, University of Edinburgh Collection of Historic Musical Instruments.
124 The Cyfarthfa Band, for example, won a set of journals in 1860, but continued to play from manuscript part books which contained many of the titles included in the journals.
125 E. A. Lodge, *The Brass Band at a Glance*, Huddersfield, 1895.
126 J. Ord Hume, *Chats on Amateur Bands*, London, 1900, Chapter 1.
127 These events are depicted in watercolours at the Cyfarthfa Castle Museum.
128 Ainscoe Collection, kindly conveyed by Arnold Myers. The surviving entrance forms for the 1861, 1862 and 1863 contests show a similar picture. The conductor of the 20th Shropshire Rifle Volunteer Corps in 1861 was 'the actuary of a savings bank'. In 1862, the Wakefield Rifle Volunteer Corps Band's conductor, George Hudson, was a 'shoddy dealer'.
129 Scott, 'Evolution of the Brass Band', p. 214.
130 Russell, 'Popular Music Societies', pp. 347ff.
131 Marr, *Music for the People*, p. 128.
132 Ibid.
133 Ibid.
134 D. J. Lamora, 'Alexander Owen 1851–1920', typescript copy at Manchester City

Library (F781 685 Owl). There is some doubt over the details of the early life of Owen.

135 *Life and Career of the Late Mr Edwin Swift*, Milnsbridge, 1904.
136 Russell and Elliot, *The Brass Band Movement*, p. 143.
137 Quoted in P. L. Binns, *A Hundred Years of Military Music*, Gillingham, 1959, pp. 27, 28. The letter is not dated.
138 University of Glasgow, Farmer Papers, MS 115, p. 13/14.
139 E. Baines, *On the Performance of Military Bands in Parks on Sundays*, London, 1856, p. 8.
140 *The Orchestral Times and Bandsman*, December 1891, p. 308.
141 Taylor, *Brass Band*, p. 21.
142 See *The British Musician*, March 1896, pp. 64–5.
143 B. Boon, *Play the Music, Play!*, London, 1978, p. 3.
144 *The Salvation War*, 1883 (Salvation Army GHQ archives).
145 The *War Cry*, 24 February 1881.
146 Boon, *Play the Music*, pp. 146–7.
147 Ibid.
148 The *War Cry*, 4 July 1885.
149 Boon, *Play the Music*, p. 173.
150 The *War Cry*, 10 March 1880.
151 *The Officer*, January 1895, p. 27.
152 *The Times*, 12 July 1860, p. 9.
153 Taylor, *Brass Bands*, p. 61.
154 The admission charge for the first day of the Crystal Palace Contest in 1860 was 2*s*.6*d*. (*The Times*, 10 July 1860). The second day cost only 1*s*. and 6*d*. for children (ibid., 10 July). The 1*s*. entrance fee with children at half price was then held for several years. Promoters also negotiated concessionary rail excursions with the railway companies.
155 'Musical Prize Fight', *All the Year Round*, 12 November 1859, pp. 65–8. The article is usually attributed to Dickens, who was the editor of the magazine. It is not proven that he wrote it.
156 *The British Bandsman*, 28 November 1908, p. 597.
157 See, for example, E. Hobsbawm, 'Mass-Producing Traditions: Europe 1870–1914' in E. Hobsbawm and T. Ranger (eds), *The Invention of Tradition*, London, 1983. See also Dave Harker, *Fakesong: The Manufacture of British Folksong 1700 to the Present Day*, Milton Keynes, 1985.

2 'What's Wrong with Brass Bands?' Cultural Change and the Band Movement, 1918–c.1964

DAVE RUSSELL

In the course of the twentieth century, the brass band movement has followed two separate trajectories. On a purely artistic level, it has made enormous strides in terms of technical competence and of range and scope of repertoire. At the same time, it has ultimately lost the powerful – in some areas central – position that it had held in popular musical culture. While this chapter is intended as a fairly wide-ranging discussion of bands in this period, its primary aim is to examine the second of these developments and to trace the process through which, by the 1950s and perhaps even earlier, the brass band had simply become yet another specialist pastime within an ever more variegated pattern of popular leisure.

What follows falls into four broad sections. The first investigates the structure of the movement in social, spatial and organizational terms, the second its musical functions and repertory. The third and largest component focuses on the processes challenging the position of the bands in musical life, while the final section attempts to locate their place within both the wider 'national' and the popular political cultures. The starting point of 1918 is really one of convenience, for some of the key changes explored here originated in the early years of the twentieth century. The early 1960s, with pop music in rampant ascendancy and the movement contemplating redemption through a new repertoire, seemed a suitable stopping point. The balance of the coverage is undoubtedly tilted towards the inter-war period. Although many of the conclusions here are intended to encompass the whole British experience, there is no denying the 'Englishness' of the geographical coverage, with particular attention paid to bands of the Pennines and the industrial North-East.

Detailed local studies will undoubtedly illustrate many subtle patterns of variation from the picture drawn here, and it is to be hoped that this preliminary survey will encourage such undertakings. The need for research is paramount throughout the whole gamut of popular musical life and not just in the sphere of brass bands. The field of popular music has been badly neglected by social historians and musicologists, but the period from 1914 to 1956 seems peculiarly uncharted. These are rich fields and deserve investigation.

I

Historians must be able to count, but counting bands is a notoriously difficult procedure. Despite the development of an increasingly sophisticated organizational structure over the period, no definitive registry of bands has ever existed and enumeration has to be based largely on the estimates of contemporaries, on the reports of local correspondents in the band press, especially in the detailed *British Bandsman*, and on the sporadically published band directories. While these sources do not allow for exact measurement, they can form the basis for some reasonable estimates of numbers at certain times, as well as illuminating some general trends.

Unfortunately, no half-way reliable estimate of the number of bands exists for the late Victorian or Edwardian eras as a context for the period under study. It is probable that the absolute numerical peak came in the 1890s and in the earliest years of the twentieth century, although it is impossible to say just how high it was. The band music publishers, Wright and Round, put forward the figure of 40,000 bands early in 1889 and 30,000 at the end of it.[1] It is not at all clear how these figures were arrived at. The great inconsistency between them hardly gives cause for confidence, and even the lower figure seems highly inflated, radiating a sense of commercial self-congratulation and aggrandizement. From about 1906 the band press does carry a definite if anecdotal body of evidence suggesting recruitment difficulty and a slightly higher rate of disbandment than in previous times.

It is easiest to deal with the issue of numbers and growth patterns from this point by considering in turn each of the sources mentioned above. The highest figures stemmed from individuals' estimates. In the inter-war period J. H. Elliot, who knew the movement well, put forward the figure of 5,000 on a number of occasions. In 1935, Arthur Bliss, a less experienced observer, claimed 4,000 in 'the north' and perhaps 6,000 altogether. Few seemed willing to hazard a guess in the post-war period, although Peter Wilson, editor of the *British Bandsman*, has suggested 2,000 as a figure for the early 1980s.[2]

Evidence from the second source, the *British Bandsman*, is worthy of very close attention. Particularly before 1939, it filled much of its space with the comments of local correspondents. What follows is a brief study based on two counties, Durham and Yorkshire, chosen because they both tended to receive particularly thorough coverage from their respective correspondents. Obviously, as is always the case with local studies, it is intended as a model for testing and not as a definitive statement.

In 1913 the *British Bandsman* recorded activity by some 230 bands in Yorkshire and 90 in Durham. These figures doubtless underestimate the total number of bands, the journal giving very little coverage to the village bands of East Yorkshire and of the more remote Pennine moorlands of both counties. They do at least give some indication of the size of the competitive *movement*, most of the bands noted because they were involved in contests of one type or another. Although such exercises are perilous, it seems useful here to try and extrapolate a national figure from the local. These figures show for both counties the existence of one band for approximately every 15,500 people. If this is extended to the national population, it would suggest the existence of approximately 2,300 bands in England and Wales (2,600 if Scotland is also included). It must be repeated that these are minimum figures but, if nothing else, they do illustrate the wildness of the 1889 claims.

By 1920, the Yorkshire and Durham 'counts' had dropped to 156 and 54, respectively. To a large extent, this fall reflects a change in the nature of the source material, in that the *British Bandsman*'s local correspondents concentrated increasingly on a smaller number of bands. (Given this element of unreliability, national extrapolation does not seem appropriate.) However, there is more to this fall in numbers than the mere vagaries of sources, and it does seem likely that some bands did not recover from the disruption of the war, especially those which had been in a weakened condition before 1914. Here then, is a probable specific moment of decline.[3]

In the course of the inter-war period, numbers seemed to have remained reasonably steady, with only a slight decline. By 1938, the Yorkshire figure had fallen to 129, the Durham one to 49. Significantly, however, most of the losses were concentrated in the period after late 1937. Broadening the geographical scope for a moment, it does appear that the late 1930s were a period of marked difficulty and quite rapid absolute numerical decline. The *British Bandsman* of 1938 contained many anxious records of disbandings. The Lancashire correspondent claimed that some fifty local bands had folded in the course of the year, including some of considerable stature, notably Perfection Soap Works and Glazebury bands. Lancashire seems to have been particularly affected, but most regional correspondents listed a greater number of problems than normal. The fall in numbers was one reason behind the calling of a convention to discuss 'What is Wrong with Brass Bands?' at the September Open in 1938.[4]

Although the Second World War caused massive disruption to bands, it does not appear to have added greatly to the overall fall in numbers. Analysis of the *British Bandsman* for 1954 gives figures for Yorkshire of 110, and for Durham of 40, a continuation of the downward trend, but not a particularly dramatic one. By the 1960s, the journal was devoting much more space to feature articles than to minute-book-like coverage of local bands and it thus becomes impossible to carry out any sort of worthwhile enumeration. Impressionistic evidence, however, does suggest that the decline in numbers was virtually continuous throughout the period from the mid-1950s, and possibly faster than at any previous period since 1938. A note of depression was certainly evident in the band press and, if the movement's collective memory is to be trusted, many bandsmen look back on the late 1950s and early 1960s as a bleak age.[5]

The final form of evidence is the directories, which are few in number and highly unreliable. Directories tend to be as much a measurement of the number of conscientious secretaries with access to a stationery account than anything else. The limited evidence they offer does, however, tend to reinforce some of the patterns suggested above. The first detailed listing of bands was probably Leo Croke's *The Standard Directory of Brass and Military Bands*, published in 1939, and essentially a guide to the band world for entertainment promoters. Croke admitted that the work was by no means definitive, and it is probable that only the better-quality bands would have been contacted or would have responded. It records 1,242 bands in Great Britain as a whole, with the main body, some 1,100, in England and Wales. Two directories published in 1981 and 1987, both of them claiming to be thorough rather than definitive, record 710 and 670 bands, respectively.[6]

Even from such a dense clutch of figures as this, the generalities are clear. First, without in any way seeking to deny the importance of the band movement, it is obvious that the number of bands in existence in the early years of the century was almost certainly a great deal more modest than many have assumed. Throughout the period under study we are dealing with four- rather than five-figure numbers. Second, in terms of total numbers at any one moment, the estimates of informed insiders like Elliot and Wilson look sensible. Finally, the fall in the number of bands appears to have been continuous, with a probable acceleration around the end of the First World War, and a definite one in the late 1930s. It is almost certain that the late 1950s and 1960s saw another period of more rapid decline. Most of the above figures suggest that the number of bands has been more than halved over the period from 1913. Explanation, or attempts at it, will follow later.

The geography of banding can be delineated in a slightly less hesitant manner. In terms of settlement type, the Victorian brass band was perhaps most often the product of small industrial villages and towns. This was almost universally the case with regard to contesting bands, and effectively remained so for the period to the 1960s.[7] With regard to geographical distribution, by the last quarter of the nineteenth century the brass band was a national phenomenon in the sense that individual bands were established in virtually every part of Great Britain. The competitive movement, however, had a rather more narrow base, with the most active participants to be found in central Scotland, industrial North Wales, the coal and steel towns of South Wales, Cornwall, the Northamptonshire shoe towns, the textile and mining towns of the West Riding and Lancashire and the coalfields of Leicestershire, Nottinghamshire, Durham and Northumberland.

The absolute heartland of the pre-1914 movement was undoubtedly formed by the West Riding of Yorkshire, especially the textile district, and industrial Lancashire. Thirty-six of the 81 bands winning prizes at Belle Vue between 1853 and 1914 and 15 of the 27 at Crystal Palace between 1900 and 1914 came from these two areas.[8] It has been argued with some justification that to base elite status purely on lists of prizewinners is to a degree misleading. Research into band repertoires in other areas shows that there were bands which could play the most taxing music of the day, yet for whatever reasons – financial ones were probably the most common – chose not to contest.[9] Nevertheless, it would still be difficult to deny these two regions a privileged status in the band world.

Undoubtedly, the period from 1918 witnessed the increased presence of bands from areas not previously at the absolute core of banding. Luton Red Cross, for example, became the first southern band to win the National championship, in 1923, while in 1927, Carlisle St Stephens became the first Cumbrian band to win.[10] Luton's victory was the prelude to the rise of a small but significant number of southern bands in the late 1920s and 1930s, most notably Callender's Cable Works from Belvedere in Kent and Friary Brewery from Guildford. Aided by the spread of brass teaching in schools and by the reorganization of the National along regional lines in 1945, the profile of bands from outside the traditional strongholds continued to be raised after the war.

However, in the final analysis, the traditional areas ultimately continued to dominate contesting and to produce a very high proportion of the leading players. While allowing for the limitations of contest results noted above, they still provide a good indication of the movement's spatial structure. Over half of the bands placed in the first six at the Belle Vue September Open between 1919 and 1938 came from Lancashire and Yorkshire, with some 14 Lancashire bands taking 42 of the possible 120 placings. Belle Vue results on their own would be a little misleading because the geographical proximity of Yorkshire and Lancashire bands to the venue gave them a huge advantage when trade depression made long-distance travel to contests less frequent. However, the National results over the same period show a broadly similar pattern, with the two counties taking one-third of the 114 top six placings in the championship section. The dent in their position, when compared to the pre-1914 results, stemmed largely from the much higher proportion of Durham and Northumberland bands contesting the National, bands from these counties taking just under one-fifth of the placings. It might have been expected that the introduction of eight regional heats into the National in 1945 would have led to a wider distribution of prizes. Certainly, there were individual years when bands from other regions did well, but in general, right until the 1960s, Yorkshire and Lancashire bands dominated, taking some 40 per cent of the prizes.

At the same time, the established areas were still central to the production of soloists. 'In many cases it is the migration of Northern bandsmen which is responsible for a considerable amount of this improvement' argued James Brier, editor of the *British Bandsman* in 1938, when discussing the rise of bands from the South and Midlands.[11] Certainly, the Luton band contained some outstanding local musicians, and was proud that ten of the 1923 band had joined as novices in 1918. However, the band's ambition and ultimate quality drew much from the appointment of northern bandmasters, J. T. Ogden from Kingston Mills as early as 1893 and Fred Mortimer from Hebden Bridge in 1912.[12]

Callender's progress in the 1920s was far more obviously based on northern talent. Shortly after the temporary closure of the St Hilda colliery in South Shields in August 1925, seven of the colliery band, undoubtedly one of the best in Britain at the time, took positions at the Callender Works.[13] Others followed throughout the next ten years from a variety of northern bands. Again, the dramatic rise of the Kettering-based Munn and Felton band, founded in December 1932, National champions by September 1935, owed much to imported soloists. Kettering undoubtedly had a deep-rooted band tradition, the band owing its foundation to the managing director's discovery that 18 of his 400-

strong workforce were bandsmen. However, despite this and the massive contribution made by the bandmaster, local cornet player and Munn and Felton
employee, Stanley Boddington, it was the arrival of soloists from Yorkshire,
Lancashire, Durham and Scotland that raised the band to and maintained it at,
championship level.[14]

Finally, it is also significant that the success of *individual* bands, Luton and
Callender's in the 1920s, City of Coventry in the 1940s and Morris Motors in the
1950s, did not generally stimulate the movement in their localities in any
dramatic way. Oxfordshire appears regularly in a tabulation of the counties of
origin of prizewinners at the National in the 1950s not because of an upsurge of
high-quality bands in the county but simply because of the continual success
of Morris Motors. While more genuinely 'national' than many other forms of
popular leisure – Rugby League and crown green bowling, for example –
throughout the twentieth century the brass band has had its deepest roots in its
earliest regional strongholds.

If geographical changes were less striking than has sometimes been suggested,
there can be no doubt that, at least at elite level, the inter-war period heralded
important changes with regard to the institutional rooting of bands. In the
nineteenth century bands emerged from a variety of sources, but by 1914 they
could broadly be placed into three categories: public subscription bands, which
were probably in a majority; works bands supported by the workpeople with
perhaps an element of support from the employers; and works bands funded very
largely by individual industrialists. Although little systematic information has
been collected, it does seem that after 1914, very few new subscription bands were
formed. The majority of new bands appear to have been works bands, or, from
the 1950s, school and youth centre bands.

There is not space here to discuss works bands in the detail they deserve,
although an extended study would make a useful contribution to the growing
literature on industrial welfare policy.[15] It is worth noting, however, that, at least
in the private sector, a new element in the history of musical patronage by
industrialists can be detected. Most of the works bands founded in the period to
about 1930 were either the products of individual paternalistic employers, such
as John Foster of Black Dyke, men with a particular love of music who wished to
add the 'sacred art' to wider schemes of social welfare, or of limited liability
companies with a pronounced interest in social welfare. Perhaps beginning as
early as the late 1930s, but certainly marked from the early 1950s, a much more
aggressively commercial spirit seemed to underpin the desire to support bands.
The period was littered with bands which were born with, or quickly given, silver
spoons, went rapidly into the championship class, only to disappear very quickly
once they had proved to be a less valuable asset than expected. Ferrodo, Clayton
Annaline, John White Footwear (although White himself was a great band
enthusiast) and Crossley Carpets, all top flight bands for brief periods between
1954 and 1962, fall into this category to varying degrees.[16] The 1950s and 1960s
form a bridge between the more deeply rooted support of the earlier period and
the minimal-involvement sponsorship, fashionable in the 1970s and 1980s.
The history of the works band thus reflects a little of the wider passage

of British capitalism from what might be termed a 'paternal' to a 'corporate' mode.

Works bands certainly came to dominate the contest field. For most of the period before 1914, despite the well-publicized success of bands like Black Dyke and Foden's, subscription bands dominated contesting. In the first four years of the National (1900–4), for example, Black Dyke was the only works band to take a prize in the championship section. From about 1910 until 1923, a balance existed between the two types of works band, on the one hand, and subscription bands, on the other, with the prizes more or less equally shared. However, in 1923, works bands took four of the first six places and in 1925 five. From this point, it was rare indeed for more than one subscription band to be among the National prizewinners. The pattern continued into the post-war period and, indeed, reached its climax in the late 1950s and early 1960s. In 1955 and again in the years 1957–61, no subscription band finished in the final placings in the National championship class.

One further point in this context concerns the institutional origin of bandsmen (and, eventually, women) as well as of bands. Schools came to play a highly important role in the training of brass players, through both the establishment of bands and the work of peripatetic teachers with individual pupils. Although individuals had played brass instruments in the many school orchestras that grew up in the period after 1880, it was not until the 1920s that any serious consideration seems to have been given to the founding of school brass bands.[17] John Borland argued the case for small six- or eight-piece school bands in his *Musical Foundations*, published in 1927, and again in a series of articles in the *Musical Times* in 1935.[18]

By the end of the 1930s a handful of bands had emerged, perhaps the first being the Marsden Senior School Band from the Colne Valley in the West Riding, founded in 1931. Another early band was that founded at Battersea Grammar School in 1938 by Harold Hind, who was later to play a major role in the movement in general and among youth and school bands in particular. A National School Brass Band Association was founded in 1952, by which time the idea of the school band was becoming widely accepted.[19] The increasing popularity of the brass band among music educators owed much to the relatively rapid results which could be obtained by beginners in comparison with novices in a traditional orchestra. There was, too, at least in areas with a band tradition, a keeness among some teachers to centre the children's musical experience in a culture that they understood or at least had some awareness of. Although there remained a general feeling that the school music 'establishment' placed a higher emphasis on orchestras than on bands, there can be no doubt that increased intervention by the local state through the medium of the school did much to help supply a form of voluntary culture that was losing its own capacity to recruit.

This process was aided from the late 1940s by the establishment of local youth bands (some sponsored by education authorities, others by individuals), which recruited from school students in a particular area. The influential National Youth Brass Band was founded in 1952 by Denis Wright.[20] By the mid-1950s,

many commentators believed that the band movement was increasingly becoming a youth movement, and not all were happy with the implications.
Certainly, the rise of the youth at the expense of the subscription band does
suggest that the brass band was becoming a specialist body, increasingly
divorced from the broader popular social life that had once sustained it.

Nineteenth-century commentators had dubbed the brass band 'the working
man's orchestra', and while the movement could not have prospered at any stage
without some assistance from outside the working-class community, throughout
the period to 1914, in terms of its players and to a very considerable degree its
audience, the movement's social base was overwhelmingly working-class. Some
commentators thought that they detected a significant change in this pattern in
the 1930s. A *British Bandsman* article in 1930, for example, claimed that: 'The
movement has so advanced in public opinion that we have now in our ranks a
great percentage of artisans, clerks, shop assistants and the many others who
years ago considered the brass band beneath their notice.'[21] Hard evidence is not
plentiful for the period but what there is does not suggest any great upward move
in the social base of the movement. It is surely significant that almost all of the
considerable discussion in the band press of the disruption stemming from inter-
war trade depression focused on the specific problems of manual workers. There
are many passing references to the large role of miners in bands, and, indeed, they
probably represented the largest single occupational group among bandsmen.[22]
Undoubtedly, given the changing demands of the economic system, there was a
limited social mobility for working-class males in this period and some sons of
working men would have obtained white-collar employment while still choosing
their leisure from within the traditionally 'working-class' sphere.[23] However,
comments like the *British Bandsman*'s almost certainly overestimated the extent of
this change as it affected bands. The movement's public spokesmen were
obsessed with presenting as desirable an image as possible and observations of
this type were invariably made with an eye to enhancing status.

The period after 1945 undoubtedly did see a more significant widening of the
social base. By the 1970s, Dobcross Band could include 'a director of a small
winding mill, five schoolteachers, an executive engineer with the Post Office and
one with the Water Board'.[24] It is not clear to what extent bands were actually
attracting directly from the established middle class or simply recruiting players
from working-class families who had been educated 'out of their class' and into a
range of white-collar professions as a result of the expanded educational ladder of
grammar school and technical college. The latter seems more likely given the
divorce of many middle-class musicians from the networks and organizations
that would have led them to the movement. Even in this period, however, the
pace of change should not be exaggerated. There was probably considerable
regional variation, but certainly in the traditional band areas the overall 'flavour'
of the movement was decidedly working class. Brian Jackson and his co-
fieldworker, Denis Marsden, certainly saw it as proletarian enough for inclusion
in their classic study of working-class Huddersfield, *Working Class Community*.
Marsden described the audience at the 1962 Open as 'almost entirely working
class' and implied the same of players and committeemen.[25] The 'cloth-cap

image' which so many writers in the 1970s claimed to be long outmoded, was undoubtedly still rooted in reality in the 1960s.[26]

The final 'structural' element demanding attention here concerns gender. 'Ladies' committees' had long been a crucial feature of the fund-raising mechanism, while women had, of course, also featured in the audience at concerts. One provincial paper even claimed that a number were present at the 1920 National contest, where the 'woman enthusiast . . . takes her knitting and makes a day of it'.[27] Whatever the validity of that comment, without any doubt the band itself was a rigidly masculine republic.

It was not until the 1930s that any shift occurred. In 1930 at a concert in Batley, in the West Riding, Stanley Band featured cornet solos by two nine-year-olds, 'Master Willie' and (in this context more importantly) 'Miss Mildred Holgate'.[28] They were almost certainly the children of local band trainer, Percy Holgate, and Mildred appears to have been part of a novelty act attached to the band rather than a member of it. Two years later, the daughter of the Gainsborough Britannia bandmaster, Harvey Nuttall, was similarly featured as soloist but then actually joined the band in 1933. In 1954, when the issue of female players was beginning to receive regular attention in the band press, Britannia happily claimed her as the first woman member of a brass band.[29] By 1938 a handful of other female players began to appear. In March a slow melody contest at Dinnington in South Yorkshire was won by thirteen-year-old cornet player, Grace Cole, of Firbeck Colliery Band, with eight-year-old Betty Anderson of Leicester Imperial on tenor horn in third place. In the same year Patricia Parkinson, aged fifteen and from Shipley in Yorkshire, became the first ever girl to play in a National final when she appeared with Canal Ironworks.[30]

In a broadcast after the 1938 National, J. H. Elliot claimed that 'young women players in brass bands have recently become quite numerous', but there is little evidence to support his rather generous interpretation, and it was the outbreak of war that gave an important boost to the opportunities for women players.[31] As bands lost players to the forces, women were quite readily accepted into the ranks although, again, numbers do not seem to have been large. A further stimulus to this first generation of women players may have been the example of the all-female dance bands which emerged in the late 1930s such as the Ina Ray Hutton Band and Teddy Joyce's Girl Friends.[32] After the war, the trickle of female players, nearly always schoolgirls or teenagers, increased again, although initially it may well be that they found more space and opportunity in either newly formed bands or school and youth bands than in the longer-established ones. The Brecknock Estate Silver Band founded just after the war included seven girls, while as early as 1954 28 of the National Youth Brass Band (about 15 per cent) were girls.[33] Most of the older-established bands contained at the most only one or two women players. Nevertheless, a base had been laid for what was to become a considerable growth of women players from the 1960s and 1970s.

The early women players were in no sense making a 'political' point – they were mostly too young to do so in any really coherent way – and neither were their families. Betty Anderson came from a banding family and says: 'It did not occur to me at that time that girls did not play in brass bands. I thought everybody did.'[34] It was, though, an unorthodox and implicitly challenging action. It is a matter of interpretation as to whether their breaking into the band world represented the achievement of any significant level of social 'liberation' by women. At one level, of course, it did, in that a tightly male world had been breached. Nevertheless, it is equally the case that their place within the bands both reflected and was constrained by male values.

When discussing female players in the journals, writers often adopted a far more overtly 'human interest' approach than they had done with males. Inevitably, this involved interrogation about their courting habits, a process which illicited such standard replies as: 'You have no time for marriage while you're playing the cornet.'[35] A similar mentality prevailed when, in 1964, the *British Bandsman* acknowledged the increasing size of the women's contingent by beginning a regular 'Bandswoman's Exchange' column. The editor noted: 'The photographs will add some welcome glamour to our pages.' Women writers illustrated broadly similar attitudes towards sexual roles. Writing in the *British Bandsman* in 1954, Edith Alston argued that it was good for women to play but stressed the need for them to maintain 'their poise and dignity' and seemed to have trouble accepting the idea of women in uniform. Such sentiments, mild as they were by the standards of the period and too 'soft' a target for detailed exposition, nevertheless serve to illustrate the atmosphere in which female players found themselves.[36]

Perhaps more significantly, there does seem to be a sense in which the movement's treatment of women mirrored their function in the wider society, as a reserve army of labour, to be used when the supply of males contracted.[37] It is no coincidence that the first trickle of women into bands around the period 1938 coincided with the recruitment problems at that time. In this way, too, any sense of women 'breaking through' is muted by the realization that they were gaining access to a male space at the very moment when it was losing status and standing within the general working-class culture. It should also be underlined that women's progress in to the elite contesting bands was (and still is for the most part) strongly resisted. In these bands, where male applicants were never in short supply, women made no headway. A woman's musical place was definitely not to be in a soloist's chair, or indeed in any chair, in a first section brass band.

Writing in the 1960s, the sociologists Jackson and Marsden were struck, as had been many before them, by the sense of purpose and mission which surrounded much band work. 'The first thing they tell you is that this is the Brass Band *Movement*.'[38] Before moving on to explore the bands' musical life it is important to consider the meaning and significance of this phrase in the post-1918 period, as it undoubtedly sheds much light on band culture and on the brass band's changing role in musical life.

Although the exact structure of the 'movement' in terms of personnel and organization was never actually delineated by contemporaries, its constituent parts are fairly obvious. At the core lay the contesting bands. Always a minority at any one time, they were nevertheless viewed as a musical vanguard, raising standards, showing banding's best possible public face. Non-contesting bands were wedded to the movement through shared musical culture, by the constant supply of talent they provided to their competitive colleagues and by the simple fact that many of them had contested in the past and would do so again after passing through a process of rebuilding, financial retrenchment or whatever.

By the 1890s, through the foundation of the first regional and local band associations formed to set rules for local contests and generally oversee the interests of bands, the movement had begun to generate a skeletal organizational infrastructure, one that grew considerably from the 1920s. The increase in the number of band associations from the 1920s, the establishment of the Alexander Owen Memorial Scholarship (1922), the National Brass Band Club (1925), the National Brass Bands Federation (1931), and the Bandsmen's College of Music (1932) all illustrate an increased tendency toward co-operation and unity. However, no one central organizing body emerged. There was no compunction to join the local associations, and bands, especially the most successful ones, showed a cavalier attitude to them, joining and leaving as and when it suited their finances and their needs. The only really effective centralizing mechanism came with the establishment of the bandsmen's registry immediately after the Second World War by the organizers of the National to settle the century-old problem of bands using borrowed players and professionals in contests. The establishment of a rigorous system of registration, at least for the most important event in the band programme, gave players the closest thing they ever had to a membership card for the brass band movement.[39]

Much of this organizational activity was generated at grassroots level. However, other key aspects, the establishment of the registry, for example, were either instigated or encouraged by commercial interests. The large role played by such interests in the development of banding must be stressed, if only to illustrate the extent to which a supposedly independent, community-based form of leisure was to a degree structured by 'external' forces. The most important group were the band music publishers, and the most important of these was John Henry Iles. Almost all of the major specialist band publishers owned a newspaper or journal, advertising their products and generally reflecting their views, but as owner of music publishing house Richard Smith and Company, publisher, through the company, of the *British Bandsman*, and controller of the two major contests, J. H. Iles exerted considerable influence on all aspects of banding. The *British Bandsman*, the only weekly publication and the one with the largest circulation, became almost the official organ of the movement. When discussing the views of the 'movement', we are often referring to Iles and his colleagues at 210 The Strand, his editors and local correspondents.[40]

The involvement of national newspapers again illustrates the influence of commercial interests in shaping events. The *Daily Herald*'s decision to introduce a system of regional heats on taking over the National in 1945 was inevitably unpopular with many bandsmen in the 'traditional' areas whose chances of reaching the finals were limited by the regional structure. The subsequent complaints were overruled. The decision to proceed with a regional structure may have reflected the stated desire to widen the geographical base of competitive banding and increase opportunities for bands in previously marginal areas. However, it should also be viewed as an outcome of the *Herald*'s marketing strategy. Publicity director Jerome Chester was fully aware that if the National was to play a part in helping the paper recapture some of the market lost to the *Mirror* and *Express* since the early 1930s, it had to win publicity across the widest possible geographical area.[41]

In general, commercial and 'voluntary' groupings were able to agree on broad principles. The essential ideals underpinning the concept of a 'movement' appear to have been a belief in the bands' capacity to educate both their own members and a wider audience, great faith in the contest as the central agency of musical progress and loyalty to a clearly defined instrumentation, playing style and repertory. There was, too, a profound, almost missionary zeal, as captured in an editorial in the *British Bandsman* in 1954.

> The brass band is something of a social phenomenon, a brotherhood, part of the British way of life. Truly amateur bands are not merely haphazard groupings of players who happen to enjoy a 'blow'. They have a more serious purpose, part of which is to give opportunity for the unfolding of artistic skill and experience in those whose daily tasks are all too often monotonous and unsatisfying, although necessary.[42]

This is not far removed from the language of the singing class enthusiasts of the 1840s. Almost Victorian ideas of rational recreation and self-improvement emerge again in this defence of the social value of youth bands by the secretary of the National Brass Band Club:

> Here may be the answer to the present increasing numbers of draped-coated, drain-pipe-trousered gangs, who roam the streets of our cities. These youths are to be pitied rather than blamed . . . brass-banding is one excellent way in which to give the coming generation an interest in life. Anyway, it is worth thinking over.[43]

There was, too, a remarkably strong emphasis on outward respectability and discipline of those already in the movement. 'Remember, gentlemen,' warned the *British Bandsman*'s 'Downside' in 1930, 'that you are but part of a great movement, and *your* conduct in public may go a long way towards raising or lowering us in the eyes of the public. See to it that you do nothing that may let the brass band movement down.'[44] The adoption of uniforms at National contests in the early 1930s, the result of a long campaign by *British Bandsman* editor Herbert Whiteley, the determined efforts twenty years later by National championship producer Edwin Vaughan Morris to make players put out cigarettes before they took the stage for the second half of the massed band concert at the National, are just two of many attempts to improve public image. All this was partly to maintain the support of moneyed supporters, but it was also hoped that the musical establishment might look a little more favourably on the movement if it was divested of its 'taproom feel'.[45]

Whether the led always took great notice of the leaders is doubtful. The interviews in Arthur Taylor's *Labour and Love* include many tales of high spirits (and sometimes just spirits), and of momentary clashes with the great men of the movement, who, if one believed the comments in the band press, supposedly had the permanent, unquestioned loyalty of their players.[46] Iles's annual attempts at conducting during the massed band concert at the National were a source of some ribaldry, while amiable but pointed calls of 'Hurry up, Henry' greeted his delay in announcing the winner at the end of the 1935 contest. At grassroots level, bandsmen could enjoy a genuine democracy. 'Joe, you're a nice fellow, but you're no bloody use as a conductor and you're sacked', are the words reputedly used by the Black Dyke cornet player, Willie Lang, when asked to express the band's views to their conductor, Joe Wood.[47]

The great significance of all this, however, lay not in these internal disagreements but in the overall sense of unity. Bandsmen had a strong sense of belonging. Initially fuelled by the location of bands in specific communities and by the large role played by the family as agent of recruitment, this feeling was made ever stronger by the rhetoric of the 'movement'. It gave bands strength and sustenance. The vitality of banding owed much (and still does) to the determined sense that something special and worthwhile was being done, something that must be continued whatever 'they' (the musical establishment, the public, the BBC, the PRS – the Kluforming Klights Klan as they were referred to in the 1920s – or whatever enemy) think. At the same time, such inner strength might have been a source of weakness, cutting players off from some of the major social and artistic changes of the period. Traditional instrumentation, repertoire and much else were clung to with a determination that annoyed many would-be reformers. In this sense, at least some of the bands' reduced position within popular musical life originated from within.

II

The brass band, although only one of many forms of popular musical society in existence before 1914, was a particularly privileged one. Especially in small industrial communities where the entertainment industry was less penetrative, it was central as an agent of both musical entertainment and education. This section investigates their changing place in local musical and social life from the 1920s.

The bands' varied musical life had fallen essentially into four activities: playing for dancing, for public ceremonies, concert work, and contesting. The dance band function was the least important of the four but it was more significant than has been realized. The history of popular urban dance in Britain has been seriously neglected but it is clear that for working-class youth in particular, dancing in a variety of locales was a major form of entertainment at least from the 1860s and probably earlier.[48] Some of the brass bands' contributions to this were unintentional. Listeners simply took the chance to dance to whatever suitable music the bands had to offer. Such displays were sometimes discouraged, especially by Nonconformist recreational reformers, being viewed as unseemly, and opposed to the rational atmosphere deemed appropriate when music was being performed. In June 1871 at Bradford's first ever corporation-sponsored park concert, the local paper noted that: 'There was some dancing going on but of a furtive and disconnected kind, it being understood that the committees objected.'[49] By the 1890s public dancing had lost some of its stigma and brass-as-dance-bands became common attractions at pleasure gardens, fêtes and a variety of other attractions, including public parks in some areas.

Engagement work of this type seemed reasonably plentiful until about the mid-1920s when brass bands were made effectively redundant by the emergence of specialist dance bands, performing American-style popular music. In 1926, when one Bradford Park Band Committee dispensed with brass bands and engaged dance bands 'proper', the first night of the new regime saw 1,500, a far larger crowd than ever attracted before, dancing to the Indiana Dance Band.[50] When Don Pedro's Mexicans were booked at the Rydings Park, Brighouse, in 1930, they drew 'one of the largest crowds ever seen in the Rydings'. The local paper expressed some disapproval that locals seemed to prefer 'jazz' bands, and foreign bands at that, to the 'excellent' local brass bands. ('Don Pedro' was in fact John Guy from Birmingham.)[51] Brass bands did continue as dance bands in certain settings, particularly at private, socially select gatherings. In 1930, for example, Brighouse and Rastrick in Yorkshire, Mere Band in Wiltshire and Poole Town in Dorset, all found themselves playing for dancing at Conservative Party fêtes.[52] How long this kind of work continued is not clear, but it is apparent that by 1930, one of the links that held the brass band in the mainstream of popular youth culture had been broken.

Concert life was more central to banding and initially more secure. In the course of the nineteenth century bands had built up a flourishing circuit of concert life. Much of this was outdoor work, usually on summer evenings and, dependent upon the strength of the local Sabbatarian lobby, Sunday afternoons. Even the smallest bands could usually be guaranteed work in their local parks, but an elite group undertook national tours of up to ten or twelve weeks' duration. In 1922, six such bands advertised themselves in the *Brass Band News* specifically as 'concert bands'.[53] From the late Victorian period major concerts in parks and on seaside promenades could sometimes attract crowds of a size more normally associated with important sporting events. One of the largest of the inter-war period came at Oldham in August 1926 when an estimated 15,000 watched Durham-based Harton Colliery. The hardship of miners at this moment of industrial conflict and a subsequent display of sympathy and practical financial assistance may have swelled the audience here, but other attendances of several thousand were common.[54]

There was, however, a continuous rumble of concern in the band press from about 1930, suggesting that these concerts were losing their audiences and that bands were losing some of their share of such engagements. Initially, there was little hard evidence, but by the late 1930s, the weight of argument had become convincing. The main concern centred on the evidence of a move by concert organizers towards a much increased use of military bands and dance bands in public parks. Similarly, seaside resorts were clearly making less use of brass bands. In 1938, Southport parks committee cut the number of brass bands it hired from ten to five, while Eastbourne council decided not to engage any at all. The *Eastbourne Gazette*, referring to the performances of what, perhaps significantly, they termed 'industrial bands', articulated an increasingly common critique of their repertoire and approach.

> It is true that these bands could well emulate their military brothers and introduce a little light variety into their programme. On the other hand, the correct presentation

of brass band music hardly lends itself to modern tastes for variety and swing. It is quite a tribute to the catholicity of style in industrial bands that many dance band trumpeters were trained in the north.[55]

By the final months of 1938, the *British Bandsman* had become concerned enough to publish a detailed investigation of the policies of seaside entertainment promoters. The problem was clearly greatest in the South of England where bands were less centrally rooted in popular musical culture, but even entertainment managers in resorts like Scarborough and Yarmouth, with a large number of visitors from the bands' heartlands, and where the top bands were still popular attractions, admitted some evidence of changing taste. The consensus echoed the *Eastbourne Gazette*. 'Stage bands', as some dance bands were termed in this performing context, and to a lesser extent military bands, gave greater variety in the fullest sense, with their novelty acts, vocalists and comedians. One manager claimed that a new generation were not content 'with sitting round a bandstand listening to 25 musicians, who are generally only on view from the chest upwards, putting over some rhapsody, which, the programme informs us, owes its birth to the Slavs'.[56]

It is significant that it was against this background that St Hilda band, professional since 1927, and probably the most commercially attuned concert band, folded in 1937. Its manager, Jimmy Southern, felt that worthwhile engagements were increasingly hard to find. That might be a comment on a particular band, but it reinforces the general pattern, and, highly significantly, coincides with the timing of the recruitment and disbanding problems noted above.[57]

Of course, the outdoor concert did not disappear in the 1930s. Elite bands did not abandon this work until the 1960s, and it forms, through the local park concert, an important element in the activity of many bands to this day. It was, though, in long-term decline. The 1950s saw the real acceleration of the trend. Falling attendances and diminishing appeal were partly accompanied, partly caused, by a new rival, so-called 'canned music', the playing of current hit records over amplification systems. 'How ludicrous it is', commented Harold Hind in 1954, 'to see a crowd of people in deckchairs, sitting round an empty bandstand containing a loud speaker emitting the latest hits'.[58] It was, though, popular with audiences and cheap for local authorities, and virtually all forms of live bandstand entertainment suffered. By the early 1960s, many bandstands were rapidly becoming more monument to past taste than focus for live entertainment. The *Daily Herald* was referring to more than simply the outdoor concert when bemoaning the decline of banding in this lament from 1956 but it was undoubtedly one of the issues in mind. 'The public demand for brass bands has fallen lamentably since the war . . . one's fear is that brass bands may eventually have to play largely for their own enjoyment'.[59]

Inevitably, bands became despondent when playing to small and not always attentive audiences. One obvious response, gathering pace from the 1920s, was simply to move indoors, and thus attract only the serious and genuine followers. Indoor concerts have indeed become a central feature of band culture. For all their value, however, especially as a showcase for music which had previously been regarded as too specialist for park and pier audiences, such concerts were never to be so frequent as the outside engagements. Moreover, they lacked the direct link into popular social life that the older-style engagements possessed. Almost imperceptibly at first in the late 1930s but gathering pace from then on, audiences increasingly had to go looking for bands, rather than simply meeting them during the course of evening, weekend or holiday social life. In this way, another link with the wider community withered.[60]

This process becomes clearer if the focus is shifted to the third category of musical function. The brass band movement's involvement in the ceremony and ritual of public communal life was established from the very earliest moments of its inception and provided it with some of its strongest linkages with the wider popular culture, especially working-class culture. Sunday school walks and processions, trade union galas, friendly society demonstrations, the opening of public buildings and other civic high days and holidays were major events in the band calendar. This is underscored by bands' emphasis on good appearance and deportment at these events, both to honour the community and to ensure a rebooking. Uniforms, not normal at the slightly more private world of the contest until the 1930s, were obligatory. Southowram Band, from a small village near Halifax, purchased a new uniform in 1920, at some inconvenience, specifically to do justice to the St Anne's Sunday School Whit walk. In 1938, Batley Band launched a uniform fund after losing a ceremonial engagement they had held for twenty years, because of their poor appearance.[61]

Quite simply, public displays of what might be termed 'civic culture' have declined significantly (or taken new forms) over the whole period, and especially since 1945. It is difficult to be precise about the patterns here, for the changing nature of recent community ritual has not as yet received any serious scholarly attention. Almost certainly, different forms underwent changes at various stages and regional variations will also have been significant. The decline of the Whit walk might, however, prove indicative. As early as 1920 one West Riding local paper commented on the reduced presence of adults on the local walk, suggesting that the excursion was rapidly taking over as a focus of popular interest on the Whit holiday. By 1937, after almost two decades of falling church attendance and increased penetration of popular social life by the expanding leisure industry, the same paper could talk of a clear decline not just in attendance but in the actual number of walks. In the 1950s, the pace of decline seems to have quickened considerably. Obviously, there were still plenty of walking engagements. The trend, however, was clear. For brass bands such changes were highly important; they had grown up within a pattern of local culture that was gradually being superseded, and could hardly avoid being hurt in the process.[62]

If the wider culture was increasingly hostile, then it was inevitable that bands took ever prouder refuge in the central ritual of their own world, the contest. The number of contests involving full bands undoubtedly fell after the First World War as travel costs and trade dislocation took their toll, but even the most cursory glance at the band press illustrates how the great events of the contest season pervaded the whole mentality of banding. The importance of the contest lay in its capacity to satisfy the needs of so many groupings within the band community.

For what one writer has termed the 'idealists', those who sought '*to make better music, to make music better*', the major contests provided the occasion for the release of the new repertoire that they believed would both raise standards and increase the respect in which the movement was held in the wider musical culture. Both this repertoire and its impact will be discussed later.[63]

For the commercial interest groups, contests offered sizeable rewards. Certainly, only a very limited number were organized with major commercial intent. Some contests were organized by local band associations. Many others were promoted in order to raise funds for a particular institution – a band, a club, sometimes a charity. However, even the smaller events were an obvious and effective location for trade stands advertising wares as diverse as musical instruments and gum for dentures. The two major national contests controlled by J. H. Iles, the National and the Open (under Iles's control from 1925) were the clearest examples of commercial motivation. Although it would be churlish to deny Iles's commitment to bands as forces of musical education and entertainment, it would also be foolish to overlook the extent to which the two big festivals were used as vehicles to publicize Richard Smith and Company and the *British Bandsman*. Competitions also provided considerable sponsorship opportunities for organizations from outside the movement. The clearest example is afforded by the involvement of newspapers. By the mid-1920s, all of the classes at the National, with the exception of the 1,000 guinea trophy, were sponsored by a paper or magazine.[64] The most celebrated press involvement came in 1945 when the *Daily Herald* took over the running of the National from Iles, whose finances had never recovered following his bankruptcy after sustaining losses in the film industry in 1938.[65]

For the players, the rewards were enormous. Apart from the artistic pleasure and the sheer excitement of performing, contesting provided chances to travel, to renew old acquaintance, and in some cases to learn. Keen younger players and junior bands especially, clearly saw contests, again particularly the major ones, as a great stimulus, a chance to sample the best of their culture. At the National, the main competitions were always followed by a concert and the battle for seats was intense. Here the leading bands and soloists became heroes, as enthusiastically welcomed and studied in this fraternity as any jazz or dance band musician was in his.[66]

Finally, contests linked bands to their local community. Most bands took some supporters to contests, although the exact number varied according to location, importance and the state of trade. They gave proceedings something of a sporting flavour, many of them wearing band colours and favours. Press commentators could not avoid the Cup Final analogy. At least until the early 1950s, victorious bands could be assured of the type of civic welcome – crowds at the railway station, 'See the Conquering Hero Comes' played by another local band, speeches from the president, a procession across town for a celebration dinner – that had become almost a cliché of social behaviour by the 1870s.[67]

Even the contest, though, was not immune to changed circumstance. The gradual loss of interest in contest performance among the wider community from the 1950s is a further significant indicator of the bands' marginalization within popular musical culture. 'Thousands', for example, gathered to greet Brighouse and Rastrick after their National success in 1946, 'one thousand' after a similar achievement in 1968.[68] This changed pattern of behaviour to an extent reflects new attitudes to community celebration but also stemmed from a reduced level of media attention. In 1946, a Yorkshire journalist noted the enormous attention given to the National by the BBC. 'The first four placings were announced by Stuart Hibberd, Frank Phillips and others nearly a dozen times in the space of six hours.' The national press often gave quite substantial coverage to the major events. Almost forty years later conductor Trevor Walmsley could argue that if 'Barnsley's left back breaks his bloody leg, it's more newsworthy than winning the National'.[69]

This emphasis on reduced status in popular musical life should not obscure bands' willingness to make use of new opportunities to reach an audience that was proving increasingly fickle. In particular, they embraced wherever possible the growing technological mass media. Black Dyke had recorded as early as 1903 and the leading bands became regular recording artists. One band discographer has talked of a 'flood' of recordings from the 1920s, with St Hilda, Besses o'th'Barn and Black Dyke especially prolific. St Hilda made some 160 '78s' up to 1937, while Black Dyke made 26 for HMV in 1938–42 and a further 23 for Regal-Zonophone from 1940 to 1943.[70] There were plentiful opportunities, too, for the leading cornet soloists such as Harry Mortimer, Jack Mackintosh and Owen Bottomley. Bands were still to find a reasonable market for the LPs in the 1950s and 1960s. Obviously, these recordings made up only the smallest fraction of the total record market but they did at least help bands counteract some of the antagonistic trends.

Bands were less happy about their relationship with the BBC, an issue which will be returned to later. For all the undoubted problems, however, from the first band broadcast (almost certainly that by Clydebank Burgh in April 1923) the BBC did provide another useful showcase.[71] The highest profile accorded to bands came during Harry Mortimer's period as the Corporation's brass and military band supervisor from 1942 to 1964.[72] His initial task was eased by the great demand for light music during the war. Broadcasts played a central role in keeping the band movement together during the war, providing a focus when normal activity was massively disrupted. The *British Bandsman* ran a weekly column on the performances, taking the medium more seriously in a critical sense than at any stage before. Mortimer was able to build on this: during one brief period in the later 1940s, he succeeded in transmitting between ten and fifteen half-hour programmes a week. There was a constant demand for more broadcasts, however, even during the best days. In 1945, for example, a petition of 10,000 names was handed to the BBC by the National Brass Band Club as part of a campaign for greater coverage. The issue has remained high on the agenda to this day.[73]

Before 1914, the brass band repertoire had served as a kind of repository of the main currents of popular musical taste (with the notable exception of music hall song and drawing room material). The need to fulfil a variety of musical functions had led to the development of an extraordinarily wide repertoire embracing, in almost equal proportions, elements of 'art', 'popular' or 'light' music, and specialist band music.[74] In essence, selections based on nineteenth-century opera had become the norm for contesting purposes, while a distinctive blend of operatic selections, musical comedy and operetta, marches, specialist solos and hymn tunes formed the basis of the concert repertoire.

This mixed repertoire remained typical of band performance right through to the 1960s, and beyond in many cases. Concentrating momentarily on concert music, the continuity is quite striking. At least until the 1950s the *structure* of the programme reflected very faithfully the shape and pattern that had been established by the Victorian bands. A typical programme invariably began with a march, which was followed by an overture and then a selection, usually operatic. At this point there was usually scope for a little variation but at least one more selection, a shorter piece such as one of the specialist tone poems, a solo usually for cornet, and finally an arrangement of a vocal item, a glee or, more commonly, a hymn, usually completed the performance. Such a relatively predictable structure clearly had advantages. Audiences knew what to expect, while the mixture gave variety to the programme, both in terms of length and mood of piece. This was a type of programme well suited to audiences with both mixed tastes and levels of interest. While most areas of musical performance have their own structures and patterns, the band concert does seem to have been slightly more standardized and ritualistic than most. The half-hour broadcast concerts generally followed this pattern, although the exact mixture might alter according to requirements. The 6.30 a.m. 'Bright and Early' slot that many bands filled in the 1950s was obviously likely to be much 'lighter' in tone than a Saturday afternoon concert.

There were obviously changes in the content of the repertoire. It is simply not possible to do justice to this topic here, but a few generalizations are useful.[75] There does appear to have been a diminution in the appetite for Italian opera over the period, with the Classical and Romantic symphonic repertoires increasingly favoured as sources for the 'serious' element of a performance. There was almost no use of the contemporary art music repertoire, a clear example of the popular–serious divorce that so many commentators debated from the 1930s. The choice of musical comedy and show music simply reflected changing taste, new works moving in and then almost as rapidly out of the repertoire. Gilbert and Sullivan, of course, remained massively popular and some musicals, such as Novello's *Dancing Years*, became brass band 'standards'.

Iles's use of Percy Fletcher's *Labour and Love* as the test piece for the 1913 National was undoubtedly a major turning point in the contest repertoire. It is sometimes argued that Fletcher was the first 'serious' composer to write for the medium, but Fletcher's standing was in fact a little lower in the contemporary hierarchy. His obituary in the *Musical Times* termed him 'a theatre conductor and composer of popular music'.

Probably the first composer of any status to write for the brass band was Joseph Parry, who in the late nineteenth century produced the *Tydfil Overture*, while Granville Bantock composed both a brass 'Festival March' and a setting for brass and voice of his wife's poem *Sons of Liberty* as part of a work composed for the twenty-first anniversary of the Independent Labour Party in 1914.[76] However, *Labour and Love* broke the hold of the selection-as-test-piece, and there was never any doubt that the event would from then on be dignified by an original commissioned piece. From the 1920s, a number of major British composers were persuaded to write works for the National, the best-known results being Holst's *A Moorside Suite* in 1928, Elgar's *Severn Suite* in 1930, Ireland's *Downland Suite* in 1932 and Bliss's *Kenilworth* in 1936.

The Open continued with the operatic selection until 1924, but when Iles effectively took over the contest in 1925, he quickly adopted his National policy, commissioning a work from Thomas Keighley. His *Macbeth* was sufficiently successful that he came to dominate this contest for several years with further pieces in 1926–8, 1932 and 1935. Apart from a period in the 1950s when the National organizers called upon Frank Wright to produce arrangements of a variety of nineteenth-century works, the major contest test pieces have been original works.[77]

Throughout the period, the brass band was undoubtedly developing its own 'canon', in the sense of a body of music specifically composed for bands, and which had gained a favoured place in the taste of bandsmen and audiences alike. This included both shorter pieces such as the cornet solos *Carnival of Venice* and *Alpine Echoes* (1928) and test pieces like Fletcher's *Labour and Love* and his *Epic Symphony* (1926), *Life Divine* (Jenkins, 1921), *Lorenzo* (Keighley, 1928), *Pageantry* (Howells, 1934) and *Resurgam* (Ball, 1950). While the best of these pieces undoubtedly stretched technique, placed heavier demands on the band as a whole rather than simply the soloists or 'cornermen', and explored the texture of band instrumentation far more inventively than before, it is also the case that the repertoire was becoming more highly specialized than had previously been the case. Much of this was music for an 'in-group'. One commentator's view that much of it was '"non-music" . . . markable music' might be harsh, but it does point up the existence of a growing gap between the maturing band repertoire and wider popular taste.[78] To a degree, the development of the band as a musical medium took place at the expense of a more general popularity.

III

Both the band movement's decline in numbers and loss of place in popular musical culture have already been touched on in a number of places and the explanation for those processes rehearsed to some extent. It is now time to consider possible explanations in real depth.

It must be stressed that the problems of the movement were not a specific creation of the years after 1918. Complaints about recruitment difficulties in particular had been prominent for several years before the war with many a lament on the preference of young men for 'sport and the pictures' over banding. The First World War added further burdens. The band press featured many stories in 1914–15 of bands enlisting *en masse*, or losing large numbers to the forces in a very short time. Most survived by drawing on young players, and by

Christmas 1919 were back to full strength.[79] Nevertheless, the count of Yorkshire and Durham bands noted above, although problematic, clearly suggests that some bands did not survive the war years. From this point, a movement already past its peak was threatened by the acceleration of the existing challenges and by the development of new ones.

Many factors have contributed to the changed status of the brass band. Rather than attempt to look at the issue chronologically, the ensuing discussion is grouped around economic, social (narrowly defined here as almost synonymous with 'recreational') and musical changes. Economic processes at both macro and micro levels have undoubtedly played a highly significant role. The few writers who have considered the twentieth-century band movement have suggested that the economic depression and chronic unemployment of the inter-war period was a major reason for the fall in numbers of bands at this time. The exact impact of the depression needs careful consideration. Economic historians now paint for us a complex view of the period 1920–39, those years during which the number of registered unemployed never fell below 1 million. Simplifying enormously, the period is now seen as one in which regional differentiation in unemployment levels was quite marked. Certain areas, especially those with an economic dependence on staples aimed at export markets, suffered appallingly. Unemployment in Jarrow reached 72 per cent in 1935; in Merthyr, it reached 62 per cent in 1934. In the new growth points of the economy, however, in electronics and consumer durables, for example, outside of the worst crisis of 1929–33, unemployment was low, sometimes negligible. High Wycombe had a rate of only 4 per cent in the mid-1930s. This was not, however, simply a matter of divisions between North and South, between 'old' industrial and 'new' industrial regions, as the above examples might be taken to imply. Towns in the heart of the old industrial North, with a mixed economy or a specialism in a particular area such as engineering, often had unemployment rates close to those of the 'prosperous' South. These variables have to be taken into consideration and generalizations about the economy and the problems of bands made reasonably localized and subtle as a result.[80]

There can be no doubt that in areas of high continuous unemployment, the period from 1920 posed severe difficulties for the movement. Some bands did fold as a direct result of economic slump. At least five Durham colliery bands – Hebburn, Woodlands, Cornsay, Esh Winning and Kibblesworth – for example, went out of existence for long periods between 1932 and 1938.[81] Economic depression does not, however, appear to have been a fundamental cause of the falling number of bands catalogued earlier. The timing of the acceleration of band closures seems crucial, occurring around 1938 after the worst impact of the depression had passed. Moreover, a town like Halifax, with a relatively low unemployment rate of around 6 per cent, lost four bands in 1938, suggesting that factors other than economic ones were in operation.[82] What it did cause were the severe organizational and financial problems that so hampered and pressurized many bands in this period. Bands were often left, in movement parlance, 'short-handed', as players left to seek work in other areas. The regional reports in the band press recorded these problems, with a level of exactness which gives events a certain poignancy, as when 'Downside', the Dorset and Wiltshire correspondent of the *British Bandsman*, noted the extreme difficulties of Bourton band, caused by the closure of the local iron foundry and the subsequent migration of several players to new work in King's Lynn. By 1938, 'Red Rose' in the *British Bandsman* could talk of a 'little army' of bandsmen lost to Lancashire over the two decades. It is likely that the hardest-hit area of all was the Rhondda Urban District, which suffered the migration of 28 per cent of its population, some 47,000 people, between 1921 and 1935.[83]

Financial problems were legion and it is not entirely surprising that a certain bitterness was directed by some bandsmen at some of the better-funded works bands, especially in the South, which were generally little affected by such difficulties. New instruments, music and uniforms were at a premium, travel became a luxury. Bands constantly found themselves appealing for funds, running raffles, collecting 'a mile of pennies' and going out playing with collecting boxes. There were impressive attempts at mutual aid when banding showed hints of moving from a purely musical to a social movement. In 1928, the North Wales correspondent of the *British Bandsman* encouraged his local bands to raise money for the 'bandsmen's kiddies' in the stricken South Wales coalfield. In the December of the same year, the paper launched a 'Find A Miner A Job' campaign, encouraging bands away from the coalfields to fill their vacancies with unemployed miners, using government migration schemes to find them work. Whether this campaign achieved much is not known, but it illustrates the sense of fraternity that sometimes broke through the pettier elements of banding activity. There were, too, many modest acts of local assistance, as when, in 1938, Stourton Memorial Band near Leeds held a concert to boost the funds of struggling neighbours, Kippax Old.[84]

Successful bands were not exempt from these problems. In 1930, the wife of the Brighouse and Rastrick president raffled a gold watch to raise money for the band to travel to the Crystal Palace. Two years later the band was again struggling to raise the £50 for travel and only reached the target at the last moment. Wingates Temperance was less successful, failing to find the money for its London appearance in 1938.[85]

Some of the smaller bands with no reserves to fall back on found themselves in disastrous situations. The records of the Idle and Thackley Band, a sixteen-strong band from a textile community on the northern edge of Bradford, make truly depressing reading, featuring as they do a number of small but decidedly unpaid bills. In 1933, the band managed to persuade Wright and Round to supply music on credit. The company acceded to this 'unusual request' (a form of words suggesting that the company neither liked or greatly encouraged this form of transaction) as 'we remember you as very old subscribers and we want to help you as much as possible in these hard times'. The band's enthusiasm for Wright and Round's assistance is undoubtedly more than partly explained by Boosey and Hawkes's anxious enquiries in the same year about 18s.10d. owed on music purchased eighteen months earlier! The band seems to have struggled on, eventually dissolving during the war.[86] Public support, too, was affected by depression. A Welsh commentator noted a marked fall in attendance between two visits by St Hilda to Caernarfon Pavilion in May and August 1930, as 'industrial matters are bad at the quarries'.[87]

It has to be said, however, that the impression of a movement battling very hard and to a certain extent succeeding in living on reduced means and with reduced expectations – like so many sections of the working class in general in this period – is stronger than that of a movement dealt any kind of fatal blow. Alongside the various strategies for coping noted above, bands showed in general a determination to survive. A Durham newspaper was impressed that Brandon Silver band could still win prizes three years after the local colliery where most of the players worked had closed down; the *British Bandsman* equally so by the efforts of some of the Rhondda bands.[88] Indeed, virtue was often made out of necessity and periods of unemployment, and indeed periods of inactivity caused by strikes and lock-outs were often used to the bands' advantage. Work was done on bandrooms, extra time was spent on practice. The *British Bandsman* commented in 1920 that the coal strike was giving bands in areas where the shift system usually militated against midweek rehearsal, unexpected opportunity to practise. The Marsden Colliery bandmaster, Jack Boddice, claimed that the band had managed an unprecedented seventy-six full rehearsals during the 1925 coal dispute preceding its success at the National. Harton Colliery undertook a twenty-six-week tour in 1926, an opportunity that would not normally have presented itself.[89]

Banding also provided a valuable source of income, both communal and individual. Some bands worked to raise money for local projects during periods of hardship. Welsh bands, in particular, were active during the strike of 1926.[90] Probably, soloists and members of the elite bands benefited the most, as banding skills provided, in the words of one contemporary, 'the means of creating an opportunity for them to earn a livelihood, which would otherwise have been an impossibility'.[91] St Hilda Colliery's decision to become a professional band soon after the temporary closure of the pit is perhaps the most extreme response of this type to adversity.[92]

Many historians have been struck by the fact that 'Working people seem to have been extraordinarily resilient, or stubborn, in the face of the depression'.[93] That determination kept the bands and other elements of the (at least in traditional manufacturing areas) rich working-class associational culture alive. At the same time, through both the mechanisms noted above and a less quantifiable artistic contribution, bands undoubtedly played their part in softening the worst excesses of the period and in allowing people to sustain their dignity and resilience.

Mass unemployment on this scale was not to return again until the 1970s, and the 1950s and 1960s were periods of relative economic prosperity. Nevertheless, large changes were wrought by the secular decline in the numbers employed in certain traditional staple industries. The geography of banding as it stood in 1914 corresponded fairly faithfully to the geography of eighteenth- and nineteenth-century industrialization. As has already been shown, the 'classic' location of bands was the small industrial town or village. As that industrial pattern altered, the place of bands shifted with it. The most striking example is provided by the mining industry. In the early 1920s 1,289,000 miners were employed in Great Britain. By 1974, that number had fallen to 246,000. The situation becomes even clearer if looked at in a local perspective. In 1923, 170,000 miners were employed in Durham. By 1939, the figure had fallen to 112,000, by 1960 to 87,000, by 1970 to 34,000. Seventy-five Durham pits closed in the 1960s.[94] Given the huge contribution made by miners to the band movement, it is hardly surprising that their falling numbers and, above all, the subsequent breaking-up of pit communities and the distinctive social life that they spawned, have contributed much to both the decline in the number of bands and their diminished role in social life.

Ultimately, however, relative affluence proved a greater threat than industrial depression and economic decline. There can be no doubt that, for those in regular employment, the period from 1924 to 1938 saw a significant and almost continuous rise in real wages.[95] Crucially, the period also saw a marked fall in basic working hours for many workers. Six and a half million workers enjoyed an average reduction of six and a half hours a week in 1919, and although this was the single largest such reduction, by the end of the 1930s, the forty-eight-hour week had replaced the pre-war norm of fifty-four hours for many workers.[94] The 1950s and 1960s were to see further extensions of these twin developments. Obviously, confident generalizations like these ride roughshod over the often massive hardships of some areas and some individuals. Nevertheless, it is clear that many people had both increasing amounts of disposable income and increasing amounts of spare time in which to spend it. The ensuing social changes undoubtedly touched the brass band world.

Bands themselves had benefited greatly from similar processes in the nineteenth century. Now they found that in an environment conducive to the expansion of leisure activities, rivals emerged. Concentrating for the moment on the inter-war period, challenges for popular commitment, loyalty and money came from a number of directions. Many of them had first emerged in the years immediately before the war, but they undoubtedly gathered momentum. One such challenge was offered by sport, especially soccer, although rugby union in South Wales, and rugby league in its various enclaves in the North of England, could attract large support, as could league cricket, and the 'new' sports of the period, especially speedway and greyhound racing.

To a degree, bands coexisted with sport, providing half-time or pre-event entertainment at many venues. Again, it must be stressed that sport could suffer quite seriously from the same economic pressures that affected bands. First-division soccer attendances fell in the height of the depression in the early 1930s, while a number of sides in depressed areas, including Merthyr, Ashington, Thames, and Durham City lost league status as crowds fell and finances crumbled.[97] Gareth Williams has illustrated how Welsh rugby suffered from the loss of players in the 1930s as top performers either turned professional with league sides or went to those West Country union clubs able to find them work.[98] Nevertheless, while such a broad view guards against simplistic analysis, there can be no denying the intensifying hold of sport in this period. Average attendance at football matches over the period as a whole rose steadily, first-division averages rising from 25,300 in 1927–8 to 30,600 in 1938–9, and peaking at 40,700 in 1949–50. The sideshow nature of band performances at soccer matches seems suitably symbolic of wider shifts in popular loyalties.[99]

The cinema, too, was blamed by many commentators for the bands' difficulties. As with sport, there can be no doubt of its hold over popular audiences. Annual cinema attendances rose from 903 million in 1934 to 1,027 million by 1940.[100] Of some importance here was the high attendance of the boys and young men that bands were so keen to recruit. Clearly, spectator sport and the cinema were easy targets, especially in a period when many commentators made much of the division between 'active' (good) and 'passive' (bad) leisure pursuits. Less commonly selected for attack, because they were normally 'active' but actually representing serious competition, were the innumerable voluntary activities that absorbed the energies of so many. The number of junior football clubs grew from 12,000 in 1910 to 35,000 in 1937; the Scout movement grew from 108,000 to 420,000 over the same period.[101] One could play football (and be a scout) and play in a band; many, including Jack Mackintosh, managed it. The point is simply that there were ever more choices, choices diminishing the bands' pool of recruits and supporters. After the war, although some of the leisure pursuits discussed here were now themselves suffering from declining patronage, a further set of social activities emerged to reshape leisure style. Television, DIY and motoring were only three of the most talked about.[102]

Without any doubt, however, the most significant threat, and probably the single most important change of any type influencing the band movement, was the massive set of changes in popular musical tastes and habits which first became apparent in the period around the end of the First World War. At the very heart of this lay three interrelated developments: the growth of the technological media; the so-called 'Americanization' of British popular music; and the accompanying rise of the dance band and a new style of dance music.[103] The term 'Americanization' is problematic, and is only used here as a working generalization, to refer to broad changes in British taste and repertoire that owed something to exposure to American influences. Similarly, 'dance band music' covers a range of evolving styles played by a variety of musical combinations, and again the phrase is loosely worn here. The significance of these changes has to be traced over a long period, at least into the 1950s, in order to be fully appreciated, but the focus for the moment remains on the inter-war years.

This sea change in taste has many strands, too complex to unravel in full detail here. Of major importance was the take-off of the dance hall. As already noted, dance halls were a feature of British popular musical culture from the mid-nineteenth century. However, they were generally deemed unacceptable by respectable middle- and working-class society and it required the relative loosening of social restraints during the First World War (coupled with an increase in purchasing power) to generate a more tolerant attitude. From about 1919–20 there was, too, an important change in the marketing and structure of the dance hall business with the establishment of the highly respectable 'palais de danse'. The earliest halls to bear this name, at Hammersmith and Birmingham, were aimed at middle- and lower-middle-class audiences (minimum admission at Birmingham in 1920 was 5*s*.) but over the course of the next decade this new style of hall became available to a far wider clientele. Together with the much larger number of venues that grew up in all manner of premises all over the country, they occupied an absolutely central place in popular social life from the early 1920s.[104]

With the new halls came new music. The older styles were not totally displaced. There was always a market for 'old-tyme' dancing among older age groups and indeed in the late 1930s there was a considerable enthusiasm for 'Gay Nineties' nights in some northern halls among younger audiences. Bolton even witnessed a vogue for *ceilidhs* in 1938 which both worried local swing bands and raised listenership to Radio Telefis Éireann.[105] American styles, however, predominated. After a brief flirtation with the jazz music of the type associated with the American 'novelty' bands that visited Britain between 1916 and 1920, British bands rapidly adopted a much lusher, sweeter style, drawing in particular on the work of Paul Whiteman. Whiteman virtually set the agenda for British dance music in the 1920s. When he allowed Bix Beiderbecke to play 'hot' solos, British bands felt able to unleash their soloists in similar fashion. Similarly, in the later 1930s American swing bands established the new canons of taste.[106]

The fact that the 'Americanization' of popular music in this period was often stimulated initially through *live* performance in dance halls, and indeed in variety theatres, is a point sometimes overlooked. So, too, is the fact that throughout the rest of the period to 1939 many first experienced new musical trends through the medium of live performance. Nevertheless, it would be hard to underestimate the key role played by the new technological media, partly the gramophone, but above all the wireless. The growth of this technology in this period was striking. By 1928 there were an estimated 2.5 million gramophones in Britain, record sales having increased from 22 million to 50 million in the previous four years. The collapse of the record industry in 1929–30 slowed this growth dramatically but a crucial base had been laid.[107] The growth of broadcasting was more significant still. In 1922, when the British Broadcasting Company (as it was then known) was founded, only one household in every 100 had a licence. By 1930, the figure had become 30 in every 100, and by 1939 it had risen to 71.[108]

The spread of new technology fundamentally altered the context in which brass bands operated. First, it undermined the bands' function as a source of musical education and dissemination in the field of art music and even in some areas of light music. It was now so much easier for audiences to gain access to various types of music in the original form. J. H. Elliot's claim in 1936 that 'the old conception of the brass band as a mirror through which the classics could be displayed to thousands who could never see the actuality is no longer valid', may have underestimated levels of previous popular musical experience as well as the continuing popularity of selections, but it underscores this fundamental change in the musical environment.[109]

Alongside this, wireless and gramophone gave massive exposure to the new, mainly American, styles of popular music. It is noteworthy that dance band record sales provided the biggest source of record company profit in the 1920s.[110] Dance band music formed a regular and popular broadcasting feature from the earliest days. The local stations that carried so many of the earliest transmissions before their absorption into the BBC regional networks from the late 1920s, regularly featured bands and did much to stimulate local groups.[111] The BBC's first national band transmission came in March 1923, and in the next month the Savoy Havana Band made the first of its many broadcasts. In 1928, the BBC formed its own dance band with Jack Payne as leader.[112] By the end of the decade, late evening dance band performances were an established feature of the schedule. From the early 1930s another source of dance music was supplied by the expanding network of continental commercial stations, which the BBC fought so persistently to destroy. Radio Luxembourg's powerful transmitter penetrated the whole country, although most of the other stations could only be clearly received in the South-East and Midlands.[113] For the few, there were also the American East Coast shortwave stations, whose jazz programmes could be received quite clearly at certain times of the year and to whose timetables the proselytizing *Melody Maker* gave considerable space.

This massively increased interest in American popular music and in dance music in general called into being a legion of dance bands. The existing literature on dance bands concentrates very largely on the top-flight professional bands but pays little attention to the huge number of bands that grew up to service the needs of local halls. It is not possible yet to talk with confidence about numbers, growth rhythms, geography or social class. First impressions suggest rapid growth, large numbers, a genuinely national coverage and a wide social mix, but still (at least at semi-professional level and below) a preponderance of working-class players. Gender issues are clear: almost all bands were male, although women players were not completely unknown.[114]

Bands playing a degree of American-style music existed in London and the provinces by 1919–20. The involvement of the dance music publisher, Lawrence Wright, in the launch of *Melody Maker* in 1926 as largely a dance band musicians' paper suggests a fairly advanced level of growth during the early 1920s.[115] By the 1930s, the dance band had become a major feature of musical life. In 1938, a local correspondent in *Melody Maker*, with an albeit ill-disguised enthusiasm for the musical prowess of his region, claimed that Bolton, Lancashire, had almost fifty 'gig' bands, with another twelve in the neighbouring district of Farnworth.[116] These would have ranged from scratch bands probably surviving for very short periods in the 'lower' end of the market, hunting for work in the private party, scout hut dance market, to the elite semi-professional bands with residencies at local halls, recording engagements and quite probably some success in the network of dance band competitions which *Melody Maker* established almost immediately after commencing publication. Most towns possessed a solid core of dance band players. Raymond Thomson's excellent study of dance in Greenock – admittedly in the post-1945 period – suggests that in a town with a population of 70,000 about 100 musicians served the fifteen local venues.[117]

The significance of the dance band in this context lay not only in its new repertoire but in the challenge it posed to the hegemony of the brass band. Here was a rival instrumental organization of real strength growing up within the community at large. The spokesmen of the brass band movement were for the most part as hostile to 'jazz', as they (like so many other commentators) termed dance music of all types, as all other defenders of musical tradition based on formal notation, formal training and a base in Western art music. They had not liked ragtime either and they assumed that jazz would be a short-lived craze, as ragtime had been for many British audiences. Even many perceptive players made the same assumption, Harry Mortimer, as he wryly remembers in his autobiography, turning down the chance to play with Jack Hylton on these grounds.[118] It says little for the grasp of popular taste among many in the movement that, as late as 1938, contributors to the band press could still proclaim: 'it will be a glad time for brass bands when this craze dies out', 'let not the bands lose heart it is only a passing phase', and 'we believe and contend that "jazz" and "swing" music is a passing vogue'.[119] Their greatest worry was that dance bands would attract brass band players. Undoubtedly they did. Indeed, at least in the provinces, the brass band not surprisingly formed the major training ground for dance band brass players. They were greeted with some suspicion by some of their new colleagues, the brass band being seen by many as a profoundly unsuitable nursery. A writer, commenting on the quality of Billy Cotton's new trombonist in 1928, was paying a compliment when he said: 'Originally a brass band man, he has left all traces of that school behind.' Jock Bain, trombonist with Roy Fox, commented ten years later: 'some aver that the thorough brass band man never shakes himself free of staccato phrasing and thin tone – especially on the trombone.' Bain concluded that it depended 'on the man behind the gun'. By now, there were many gunslingers.[120]

In 1926 the *British Bandsman* presented the issue in simple terms of loyalty to a pure movement against short-lived financial gain:

> Is it worthwhile sacrificing all the comradeship, and maybe the healthy rivalry of brass banding, for a temporarily more lucrative spare-time occupation, which, in a year or two's time, the caprice of a fickle public may (as likely as not) have relegated to the limbo of forgotten things?[121]

Whatever the bandsman's musical taste or sense of loyalty, at that exact juncture the financial rewards were extremely high, as indicated by rumours that due to the huge demand for trumpet and trombone players for work of this type, theatre musicians were being paid ten times their normal fee to take dance engagements.[122] Throughout the 1930s, dance band work undoubtedly offered reasonable remuneration, and probably higher than that available to most bandsmen.

Unquestionably, some players were lost to the movement in this way. These ranged from soloists such as George Swift, who went from St Hilda to Jack Hylton, to rank and file players.[123] However, bands had always suffered the loss of personnel, whether to symphony orchestras or ice rink bands, and it is probable that much of the contemporary complaint about heavy losses was exaggerated. Bandsmen had a long tradition of combining loyalty to their bands with semi-professional work and this pattern probably continued over this period in the shape of men like Frank Wilby, cornet with Brighouse in the 1930s and trumpeter with the New Imperial Dance Orchestra in Huddersfield; Cliff Ward, conductor of Llanelly Silver and leader of Len Colvin and his Denza Players; and the cautious A. L. of South Shields, cornet player with a first section band, who wrote to the *Melody Maker* asking for advice about mouthpieces for dance band trumpeters who did not want to spoil their brass band work.[124]

This dangerously 'divided interest' worried band commentators almost as much as defections. They claimed, probably with some justification, that dance band engagements kept players away from rehearsals, and, less convincingly, that they developed in the dance hall 'a slipshod way of playing' that was undermining the movement's musical standards.[125] In the final analysis, however, probably more crucial to the long-term future of banding was that dance bands recruited a new generation of musicians that might otherwise have gone into brass bands and that this massive injection of new musical experience fundamentally shifted the taste of the younger generation.

The first point is difficult to substantiate, but there is no doubt that the 1930s in particular saw a rise in the sale of previously relatively unorthodox instruments, most notably saxophones, but also accordions, guitars, mandolins, and many others. Musical instrument dealers were quick to respond to the new market opportunity, offering most of these instruments at weekly hire-purchase rates of between 2*s*. and 2*s*.6*d*. per week.[126] On the second point, there can be no denying the massive appetite for American-influenced dance music in this period. Dance band programmes were consistently shown to be among the most popular form of radio entertainment, especially among younger audiences. In their 1939 study, *Broadcasting in Everyday Life*, Jennings and Gill noted that when asked to name their favourite band conductor as a test of knowledge and discrimination, while 'the elder women showed complete indifference', 57 per cent of young women and 89 per cent of children put forward a name. The authors also noted the debate that took place within the community over interpretation of individual tunes by different bands, admitting with a little reluctance that 'even in homes where dance music flows on for hours at a time, a certain amount of discrimination is exercised'. They recorded, too, that national band leaders were hero-worshipped and that even local players gained enhanced status in their communities.[127]

This major set of changes in popular taste obviously accounts for some of the lost public engagements of the late 1930s and earlier. It must also have been central to the recruitment problems which were emerging just before the war. By the late 1930s, bands were having to draw from the first 'youth culture' that had been fully exposed to the new technological media. The changed taste of youngsters was a commonly cited reason for the bands' problems. When Southowram Band folded in February 1938, the decision hinged on the fact that it was hard 'to get youths to take up the instruments'. In the same month Crookes band in Sheffield, the third band to fold in the city in twelve months, claimed that 'they could not get youths to take up the instruments'. In the next month, when Barton's band in Preston 'simply faded out', the *British Bandsman* claimed: 'The bands in the Preston district are getting concerned about the lack of interest which is beginning to show itself in the general public. They seem to be more interested in military bands and jazz combinations.'[128]

To an extent, some bands attempted to fight back with changes in repertoire and performance structure. Jazz pieces occasionally appeared in the publishers' journals, Munn and Felton making effective use of Feldman's brass band arrangement of the Original Dixieland Jazz Band classic, *Tiger Rag*, at the 1938 National concert. Played as an encore for *Labour and Love*, 'it caught the audience by surprise by its unexpectedness, but after the initial shock (as it were) everyone settled down to enjoy it, especially the drummer's effects.'[129] More common was the increased use of vocal or non-brass instrumental items, although such performers usually worked within the 'popular classic' rather than the 'popular' idiom. Probably the most successful of these acts was Roland Jones, euphonium soloist with Black Dyke and, from 1939, Bickershaw, who was regularly featured by his bands as an operatic tenor. Indeed, he went on to join Sadler's Wells as principal tenor in 1947. Ultimately, however, these tactics provided little defence. Although the *British Bandsman* writer who claimed in 1938 that brass bands 'couldn't swing' may have underestimated their potential for change, he nevertheless captured their limits in the new environment.[130] Under the impact of the 'Americanization' of popular music the brass band, that most British of musical institutions, had lost its privileged position in the popular musical culture of industrial Britain.

It may seem perverse to have spent so much time looking at the inter-war period, a time during which the bands' declining status in popular musical life was only just becoming apparent. However, it does seem that this period saw the establishment of new patterns of musical style and consumption that increasingly cut brass bands adrift from the wider community and, more particularly, the younger performers and consumers. The problems experienced in the 1950s and 1960s to a large extent simply represented the working-through of the previous thirty years of social and cultural change.

The 1940s and 1950s certainly continued the process of change. The presence of American servicemen in Britain during the war further stimulated the popularity of swing. Revivalist jazz from about 1946 and the 'trad' jazz boom of the late 1950s and 1960s may have represented a further challenge to the supply of brass players. Absolutely fundamental was the great change in the popular musical tastes of the young, beginning in earnest in 1956 and establishing a whole new pantheon of musical rivalries, rock 'n' roll, skiffle, and jive, words which, like jazz before them, many band writers could only bear to write down if sanitized by inverted commas. With jazz and dance music there could be coexistence, at least at the level of shared instrumentation and personnel. With the guitar-led 'pop' culture there was very little overlap. It can have been little consolation that the old rivals, the dance bands, were also damaged by the change.[131] Television theme tunes, selections from shows like *South Pacific*, coupled with the not inconsiderable audience they retained for the standard band repertoire, still gave brass bands a footing in the wider popular musical culture. None the less, by the late 1950s they had become effectively divorced from the mainstream culture of popular *youth* culture. The passage from somewhere near the centre to the margin of popular culture had reached the point of no return.

A final consideration in this study of decline concerns the style of band culture. As early as the 1930s but perhaps particularly from the 1950s, it may well have been the brass band's image and overall culture, as much as its music, that made it unattractive to new generations. Bands had always operated under a very tight discipline. Conductors or bandmasters who had won the respect of their players, usually through artistic achievements, could exert the authority of an officer over the ranks. Sometimes that discipline was natural, considerate and unforced, other times almost cruel. Tom Morgan, conductor of Callender's and indeed an ex-military bandmaster, could generate an atmosphere in which 'sometimes you'd actually be sweating with fear'. J. A. Greenwood was another with a tendency to hardness.[132] All bandmasters placed high emphasis upon an almost military cleanliness, formality and neatness. Black Dyke bandmaster, Arthur O. Pearce, stressed these elements very forcefully. In the late 1940s, solo cornet Willie Lang, forgetting his overcoat for a park engagement, was saturated in a subsequent downpour when Pearce refused to allow him to borrow a replacement. Afterwards, it was Lang who apologized for his improper dress.[133] At about the same period at the beginning of a park concert on an exceptionally hot day, Pearce, tunic over arm,

> addressed the audience and asked them if the players could play with their tunics off. An immediate 'yes' was voiced by the audience, so in coloured shirts and with caps on they played to a delighted crowd. This is a good exhibition of discipline and will be remembered for a long time.[134]

Generally, those brought up in the movement seem to have accepted and indeed been proud of this discipline, but it must have appealed less to new recruits, especially as there were now attractive alternatives. Dance bands from the 1920s and pop groups from the 1950s, although in a sense adopting uniforms of their own, had an altogether more fashionable image. Interestingly, some of the uniform manufacturers who had serviced brass bands were quick to respond to the new opportunity, Beevers of Huddersfield, one of the oldest uniform firms, offering 'styles of the moment for dance bands'.[135] Again, although many were run in a fairly hard-headed way, there was a slightly more democratic feel about dance bands and groups. There was, too, an element of responsiveness, bands picking up rapidly on new styles and new repertoire. Brass bands were much more at the behest of publishers, contest organizers, conductors and the sheer weight of tradition. Certainly by the 1950s, in an age when, for young men, uniform and discipline meant National Service, the essentially Victorian brass band sub-culture must have appeared somewhat anachronistic. It seems suitable that the brass band's major contest should have been sponsored by a daily paper, the *Daily Herald*, that was very much associated with the older generation of the 'traditional' working class.[136]

IV

For most of the period to about 1930 the band movement felt itself hugely neglected and underestimated by the musical and, indeed, the entire artistic 'establishment'. There were good grounds for this view. The 1927 *Grove* almost ignored the movement altogether and even the *Musical Times* failed to notice either Holst or Elgar's test pieces in 1928 and 1930, respectively. When bands were mentioned much of what was written was inaccurate and ill-informed. Probably the most infamous example of this is afforded by Beecham's speech to a luncheon club in Leeds in 1928 when he referred to the brass band as 'that superannuated, obsolete, beastly, disgusting, horrid method of making music'. This attack formed only part of a wild tirade against many aspects of British musical life and some, like Iles, felt able to dismiss it as mere publicity-seeking or as simply another example of Beecham's idiosyncratic beliefs. 'I cannot take anything Sir Thomas Beecham says about music seriously', the editor of the *British Bandsman* told his readers. Others were furious and lengthy criticism of Beecham filled the band press for some weeks.[137]

As the twentieth century progressed, many leading figures within the brass band movement began to entertain great hopes that through its alliance with 'serious' composers, the brass band would attain the *kudos* previously denied it and take its rightful place in the mainstream of serious musical culture. Large claims followed each new test piece commissioned from 'outside'. Hubert Bath's 1922 test piece, *Freedom*, was deemed the first brass band symphony, the appearance of which 'marks an epoch in the history of the movement, and the year 1922 will become a date of outstanding importance in the world of music'. The 'capture' of Elgar in 1930 was greeted with particular rejoicing, well illustrated by Iles's strangled hyperbole as he made the announcement in the *British Bandsman*: 'The upward progress in our ambitions and aims for thirty years past is disclosed in the grandeur of our attainments today.'[138] By 1938, the *British Bandsman*'s editor, James Brier, could write: 'Bands have always been popular with the working-class people, but since our great composers began to realize the merit of our working-class brass bands they have risen to the dignity of professional orchestras in some cases.'[139]

Although these declamations – 'movement' rhetoric at its most extreme – were hopelessly exaggerated, bands undoubtedly received greater attention from about the early 1930s. If the specialist music press failed to notice Elgar's *Severn Suite* the national press certainly did not and the ensuing publicity helped launch a modest 'discovery' of the movement. Two *Musical Times* articles by Denis Wright on 'Scoring for Brass Band' in 1932, later expanded into a book, continued the process, followed by Harold Hind's technical treatise *The Brass Band* (1934), Bliss's inclusion, albeit briefly, of a positive comment on bands in his 'A musical pilgrimage of Britain' for *The Listener* (1935) and J. F. Russell and J. H. Elliot's pioneering history, *The Brass Band Movement* (1936). Apart from the stimulus provided by Elgar, these publishing events also reflected a mild flurry of competition among music publishers for a potential new market and, more importantly, a small part of the much wider 'discovery' of working-class culture that so marked the 1930s.

This flurry of anthropological endeavour encompasses the investigative journalism of Orwell, the documentary film movement, the establishment of Mass Observation and much else. Some of the impetus for this investigation stemmed from sympathy with the plight of the unemployed, while much else reflected the contemporary debate over the 'Americanization' of British culture. Increasingly, especially among certain elements on the political left, the working class suddenly appeared a homely bulwark against the worst excesses of a shadowy and rarely tightly defined Americanism.[140] Some composers enthusiastically embraced the bands as a refuge against the American invasion. The clearest statement of this type came from Hubert Bath, writing about the 1930 National:

> It was a joy to me as a musician to know that the musical backbone of our country, north of Luton, is not and, it is hoped, never will be at the mercy of the American invasion. The breath of our good, honest, fresh brass air from the north was, and always will be, an invigorating tonic to the jaded, Americanised southerner.[141]

After about 1940, composers and musical commentators could less often, and less glibly, admit their total ignorance of bands. An outburst like Beecham's of 1928 would have been inconceivable in 1948; indeed, in February 1947, he conducted a mass band concert at Belle Vue.[142] Certainly, between approximately 1930 and 1955, the national press gave the movement more coverage than previously. Alexander Owen's death in 1920 received almost no mention, whereas Fred Mortimer's in 1953 even earned an obituary in some editions of *The Times*.[143]

The emergence of the brass band as a 'serious' artistic force was not, though, to become a reality. Very few composers ever produced more than one piece for bands and fewer still entered into anything resembling long-term relationships with them. To a degree this simply reflected the class base of the British musical elite. The band movement occupied a social position beyond the experience of most contemporary composers. Probably more influential, however, was the bands' rigid, almost ritualistic adherence to a specific instrumentation, one both alien to most formally trained musicians, and appearing restricted in scope to those who did discover it.

From about 1950 the movement thus passed from hopeful enthusiasm about its possible elevation in the artistic hierarchy to the ambivalent attitude it perhaps still shows. The musical and artistic 'establishment', especially the Arts Council, was increasingly viewed with suspicion and sometimes worse, and yet there was great pride in those bandsmen who graduated into symphony orchestras, and affection toward those composers and conductors who paid the movement some attention.[144] There was, too, an inferiority complex, reflected in a desire to be flattered by the elite musical community, and to flatter it. Jack Howard's 'appreciation' at the beginning of Frank Wright's *Brass Today* (1957) illustrates this well. Howard, the managing director of Bessons, claimed that it would be 'invidious' to single out any of the many contributors for special mention, but then did exactly that, selecting first Sir Adrian Boult, and then Karl Rankl, former musical director of the Royal Opera House, Covent Garden. Both men had done much for bands, especially Boult, both as a guest conductor and through his work at the BBC, but it is highly significant that Howard felt obliged to emphasize their achievements, rather than those of some of the other contributors, many of whom had over thirty years' 'frontline' service.

Similarly, despite the heightened level of media coverage from the 1930s until approximately the mid-1960s, bands were never really able to hold a strong

Plate 6(a), (b)   Two images of the 1937 National contest, illustrating the essentially light-hearted treatment often accorded to bands by the media. (*Source: Hulton-Deutsch Collection.*)

position in the general popular culture. In their strongholds they were often respected and capable of generating quite considerable degrees of local and regional patriotism. The *Shields Daily Gazette* used St Hilda's national victory of 1920 for a strong defence of the cultural vitality of the North:

> The southerner is apt to regard the northman – especially if the latter hails from an industrial or coal-mining area – as a somewhat grim and hard being, who has little use for the refining graces and arts of life. As a matter of fact, the North is, we believe, more musical than the South; that is, musical inclination and aptitude are commoner possessions of the people. The fame of its bandsmen, recruited almost entirely from the ranks of labour, affords one proof of that; its celebrated choirs and musical societies supply others.[145]

There was something of this almost missionary spirit behind the annual pilgrimage to London for the National, a northern cultural 'invasion' of the unenlightened South.

In general, however, in most parts of Britain outside of the band heartlands, and eventually even there to a degree, a strikingly different image of bands and industrial musical culture emerged. Ultimately, much of this stems from the representation of bands by a national press that often did not understand the culture it was portraying. Ignorant of the specialist nature of the music, reporters sought for 'human interest' – inevitably, given that this became the unifying element of so much journalism from the 1930s. In general, treatment of bands was light-hearted. 'Characters' and atmosphere dominated. This was most noticeable in the use of photographic imagery. A set of clichés evolved, a favourite involving a very young player invariably featured either holding the largest instrument, or conducting the rest of the band (or, even better, older members of his own family) in some impromptu concert (see Plate 6 (a), (b)). The adjudicators' box was another object of interest and humour. Did they really stay in there that long and what happened when they wanted to . . . ?[146]

This generally humorous, light-weight treatment, which might usefully be termed the 'oompah-syndrome', was reinforced through a variety of other representations, such as the use of bands in adverts for breweries. As a result of this, the brass band began to emerge from at least as early as the 1930s as a convenient symbol for a rather comic-book northernness. Dennis Potter captured this in a *Daily Herald* review of 'Man of Brass', a 1963 BBC TV play by Ron Watson, starring Jimmy Edwards as a double Bb bass player named Ernie Briggs, who preferred his band to married life. This 'northern saga', commented Potter, 'grimly celebrating slate-grey rain and polished euphoniums, was firmly in the eeh-bah-goom heritage of lazy so-called North Country humour'.[147]

Much of this satire was understandable. In an ever more style-conscious age the bands' use of uniform and their maintenance of often clumsy Victorian names gave them a rather antiquated image in many eyes. There were also, of course, other more positive images, including the rather heroic 'dignity of labour through art' or 'sacrifice of labour for their art' depictions usually found in left-of-centre representations. The *Daily Herald* usually included one such item in its pre-National coverage, as in 1947, when the contest took place during a chronic fuel crisis. The paper noted: 'The musicians of the miners' bands had worked two shifts without rest last Thursday, to avoid a drop in production while away.'[148] (While this style of description tended to be overblown, it is hard not to be impressed by that particular act.) In general, though, comedy won out.

There was more to this than the simple use of bands as slight comic relief. It also represented the marginalization and even denigration of provincial culture, and more especially Northern (the strong Celtic band tradition was little noted) working-class culture. In an age when, especially as a result of the BBC's centralizing tendencies, the metropolis was increasingly assumed to be the centre of British culture, and when an expanding media emphasized the international, the brass band appeared decidedly parochial.

The BBC's policy of 'cultural uplift', its desire to raise standards of taste, for the most part added to the problem. The brass band was often treated as a rather deviant form in need of being 'taken in hand', as *The Listener* once put it. The BBC did consider establishing its own band in the 1930s but the idea did not come to fruition. In effect, Callender's served as the BBC house band at least until Mortimer's arrival in 1942, making its 150th broadcast in January 1938.[149] The band was eminently suited to the role. Angry at missing out on the first prize at Belle Vue in 1928, it refused to compete there again and threw away all their Smith and Company arrangements, subsequently proving highly sympathetic to the rather technical and specialist works that some BBC personnel felt bands should be playing. This combination of musical 'correctness' and hostility to the contesting world (combined with proximity to London) may have benefited Callender's, but other, more mainstream bands, were regularly measured against the band in such places as the wireless notes of *Musical Times*, and found wanting. Conversely, when it suited programming needs, bands were made to look comical and unsophisticated, as when Lostwithiel Band was asked to play '*Flora* [sic] *Dance* at a much increased tempo so as to fit the time block' allocated to it on a particular programme.[150]

The ultimately rather cosy image of the working man at play that emerged from so many of these presentations allowed the brass band, rather in the way that George Formby and Gracie Fields operated in a much larger arena, to be appropriated by the media as a symbol of the working class in amiable, domesticated form.[151] In times of conflict, the bands were used to remind the middle classes of the essential 'decency' of the working class. In 1920, a reporter on the *Croydon Advertiser* revealed much when informing readers: 'It was a delightful contrast to the dreadful strike of the miners that . . . many brass bands from colliery districts assembled at the Crystal Palace and joined in the competition'. The Victorian notion of music as the civilizing art clearly still had purchase; brass instruments made striking miners safe.[152]

The relationship between the band movement and popular political culture raised here is a key one. Before 1914 bands for the most part adopted a self-consciously non-political stance, seeking, for 'the good of the band', to appeal to and serve as wide a community as possible. This tendency remained equally marked in the period studied here. The movement's spokesman continued to stress the need to avoid controversy, and the band press remained generally mute on all major domestic political issues.[153]

Obviously, some chose a different path. In certain areas, especially in mining districts, relatively strong organizational and financial links were forged with trade unions. The Durham coalfield provides particularly strong evidence of this, with a number of lodges adopting and funding bands. The annual miners' gala in July became one of the great festivals in the band as well as the union calendar. Some bands were prepared to display public loyalty to lodge politics. In 1922 St Hilda, Harton and Marsden Colliery bands headed a procession for William Lawther, the Labour Party general election candidate for South Shields.[154]

In 1928, at a time of particular tension within the Durham miners' movement, two Durham colliery band conductors, W. R. Straughan, in charge of both Hetton and Houghton bands, and R. C. Lander of Lumley band, claimed that they had been sacked by their bands because their political views were not acceptable to the Durham Miners' Association.[155] A letter from the Hetton secretary denied the charge, admitting to 'a little trouble between the union officials and Mr Straughan' but claiming that Straughan's sacking was the result of his being too busy with other bands.[156] Lumley's officials responded to the political charge by arguing that Lander was dismissed because of his 'reckless' use of money when engaging players and buying instruments. 'Mercato', the *British Bandsman*'s Durham correspondent, and Lander seem to have been one and the same person. In his last piece for the paper before he moved south after the collapse of his small business, 'Mercato' lay the accusation of corruption alongside that of socialism. 'So long as a conductor will sing the *Red Flag* and ask no questions as to what's happening with the £8 or £10 a month subscribed by the colliery workmen he is all right, but as soon as he wants a little information no time is lost in getting rid of him.'[157] While there is not really enough evidence to reach the essence of these disputes, it is obvious that some bands and their officials were anxious to defend the ideals of the labour movement within the wider mining culture.

In general, however, such events were the exception that prove the rule. It is significant that the bands which marched for Lawther in 1922 felt it necessary to defend themselves against a hostile letter in the local press on the grounds that their action was simply an extension of their general community service function. Harton's secretary argued: 'We did what we thought was our duty, the same as we did when we paraded the town for the Mayor's Catillon Fund, the Ingham Infirmary Fund, the Buffs memorial day, and various other objects.'

St Hilda's Jimmy Southern, while pointing out that 'St. Hilda's Lodge, through their generous weekly subscription rightly demands a claim on our services', offered his opinion that such parades did little to change people's minds and stressed that 'we rely upon the support of all sides and hope to meet a continuance of the same'.[158]

More important perhaps in this context were the links that were forged between bands and colliery management and owners. A number of bands received important financial assistance from these sources, including some of the lodge bands. St Hilda band was given £100 after winning the National in 1920, probably a fairly small cost for the publicity the company received.[159] Moreover, there must have been very close liaison between bands and managers in order to secure the often very substantial periods away from work required for contest and, above all, concert tours of the type undertaken by St Hilda and Harton. Management could also exert a powerful hold over individuals; in the 1920s Bill Blackett of Harton Colliery was threatened with dismissal if he played for another band. For an individual who stood to make £3 a week during band tours as opposed to his normal rate of £1.17s.0d. as a platelayer, such threats had real force.[160]

Evidence of similar barriers preventing the bands from becoming a more central element of the labour movement can be found all over the country. There were in fact incidents that placed bands in confrontation with individual unions. The pre-war battle with the Musicians' Union over bands and bandsmen undercutting union rates persisted at least into the early 1920s. Some unions objected to band's recruiting policies, several members of Horwich RMI Band losing their jobs in the early 1930s after railway unions complained that long-serving employees were being laid off at the expense of recently appointed bandsmen.[161] In general, the old-established 'business' mentality persisted, bands taking any engagement that would not alienate the local community, and taking necessary action where needed to distance themselves from controversy. St Hilda was reputed to have dropped 'colliery' from its title after the General Strike in order not to alienate potential customers. Gravesend Workers' Band changed its name in the same year, believing 'Workers' to be 'acting as a deterrent. Although, taken literally, this should not be the case, the existing prejudices of political opinion cannot be totally ignored.'[162] All the examples here stem from the inter-war period, but there is little evidence of any great shift after 1945. Indeed, the incorporation of colliery bands into welfare schemes after nationalization may have intensified this pattern.

It is instructive that neither the industrial nor political wings of the labour movement ever really made serious efforts to encourage bands either politically or artistically. *The Miner*, the official paper (1926–1930) of the Miners' Federation of Great Britain, for example, did much to encourage literary and artistic expression through 'Black Diamonds', its weekly page devoted to reader's contributions, yet barely mentioned bands despite their centrality in the musical culture of many miners. In general, the labour movement's emphasis was much more on the creation of an oppositional popular culture, based on specifically created workers' sports clubs, theatre groups, cine clubs, choirs, and so forth, rather than on attempts to reshape or use existing configurations.[163] Such an attitude suggests many possibilities. Labour leaders may simply have been acknowledging the fact that they were dealing with a long-established associational culture with an essentially non-political approach that was not easily changed. It does also suggest a lack of confidence in and perhaps, in the case of the intelligentsia on the political left, an ignorance of, the strength of the indigenous working-class culture. Whatever the reasons, an emphasis on 'politically correct' forms of high art generally formed the preferred vehicles for struggle through culture.

I have suggested elsewhere, with reference to the period before 1914, that banding helped reinforce some of the more conservative – perhaps consensual is a better term – forces within society.[164] A similar case could be made for this period. At the very least the tendencies of the less politically aware bandsmen were likely to have been reinforced by their absorption in this largely non-political culture. Moreover, musical activity directly rivalled politics for precious (although perhaps less precious than before 1914) resources of time, money and energy. Most important of all, banding offered considerable artistic, emotional, social and, to a lesser extent, economic rewards. The sense of belonging to a movement, a sense quite possibly stronger after 1914 than before, had special importance here. It gave bandsmen a feeling of purpose, achievement and collective identity, which otherwise might have found an outlet in the political sphere – particularly in the labour movement. To an extent, through their musical activity, band members found satisfactions denied them elsewhere and which limited their recourse to the political arena.

It is also worth considering whether the strict discipline, the respect for authority, the great emphasis on hard work that bandsmen had imposed upon and emphasized to them so often, shaped some individuals' world view so as to prepare them better for service to the needs of the modern industrial state. Pushed to extremes, the belief that political consciousness can be defined by the structures and patterns of particular leisure pursuits tends not only towards mechanistic readings of social behaviour, but ignores the fact that the intellectual and attitudinal needs of capitalism are sometimes also those of political and industrial radicalism.[165] Socialists and trade unionists need discipline, an appetite for hard work, and so on. Nevertheless, it is hard to imagine either a works manager or a recruiting sergeant being unhappy with the precision of a band in full flight.

V

This chapter has dealt mainly with decidedly negative aspects of banding and it would be unfortunate if this emphasis masked completely the many achievements of bands over this period. The improvement in standard has been alluded to on a number of occasions; Brian Jackson's informant may not have been far wrong when claiming in the early 1960s: 'These big bands, it sounds funny to say it, like the Lindley Band that won the Belle Vue Championship in 1900 – well they wouldn't have been able to *play* some of the stuff that our local band plays now.'[166]

Given the shrinking audience for band music, much of this endeavour was only appreciated by specialist audiences. A much wider public, though, benefited in the sense that the brass band remained throughout the period the single most important training ground for brass musicians of many different styles and persuasions. Maurice Murphy is perhaps the best known of those who maintained the long-established line of supply to the symphony orchestra; Eddie Calvert, Ted Heath, Kenny Baker, Joan Hinde and Dawn Heywood are just a few of the many in the fields of jazz and light music who owed at least some of their training to brass bands.[167] There was too the great contribution that bands made to the *social* as well as the artistic life, particularly of their members, but also of the wider community. It must never be forgotten that a great deal of band work was a source of enormous fun and enjoyment.

Their decline in popularity is not, of course, peculiar to brass bands. It forms a small part of that massive process which we describe as 'the decline of "traditional" working-class culture'. Dangerously misleading in that it implies the existence of a static culture in the period from about 1880 when this traditional pattern began to emerge, in the context of popular leisure it does at least serve as a shorthand for the falling popularity of professional soccer, the music hall, certain types of seaside holiday, and so on. The very specific problems of the band illustrates how careful we have to be with blanket phrases: the movement was clearly in some difficulty before 1939, although the 'decline' of working-class culture is normally regarded as having its roots in the 1950s. Brass bands were an early victim because they lacked the absolute centrality in the total working-class culture of some of the other institutions that experienced difficulties from the 1950s and because they were especially vulnerable to the changes in taste and attitude that were eventually to mark so much of British social life. The band movement showed early, and in revealing microcosm, the combined impact of an economic shift from a manufacturing toward a service-based economy, rising living standards and greater consumerism, and the nationalization and internationalization of popular taste made possible by a powerful, largely commercially controlled technological media.

Acknowledgements

I would like to thank Joe Pope for assistance with secondary sources at an early stage, Trevor Herbert for his appraisal of the first draft of this essay, the series editors for helpful comments on the final draft, and Lynne Hamer for some last-minute help with typing.

Notes

1 *Wright and Round's Amateur Band Teachers' Guide*, 1889; *Brass Band News*, November 1889.
2 *Musical Times*, October 1936; *The Listener*, 4 November 1935; A. Littlemoor (ed.), *The Rakeway Brass Band Yearbook*, Cheadle, 1987, p. 43.
3 See, for example, article on Almondbury Band, *British Bandsman*, 9 December 1922.
4 *British Bandsman*, 31 December and 17 September 1938.
5 A. Taylor, *Labour and Love. An Oral History of the Brass Band Movement*, London, 1983, p. 17; Littlemoor, *Rakeway Yearbook*, p. 3.
6 British Federation of Brass Bands, *Directory of British Brass Bands*, York, 1980–1, pp. 51–63; Littlemoor, *Rakeway Yearbook*, pp. 385–409.
7 D. Russell, *Popular Music in England, 1840–1914. A Social History*, Manchester, 1987, pp. 165–8.
8 All figures relating to contest success are based on an analysis of the contest results in A. Taylor, *Brass Bands*, St Albans, 1979, pp. 258–99.

9 T. Herbert, 'Victorian Brass Bands', lecture given at Brass Roots Exhibition, Bradford, 1989.
10 The short-lived (1860–3) National 'contest' was won by Dorset-based Blandford Band in 1863.
11 *British Bandsman*, January 1938.
12 Ibid., 8 March 1947; Russell, *Popular Music*, p. 168.
13 Taylor, *Brass Bands*, p. 129; Taylor, *Labour*, p. 57.
14 *Northamptonshire Evening Telegraph*, 2 January 1933; *Brighouse Echo*, 7 September 1934; *British Bandsman*, 12 March 1938 and 9 January 1954, for examples of northern soloists going to Kettering. This is, of course, not to ignore a flow in the opposite direction. Leading northern bands took young players from all over the country to help maintain their success.
15 See especially Robert Fitzgerald, *British Labour Management and Industrial Welfare 1846–1939*, London, 1988.
16 Taylor, *Labour*, pp. 157–9.
17 For school orchestras, see Russell, *Popular Music*, pp. 46–7.
18 *Musical Times*, September, October and November 1935.
19 Information from interview with Ron Massey, Honley, Huddersfield; V. Brand and G. Brand, *Brass Bands in the Twentieth Century*, Letchworth, 1979, p. 167.
20 E. Howarth and P. Howarth, *What a Performance. The Brass Band Plays*, London, 1988, p. 203.
21 *British Bandsman*, 18 January 1930.
22 For example, *Shields Daily News*, 28 September 1925.
23 D. Glass, *Social Mobility in Britain*, London, 1954, pp. 98–159.
24 H. Livings, *That the Medals and Baton Be Put on View*, Newton Abbot, 1975, p. 35.
25 B. Jackson, *Working Class Community*, London, 1972 edn, pp. 22–39, for a provocative view of banding and its place in working-class culture.
26 See, for example, *Sounding Brass*, editorial, Winter 1973–4.
27 *Yorkshire Evening Post*, 30 October 1920.
28 *British Bandsman*, 23 August 1930.
29 Ibid., 24 July 1954.
30 Ibid., 26 March 1938; *The Times*, 26 September 1938.
31 *British Bandsman*, 8 October 1938.
32 For an example of wartime opportunity as exemplified by Mrs Otter of Devon, see ibid., 3 March 1945. On female dance bands, see *Melody Maker*, 22 January and 7 May 1938. Gracie Cole's move from brass to professional dance and show band work was partly facilitated by a spell with Rudy Starita's All Girl Band. See *British Bandsman*, 7 July 1945.
33 Ibid., 25 October and 10 July 1947.
34 C. Bainbridge, *Brass Triumphant*, London, 1980, p. 92.
35 *British Bandsman*, 26 June 1954.
36 Ibid., 25 April 1964.
37 P. Summerfield, *Women Workers in the Second World War*, London, 1984.
38 Jackson, *Working Class Community*, p. 22.
39 In recent years, the registration card has effectively become a membership card. Players retain their cards for three years after they end their registration with a band so that they 'still belong to the movement'. I am grateful to Ethel Beahan of the Registry for this information.
40 For a brief biographical sketch, see P. Gammond and R. Horricks, *Music on Record 1. Brass Bands*, Cambridge, 1980, pp. 76–7. This useful book carries outline biographies of many of the key figures mentioned in this chapter.
41 For the *Herald*'s marketing problems, see H. Richards, 'The *Daily Herald*, 1912–1964', *History Today*, December 1981, p. 15.

42　*British Bandsman*, 20 February 1954.
43　Ibid., 15 February 1958.
44　Ibid., 9 August 1930.
45　Taylor, *Labour*, p. 67, p. 114.
46　Ibid., pp. 161–4 for one player's not exactly flattering view of Alex Mortimer.
47　*Northamptonshire Evening Telegraph*, 30 September 1935; Taylor, *Labour*, p. 128.
48　For a marvellous – albeit highly coloured – view of Victorian dance hall, see J. Burnley, *Phases of Bradford Life*, Bradford, 1871, pp. 157–68.
49　*Bradford Observer*, 5 June 1871.
50　*British Bandsman*, 10 July 1926.
51　*Brighouse Echo*, 20 June 1930; *British Bandsman*, 5 June 1926.
52　*Brighouse Echo*, 1 August 1930; *British Bandsman*, 9 August 1930.
53　*Wright and Rounds' Brass Band News*, 5 May 1922. The bands were Foden's, Harton Colliery, Horwich RMI, Irwell Springs, St Hilda Colliery, and Wingates Temperance.
54　*British Bandsman*, 7 August 1926.
55　Ibid., 29 January 1938.
56　Ibid., 31 December 1938.
57　Taylor, *Brass Bands*, p. 132.
58　*British Bandsman*, 15 May 1954.
59　Taylor, *Labour*, p. 109.
60　We should not exaggerate the good behaviour of earlier generations of spectators. One reviewer commented in 1897: 'The selections abounded with hidden melodies – hidden by the noise of the children playing round the bandstand' (*Keighley Labour Journal*, 5 June 1897).
61　*British Bandsman*, 1 May 1920; 9 April 1938.
62　*Brighouse Echo*, 28 May 1920, 14 May and 21 May 1938. Whit Friday is, of course, still the scene of a number of quickstep contests in villages along the Lancashire and Yorkshire border, contests which in some areas can be traced back to late Victorian patterns of Whitsun celebration.
63　Jackson, *Working Class Community*, p. 26.
64　The sponsors were the *Daily Telegraph, Daily Express, Daily Graphic, Daily Mirror, Pearson's Weekly, The People*, and *Cassell's Journal*.
65　*British Bandsman*, 27 January 1945.
66　Taylor, *Labour, passim*.
67　See, for example, St Hilda's homecoming described in the *British Bandsman*, 9 October 1920.
68　*Brighouse Echo*, 25 October 1946; 18 October 1968.
69　Taylor, *Labour*, p. 262.
70　See Frank Andrew's marvellous discography in Littlemoor, *Rakeway Yearbook*, pp. 284–99; Tim Munton, in Brand and Brand, *Brass Bands*, p. 175.
71　Taylor, *Brass Bands*, p. 125.
72　H. Mortimer with A. Lynton, *Harry Mortimer on Brass*, Sherborne, 1981, p. 119.
73　*British Bandsman*, 3 March 1945.
74　Russell, *Popular Music*, pp. 185–94.
75　The *British Bandsman* gave quite extensive coverage to individual band repertoires, especially after 1945, and provides, as in so many areas, a useful source. Obviously, the discussion here revolves mainly around bands of a fairly high standard.
76　*Musical Times*, October 1932; T. Herbert, 'Repertory of a Victorian brass band', *Popular Music*, vol. 9, no. 1 (1990) p. 119; *British Bandsman*, 11 April 1914.
77　Taylor, *Brass Bands*, pp. 277–95.
78　Jackson, *Working Class Community*, p. 39.
79　See *British Bandsman*, 13 November 1920 for the bandsmen's roll of honour.

80 The best brief introduction to this topic is S. Constantine, *Unemployment in Britain Between the Wars*, London, 1980.
81 *British Bandsman*, 19 March 1938.
82 The bands were Southowram, Norland, Rishworth and Ryburn and Friendly (which soon recovered, in fact).
83 *British Bandsman*, 9 August 1930; 31 December 1938; Constantine, *Unemployment*, p. 22.
84 *British Bandsman*, 10 November and 22nd December 1928; 5 February 1938.
85 *Brighouse Echo*, 12 September 1930; 16 September 1932; *British Bandsman*, 22 October 1938.
86 Records of Idle and Thackley Brass Band, Bradford Archives, 54D 80/1/32. The band had gone bankrupt once before in the first decade of the twentieth century.
87 *British Bandsman*, 23 August 1930.
88 *Durham County Advertiser*, 26 April 1928; *British Bandsman*, 17 November 1928.
89 Ibid., 30 October 1920; *Shields Daily News*, 30 September 1925; *British Bandsman*, 7 August 1926.
90 *British Bandsman*, 19 June, 26 June and 24 July 1926.
91 Ibid., 31 December 1938.
92 Taylor, *Brass Bands*, p. 129.
93 Constantine, *Unemployment*, p. 43. For a stimulating discussion of the relationship between associational culture and unemployment, see R. McKibbin, 'The "social psychology" of unemployment in inter-war Britain' in P. J. Waller (ed.), *Politics and Social Change in Modern Britain*, Brighton, 1987, pp. 161–91.
94 M. Bulmer (ed.), *Mining and Social Change*, London, 1978, p. 22; C. Jones, 'Coal, gas and electricity' in R. Pope (ed.), *Atlas of British Social and Economic History since 1700*, London, 1989, p. 79.
95 S. G. Jones, *Workers at Play*, London, 1986, pp. 10–14, especially Table 1.2, p. 13.
96 Ibid., pp. 15–20.
97 P. Soar, *The Hamlyn A–Z of British Football Records*, London, 1985 ed., pp. 142–43.
98 G. Williams, 'From Grand Slam to Grand Slump: Economy, society and Rugby Football in Wales during the depression', *Welsh History Review*, vol. 11 (1983).
99 For attendances, see N. Fishwick, *English Football and Society, 1910–1950*, Manchester, 1989, pp. 48–9.
100 J. Richards, *The Age of the Dream Palace*, London, 1984, p. 11.
101 J. Springhall, *Youth, Empire and Society*, London, 1977, pp. 138–9.
102 A. Marwick, *British Society Since 1945*, London, 1982, has useful material.
103 For an invaluable introduction, see C. W. E. Bigsby, 'Europe, America and the cultural debate' in Bigsby, *Superculture*, London, 1975; S. Frith, 'Playing with real feeling – jazz and surburbia' and 'The pleasures of the hearth – the making of BBC light entertainment' both in Frith, *Music for Pleasure*, Oxford, 1988.
104 This paragraph draws extensively on M. Hustwitt, 'Caught in a whirlpool of aching sound: the production of dance music in Britain in the 1920s', *Popular Music*, vol. 3 (1983).
105 *Melody Maker*, 25 June and 30 April 1938.
106 Hustwitt, 'Caught', p. 16.
107 Ibid., pp. 16–22.
108 M. Pegg, *Broadcasting and Society, 1918–1939*, London, 1983, p. 7.
109 J. F. Russell and J. H. Elliot, *The Brass Band Movement*, London, 1936, p. 200.
110 Hustwitt, 'Caught', p. 16.
111 *Melody Maker*, 29 January 1938.
112 A. McCarthy, *The Dance Band Era*, London, 1971, p. 50.
113 Pegg, *Broadcasting*, pp. 116–26, 140–6; R. Nichols, *Radio Luxembourg. The Station of the Stars*, London, 1983, pp. 12–47; R. Plomley, *Days Seemed Longer. Early Years of a Broadcaster*, London, 1980.

114 *Melody Maker* provides a rich starting point for primary research.
115 C. Ehrlich, *The Music Profession in Britain since the Eighteenth Century. A Social History*, Oxford, 1985, p. 203.
116 *Melody Maker*, 19 February 1938.
117 R. Thomson, 'Dance bands and dance halls in Greenock, 1945–55', *Popular Music*, vol. 8 (1989).
118 Mortimer with Lynton, *Mortimer on Brass*, p. 106.
119 *British Bandsman*, 26 February and 2 April 1938.
120 *Melody Maker*, January 1928; 5 March 1938.
121 *British Bandsman*, 31 July 1926.
122 Ehrlich, *The Music Profession*, p. 203.
123 Admittedly, by the time of Swift's departure, St Hilda was a professional band anyway. See *British Bandsman*, 2 July 1938.
124 *Brighouse Echo*, 7 September 1934; *Melody Maker*, 16 July and 6 August 1938.
125 *British Bandsman*, 31 December 1938.
126 *Melody Maker* advertisement columns provide an excellent source.
127 H. Jennings and W. Gill, *Broadcasting in Everyday Life*, London, 1939, pp. 16, 18. Admittedly, most of their detailed research was based on a study of a working-class district of Bristol and some caution must be exercised when applying their findings to the national situation. Bristol did not, for example, have a strong brass band tradition.
128 *British Bandsman*, 5 February, 26 February and 19 March 1938.
129 Ibid., 1 October 1938. *Tiger Rag*, of course, hardly represented the most modern element of popular music by 1938.
130 Jones began his career with Gwauncaegurwen Band. On his vocal career, see *British Bandsman* 2 April 1938; 7 February 1964; *Leigh, Tydlesley and Atherton Journal*, 14 November 1947. *British Bandsman*, 29 January 1938. In some areas, another type of 'jazz band', the comic bands armed with kazoos, watering cans, funnels, mouth organs and all manner of instruments, might have also presented a challenge. They were certainly popular attractions at carnivals and processions. See E. Bird, 'Jazz bands of North East England. The evolution of a working-class cultural activity', *Oral History*, vol. 4 (1976); R. Wharton and A. Clarke, *The Tommy Talker Bands of the West Riding*, Bradford, 1979.
131 Thomson, 'Dance bands', p. 154.
132 Taylor, *Labour*, pp. 84, 49.
133 Ibid., p. 126.
134 *British Bandsman*, 6 September 1947.
135 *Melody Maker*, 1 January 1938.
136 Richards, *The Age*, pp. 15–16.
137 See the *British Bandsman*, 6 October 1928, for the speech and Iles's and Whiteley's response. The 13 October issue contained two pages of letters on the incident.
138 Ibid., 12 August 1922; 16 August 1930.
139 Ibid., 8 January 1938.
140 C. Waters, 'The Americanisation of the masses: Cultural criticism, the national heritage and working class culture in the 1930s', *Social History Curators Group Journal*, vol. 17 (1989–90).
141 *British Bandsman*, 18 October 1930.
142 Ibid., 16 February 1947.
143 Ibid., 7 August 1947.
144 It was proudly recorded in ibid., 9 March 1957, that the trombone section of the Royal Opera House orchestra, Derek James, Harold Nash and Haydn Trotman, all came from bands in South Wales.
145 Ibid., 23 October 1920. See also *Shields Daily News*, 29 September 1925.

146 I am extremely grateful to Angela Cartledge of Bradford Art Galleries and Museums for drawing my attention to these illustrations.

147 *British Bandsman*, 7 December 1963.

148 *Daily Herald*, 3 November 1963.

149 Quoted in *Musical Times*, January 1936; *British Bandsman*, 29 January 1938.

150 Admittedly, this example does come from a later period when the bands were generally better treated by the BBC music department. *British Bandsman*, 31 May 1958.

151 Richards, *The Age*, pp. 169–206.

152 *British Bandsman*, 23 October 1920.

153 Russell, *Popular Music*, pp. 238–9.

154 *British Bandsman*, 2 December 1922.

155 The Durham coalfield witnessed some conflict between the Durham Miners' Association and the break-away Durham Miners' Non-Political Union between 1928 and 1930. See R. Waller, 'Sweethearts and scabs: irregular trade unions in Britain in the twentieth century' in P. J. Waller (ed.), *Politics and Social Change in Modern Britain*, Brighton, 1987, pp. 213–28, for the wider context; and, more specifically, W. R. Garside, *The Durham Miners, 1919–1960*, London, 1971, pp. 232–34. On the sackings, see *British Bandsman*, 28 April, 2nd June and 1st December 1928.

156 *British Bandsman*, 12 May 1928.

157 Ibid., 15 December 1928.

158 Ibid., 2 December 1922.

159 Ibid., 30 October 1920.

160 Taylor, *Labour*, p. 62.

161 Taylor, *Brass Bands*, pp. 123–4; Taylor, *Labour*, p. 46.

162 Brand and Brand, *Brass Bands*, pp. 101–2; *British Bandsman*, 21 August 1926.

163 S. G. Jones, *Film and the Labour Movement*, London, 1987; S. G. Jones, *Sport, Politics and the Working Class: Organised Labour and Sport in Inter-war Britain*, Manchester, 1989; R. Samuel, E. MacColl and S. Cosgrove (eds), *Theatres of the Left*, London, 1985.

164 Russell, *Popular Music*, pp. 235–41.

165 For an extreme view, which nevertheless raises interesting questions, see J. M. Brohm, *Sport. A Prison of Borrowed Time*, London, 1978.

166 Jackson, *Working Class Community*, p. 33.

167 Frank Wright (ed.), *Brass Today*, London, 1957, p. 116; *British Bandsman*, 28 March, 25 April and 27 June 1964.

3   Brass Band Contests: Art or Sport?

CLIFFORD BEVAN

Origins of contests

In 1835, at a time when brass instruments were rapidly developing into their modern forms,[1] the Municipal Reform Act resulted in the dismissal of the few remaining civic musicians, the waits. At the same time, rural church bands were being superseded by harmoniums and pipe organs. During this period, too, the Industrial Revolution had reached a stage in Britain where not only had temperance groups, friendly societies and other workers' organizations founded bands but those of higher social status with the welfare of the 'labouring poor' at heart had begun to offer practical assistance.

There had, however, already been an amateur working-class band presence for fifty years or more. What were the 'grand band of music playing "God Save the King"' that accompanied the 'effigy of Thomas Paine . . . drawn on a sledge from Lincoln Castle to the gallows' in 1792;[2] the band that played *Ça Ira* and the *Marseillaise* in a triumphant procession of workers at Nottingham in 1802;[3] or the bands associated with workers' demonstrations and meetings in 1819, the year of Peterloo, itself marked by the presence of many 'bands of music'?[4] They consisted neither of municipal nor military musicians, but fulfilled an important and historic band function. We know something of their repertoire but we do not know their origins or instrumentation, nor do we know how or where the instruments were obtained or who taught the players.

Early bandsmen had, at least in some circles, a high reputation for musicianship. Enderby Jackson[5] claimed that often the members of the new all-brass bands had served a comprehensive musical apprenticeship:

> North country bell ringers had long maintained their reputation of being good readers of music, the members of the [bell-ringing] bands usually forming the village and church choirs of the places of worship in their districts. Clubs of glee singers abounded amongst them, with madrigal societies . . .

In northern England choral singing had long been the 'chief rational form of entertainment of the manufacturing population.'[6]

Lancashire and Yorkshire weavers were renowned for their knowledge of oratorios by Bach and Handel. James Kay noted in 1840 that young people employed in factories 'were accustomed to sing at their work in spite of an absence of early musical training'.[7]

Possibly Jackson's enthusiasm led him to overstate his case as he described the character of these remarkable musicians: 'These industrious, hard working, bell ringing, glee singing, passionate lovers of music formed the "golden ore" from which our noted world known amateur brass bands were formed'.

In considering the origins of brass band contests the importance of bell-ringing should not be ignored. Prize-ringing contests were certainly being held by 1745.[8] In the late eighteenth century contests were frequent, each band of bell-ringers performing from ten to fifteen minutes. The prizes were often provided by local innkeepers for reasons which are not difficult to deduce. It seems natural that brass bandsmen who had developed their musical skills through bell-ringing, with its active contesting activities, should seek to compare their brass-playing abilities through similar means.

But there is another factor which ought not to be overlooked, the more so as there are at least two disparate references to it. The first appears in a letter written by 'M' on 24 February 1837 and published in the *Musical World*.[9] He refers to the town in which he lives:

> Like most other towns, and even villages, this one possesses a band of wind instruments, comprised principally of mechanics, under the direction of a military pensioner, of whose proficiency but little can be said in praise. The band has been seldom heard, except at elections, and on similar riotous occasions where noise alone is required.

One of M's suggestions for improving the standards of bands was that 'annual prizes for competition should be given by towns adjacent (as in France) for the purpose of exciting emulation.'

The first contest of which we have a full account was held eight years later in the Deer Park in the grounds of Burton Constable, eight miles from Hull.[10] Sir Clifford and Lady Constable organized various rustic celebrations of the Magdalene Feast in the morning followed by 'an afternoon's rivalry of brass bands'.

Enderby Jackson, who was present, twice refers to a French connection. 'This perfect novelty on English soil was introduced by the Ladies Chichester, suitably planned from similar competitions they had witnessed in Southern France', he writes, later referring to 'Lady Chichester's French novelty.' Possibly brass bands have even more to thank the French for than their system of notation and the bulk of their instruments.

Jackson gives a detailed account of the Burton Constable Contest. Bands were limited to a maximum of twelve players, and drums were not allowed. The judge, Richard Hall (organist of St Charles, Hull) was in a small tent to one side of the platform. The order of play, decided by drawing lots, was as follows:

1 Lord Yarborough's Brocklesby Yeomanry Band (leader J. B. Acey): four cornopeans, two Sax tenors, three trombones, one Sax bass, two ophicleides. Selection of Sir Henry Bishop's works.

2 Holmes Hull Tannery Brass Band (leader Tom Martin). Similar instrumentation, but the leader played a Sax cornet-à-pistons. Selection from Mozart's Twelfth Mass.

3 Hull Flax and Cotton Mills Band (leader James Bean). Bean also played cornet-à-pistons. *Hail, Smiling Morn.*[11]

4 Malton & Driffield Band, entered as Wold Brass Band (leader James Walker). Walker played Db soprano cornet. The other instruments were one Sax cornet-à-pistons, two cornopeans, two valved French horns, three trombones, one ophicleide, one solo valved bass and one valved tuba. Music from Rossini's *Barber of Seville.*

5 Patrington Band (leader James Dalton): three cornopeans, one trumpet, two trombones, one ophicleide and three serpents. A pot-pourri of country airs.

Hull Flax Band was 'so bad even its supporters gave only a little applause', but Holmes Hull Tannery was requested to play a secular piece (*Prayer* [sic] and selection from *Der Freischütz*) and Patrington a sacred piece, Handel's *Hallelujah Chorus.* Wold was then placed first, with a prize of £12, and Holmes Tannery second with £8. The remaining £16 was divided among the other bands, 'the odd sovereign to be given to the judge'.

Thus ended the first recorded brass band contest which already demonstrated many features that were to become accepted practice in future years: a draw for position of play (to draw number one and have to play first is widely considered disadvantageous), the judge hidden from sight of the bands (still an almost sacrosanct arrangement), and no percussion allowed (a rule that was to be applied rigorously for 130 years). How many contests had been held prior to this it is impossible to say. Stalybridge Old Band, formed in 1814, is said to have competed at Sheffield four years later.[12] Besses o' th' Barn is reputed to have won a contest arranged on the spot between several bands waiting to take part in a parade on the occasion of George IV's coronation in 1820. They performed *God Save the King.*

At that time bands included woodwind as well as brass. In 1838 when Besses o' th' Barn was awarded a crown as first prize in a contest at Dixon Green, Farnworth, celebrating Queen Victoria's coronation, there were still another fifteen years to go before it became a completely brass band. As late as the 1897 Reading contest some bands used clarinets either to double solo cornet parts or play difficult passages.

History of contests

Enderby Jackson (1827–1903) was eighteen years old when he played with the lacklustre Hull Flax Band at the Burton Constable Contest and foresaw the considerable potential of this type of activity. The prime reason for promoting contests was not hard to find. As Harold Hind wrote in his seminal work of 1934, *The Brass Band*: 'Only by competing against neighbouring bands can the true level of the attainments of a particular combination be ascertained.'[13] He further commented: 'many bands have found their first contest to be a humiliating experience, their faults only becoming apparent [to them] by comparison with other contestants'.[14]

With travel expensive and inconvenient, the bell-ringing contests of the eighteenth century had been restricted to bands from relatively small areas but by the 1840s the rapid development of the railway system (see the following map) indicated that these problems would not long continue. The final barriers to proletarian travel fell in 1851 when workers from all parts of the country travelled at excursion rates to London to see the results of their labours at the Great Exhibition. That they also saw instruments made by the leading European makers seems almost irrelevant when the number of 'Sax' instruments played at Burton Constable is recollected, but certainly the presence among the exhibits of Continental instruments (available in the shops at cheaper prices than indigenous makes) was important, just as were performances by such as Herr Sommer, the inventor of the euphonium.

Jackson was not slow in later years to take credit for approaching the railway companies and arranging for them to run special trains to major contests.[15] Following a trial drum-and-fife band contest, on 5 September 1853 the first brass band contest was held at Belle Vue, a zoological garden and entertainment complex which had stood in the Manchester suburb of Gorton since 1837. The idea came apparently from Jackson, James Melling[16] of Stalybridge and Tallis Trimnell[17] of Chesterfield. Belle Vue had had its own brass band since 1851, implying some enthusiasm on the part of the manager, John Jennison. Eight bands participated, all from the North of England and each required to play two pieces of its own choice. The average number of players was twelve and the winner was Mossley Temperance Saxhorn Band, led by William Taylor. There is little doubt that it won on sheer quality of sound: a matched blend contrasting favourably with the various timbres of keyed bugle, french horn, trumpet and ophicleide common in bands of the time. There were said to have been 16,000 spectators: clearly a successful day for the railway companies.

At the 1854 contest there were 20,000 spectators, and the following year all bands were required to play a test piece, the overture *Orynthia* by Melling, as well as their own choice of work. Contests were held annually until 1859 when there were only three entrants and the event was cancelled. From 1860 until the closure of Belle Vue in 1982 the British Open Championship was held there regularly each September. (Subsequently the event moved to the Free Trade Hall, built appropriately on the site of the Peterloo Massacre.)

Jackson had promoted a major contest at Hull Zoological Gardens in 1856 for which he composed his own test piece, *Yorkshire Waltzes*. He followed this with similar events throughout the Midlands and the North. It seemed inevitable that these successful functions, having been tried out like any other show in the provinces, should next appear in the capital.

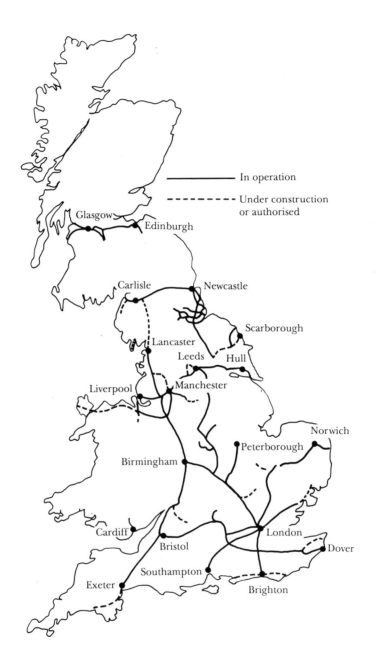

In operation

Under construction
or authorised

Glasgow
Edinburgh
Carlisle
Newcastle
Scarborough
Lancaster
Leeds
Hull
Liverpool
Manchester
Norwich
Peterborough
Birmingham
Cardiff
London
Bristol
Dover
Exeter
Southampton
Brighton

Sketch map showing railways in Britain, 1845.
(Based on Cheffins's map of the English and Scotch Railways, 1845.)

When he approached R. K. Bowley, the manager of the Crystal Palace in South London, Jackson found less confidence in the contest formula's attractions for metropolitan audiences. He therefore agreed to promote a more modest type of contest:

> My first public appearance at the Crystal Palace, Sydenham, in 1859, was as the organiser and conductor of a contest of 12 picked bands of our very best handbell ringers [from Lancashire and Yorkshire]. This admitted novelty formed the first musical contest held in the Sydenham Crystal Palace . . .[18]

Once again bell-ringers were to prepare the way for brass. The first National contest open to all volunteer, yeomanry, rifle corps and amateur brass bands was held on 10 July 1860. The Sydenham Amateur Band Contest for ensembles that had won less than £20 in the previous year took place the following day.

Financially attractive prizes secured entries of forty on the first day and seventy on the second, with the most successful bands from the North of England. Southern bands appeared in increasing numbers during the next two years and Blandford Band from Dorset won in 1863. But the project, despite being a total success, was short-lived. This was the final year of Jackson's Crystal Palace contests and in 1868, appropriately in Hull, he promoted his last ever contest, having turned to the theatre as his new interest.

Meanwhile, in 1861, bands from the South had appeared at Belle Vue for the first time. In 1864 the number of spectators rose to 25,000. Seven years later the management made efforts to overcome the problems of players appearing with more than one band when it decreed that the name and address of each member should be submitted (for publication) a month before the contest. The 'own choice' piece was abolished, a test piece only (in this case Rossini's *Il Barbiere*) being used as the basis of comparison.

Communications among bands were significantly improved with the appearance of the bandsman's first newspaper, a monthly, in October 1881 – Wright & Round's *Brass Band News & Musical Contest Advertiser*.[19] It lasted until 1985. *The British Brandsman*, founded by Sam Cope in 1887, is still in publication.

In 1886 a July contest was introduced at Belle Vue. By this time a number of bands existed which were clearly in a super league, a situation discouraging to those not so fortunate. Any band that had won a prize in the September Contest during the previous four years was barred from the July event and only those which secured the top places in July were allowed to compete in the following September.

Three years later other rules were introduced, helping consolidate the *modus operandi* of contesting. Among the most important of these were the banning of professional musicians (including service personnel); the prohibition of the performance of a test piece in public before the day of the contest; and conductors (who could be professional) being allowed to direct more than one band but not permitted to play. An interesting rule stipulated that slide trombones only should be used. This resulted from the occasion in 1873 when Phineas Bower of Black ·Dyke won both euphonium and trombone instrumental prizes, utilizing a valve trombone for the purpose.

Belle Vue retained its popularity, with large numbers of supporters attracted regularly year after year, not least, one suspects, because the venue offered a full range of entertainment. But it is important to realize that it was only the apotheosis of an activity which was popular in the truest sense of the term. Town councils, a wide range of institutions and bands themselves promoted contests. Prize money was raised from audience admissions, and it was rare (though not unknown) for a financial loss to be made. Very often a contest was followed by dancing accompanied either by the winning bands or the band which had arranged the event.

During the last quarter of the century until almost the outbreak of the First World War banding was at its most active. In 1895 it was stated (with dubious accuracy) that there were some 40,000 brass or brass and reed bands in the United Kingdom. Richardson's *Cornet Brass Band Annual* reported that in 1895 1,662 bands had taken part in 184 contests. This is certainly an underestimate, although it is remarkable how often the same bands (of all classes) appeared frequently in different contests. (Leeds City Band won most prizes in the 1896–7 season: ten firsts, seven seconds, one fourth and one fifth.) Sometimes bands, divided into smaller units, competed against themselves and up to the end of the nineteenth century 'military' and brass bands competed in the same class at many contests.

While the annual event at Belle Vue was professionally run, more democratic organizations fulfilled co-ordinating and promotional roles at a local level. These were the associations, groupings of bands primarily for the purpose of contesting. They might cover regions, counties, cities or often, as in the case of Ryburn Brass Band Association which was for bands within a four-mile radius of Sowerby Bridge Town Hall, much smaller areas. Their functions, particularly that of regulation, were taken extremely seriously and there were frequent instances of bands being disqualified for contravention of rules – most often that of fielding players who did not meet the definition of bona fide members. In some instances there was even litigation, such as the case heard at Sheffield County Court in 1893 when a difference in the interpretation of the rules between Rotherham Borough Temperance Band and Newhall Brass and Reed Band resulted in the latter, the contest promoter, having to pay damages of £10.6*s.*6*d.* to the former.[20]

The associations occupied an important middle ground between the small events organized by individual bands with sometimes only two or three contestants, and Belle Vue. There was a long tradition of the establishment and operation of societies within the working classes, particularly trades unions (which had successfully overcome the various Combination Acts) and friendly societies.[21] With the involvement of a greater number of bands, through an association, it was possible to offer larger prizes, a crucial factor in attracting contest entries.

In 1893 the British Amateur Band Association met for the first time. Among other things, its rules stipulated a maximum of twenty-four players per band in contests (twice as many as at Burton Constable); an agreement to engage only adjudicators approved by the Association; the names of the members of each band to be submitted to the Association; and players not to be allowed to register with more than one band. Despite the regulations introduced at Belle Vue in 1868, the practice of musicians playing with more than one band was still widespread.

The Scottish Amateur Brass Band Championship, which had two sections, was first held in 1895. For twenty years the leading bands from the North of England had invaded the more important contests north of the border, giving local bandsmen scant encouragement as they regularly travelled back south with the prizes. This was therefore a timely move, the more so as lowland Scotland was home to many flourishing bands.

In 1900 the businessman and entrepreneur, John Henry Iles, promoted the first National Brass Band Championship at the Crystal Palace, Sydenham, with the Crystal Palace National Challenge Thousand Guinea Trophy as prize. A recent convert to brass bands, Iles (1871–1951) had purchased both the *British Bandsman* and the publishing company of R. Smith & Co. Ltd in 1898 and was to occupy an important position in band circles during the entire first half of the twentieth century.

Supported by Sir Arthur Sullivan, this attempt to make the Crystal Palace the national base for contests was to prove successful. The first attracted twenty-nine entries in three sections. The test piece for the championship section was appropriately *Gems from Sullivan's Operas No. 1*, arranged by J. Ord Hume and given the best performance of the day by Denton Original Band, conducted by Alexander Owen.

While the three sections conferred greater fairness in enabling like to compete with like, Iles's plans for regional qualifying contests in 1902 were abortive. New rules introduced in that year, however, approached still further the modern concept of contesting. Championship section bands had to play in uniform; this was an attempt to improve the image of these occasions (bands had previously played in shirt sleeves). In addition, all players had to be members of at least three months' standing of the bands with which they appeared. As at Belle Vue and elsewhere, they were prohibited from playing with two bands in the contest, and no professionals other than conductors were allowed to take part.

With the new century Belle Vue found that for the first time since 1859 the number of entries was diminishing. Perceiving the reason to be the discouragement of the less successful bands, despite the grading implicit in the July contest, the July event was further divided, with a successful May contest result conferring the right of entry in July. At the time five sections were competing simultaneously at the Crystal Palace.

In 1923 a revolutionary rule decreed that bands in the championship section should sit while performing, thus adopting the same formation for contesting as was used in concerts. This rule applied to all participating bands the following year. Iles became managing director of the Belle Vue Company two years later and thus found himself in the position of controlling the two major contests, one of the most important brass band music publishers and one of the movement's leading newspapers.

Fire destroyed the Crystal Palace in 1936 so the next two contests were held in the Alexandra Palace. The outbreak of the Second World War led to the cancellation of the 1939–44 events. Belle Vue continued, as it had during the First World War, despite the reduced number of bands and problems connected with active service, war work and difficult travelling conditions which effectively diminished the area from which bands were drawn. Marching contests, of the type frequently held alongside performing events in the nineteenth century (usually called quickstep contests) and still popular in Australia,[22] were presented at Belle Vue during the war and for some years afterwards.

By 1945 Iles's financial situation was insecure and the *Daily Herald* was invited to sponsor the National Brass Band Festival. Following their agreement a contest was held in the Royal Albert Hall with 20 bands in one championship section followed by a massed band concert.

The public relations expertise of a national daily newspaper was invaluable, particularly when it produced Edwin Vaughan Morris who was both capable and enthusiastic. By 1946 a sophisticated system of regional qualifying contests had been established based on eight regions throughout the British Isles. Each regional contest had four sections and bands winning first and second place in their section went on to the National finals. To overcome the problems of 'borrowed' players a National Registry of Brass Bandsmen was established which by 1957 contained around 90,000 names.[23]

The *Daily Herald* went out of existence in 1964. Morris, however, retained his position, while financial responsibility for the National Brass Band Championships was transferred to a Sunday newspaper, *The People*. Following a period of some uncertainty, Vaughan Morris himself acquired the championships, which he continued to run from 1966 until his retirement in 1971. After a bewildering number of changes in ownership and management the NBBC became the responsibility of Boosey & Hawkes Band Festivals Ltd, with the support of various sponsors.

Aware of the increasing number of Continental brass bands, Vaughan Morris had instituted a world championship in 1969. This was not as great a global explosion as the title implies, for what actually occurred was that a Dutch band was invited to join in the National finals. Since Brighouse & Rastrick won they became world champions. In 1970 a Danish band (Concorde) was similarly involved and Black Dyke became world champions. GUS (Footwear) were world champions the following year, after which it became obvious that, as British bands were far and away the best, it was perhaps prudent to abolish the concept of the world championship.

It is surprising that true world championships did not take place at a much earlier period, when there were many links between bands in Britain and the Antipodes. The national championships of New Zealand were first held in Christchurch in 1880. In 1888 the music publishers, George Vassie & Co., began *The Australasian*, a series of pieces published simultaneously in London and Sydney, and before the First World War J. Ord Hume and others went from England to adjudicate the Australian National Brass Band Championships. The Newcastle Steel Works Band from Australia came third at Crystal Palace and first at Belle Vue in 1924.

The European Brass Band Championships, established in 1978, have continued successfully, with invited bands from different countries competing.

The decline in the popular appeal of brass bands, which began before the First World War, has reduced the number now in existence in the United Kingdom to somewhere in the region of 2,000, despite the remarkable resurgence initiated by local education authorities around 1960. Paradoxically, however, it would appear that the annual number of contests is now significantly greater than a hundred years ago. *The Rakeway Brass Brand Yearbook* of 1987 lists 232 in the year to August 1986, which, when compared with the estimate by Richardson's for the number in 1895, would appear to indicate an astronomical growth in the contesting rate of bands. Even taking into account the much greater accuracy of the Rakeway survey the figure of one contest for every 8.62 bands is remarkably different from the 1895 rate of one contest for every 217.39. While the specialist nature of contests has tended to remove the brass band competition from the area of general entertainment there is in existence a vast and flourishing contest movement.

Since the early post-war years there have been attempts, some remarkably successful, to broaden the appeal of contests. In 1949 one was promoted in Morecambe, Lancashire, by businessman Alec Avis in which bands performed a short programme of pieces in contrasting styles and then marched down Morecambe Promenade. To make their assessment the adjudicators sat in view of both bands and spectators, a break with tradition which caused much distress among the less progressive.[24] The huge prize of £250, more than three times the top prize at Belle Vue that year, attracted competitors but the event was only repeated once before both prize money and trophies were stolen.

New media brought brass bands before the people as never before through an attractive and entertaining format. Granada Television in 1972 initiated the Band of the Year Contest, the idea of Bram Gay, sometime solo cornet with Foden's Motor Works Band and later orchestra director of the Royal Opera House. The producer was Arthur Taylor, thus introduced to a medium which subsequently inspired him to write two important books on bands.[25]

The idea of this 'entertainment contest' was that each of the invited bands would perform a half-hour programme which was balanced, attractive and well presented. (The terms of reference implicit in the description 'entertainment contest' quite accurately imply that the conventional contest is not entertaining, however gripping for the connoisseur.) Subsequently the BBC North West Region introduced a contest for the area's eight best bands and a national 'Best of Brass' series was run on similar lines.

These programmes reintroduced an awareness of bands to a large part of the population and probably brought bands for the first time to the attention of many younger viewers. It also fulfilled one of the most desirable functions of a contest: that bandsmen (and, increasingly, bandswomen) should benefit from hearing (and in this case seeing) better performers. The lively debate about some of the compositions included was further proof of the stimulus introduced through this revolutionary approach.

Rothmans Brass in Concert Championship, whose foundation in 1977 was marked by the appropriately named test piece, *King Size March*, by musical adviser Roy Newsome, has similar aims. There are normally twelve competing bands and in addition to the championship trophy there are separate competitions for best soloist and best band in the entertainment section (prizes in these two categories being donated by trades unions). There are now an increasing number of entertainment contests.

Many local radio stations, in both the BBC and independent sectors, have instituted contests for bands within their regions. New technology has also made possible awards like the BBC Radio Band of the Year, adjudicated on the basis of tapes of the year's *Bandstand* programmes. The 'contest' thus combines aspects of entertainment, programming and performance standards. Furthermore, hasty decisions are avoided as the entrants can be heard in detail as many times as required.

One of the most impressive aspects of contemporary contest promoters is their sheer variety: holiday camps, local authorities, festival committees, the National Union of Mineworkers and many more have joined the band associations in holding these events.

Effects of contesting

Repertoire

The implications of Besses o' th' Barn winning a contest in 1820 with *God Save the King* and others offering simple pieces like *Hail, Smiling Morn* as late as the 1880s are clear: there have always been bands which appear in public while still at only an elementary stage in their musical development. But it is important to realize that players in the early nineteenth century were unsophisticated, rarely exposed to better performing standards (until contesting provided this opportunity) and in many cases barely literate. The technical progress made by 1845, therefore, when at the Burton Constable Contest bands offered selections from operas is quite remarkable.

In early contests bands were able to choose their competition piece. This had certain advantages over the set test piece which became the norm in later years. Since each band's instrumentation was different from that of its competitors the music had to be arranged, usually by the leader or teacher. This gave opportunities to feature the stronger players and give the weaker members parts with which they could cope. Outstanding soloists could be allowed to demonstrate their skills.

Reginald Nettel, the musicologist, remarked in 1946 that 'the failure of brass bands to become musically great in spite of their fine technique is historically interesting'. He suggested that it was their 'association with processions of working-class organisations that stood in the way of their fuller recognition'.[26] Howard Snell, the band conductor and arranger, stated some forty years later: 'If the brass band movement could improve its repertoire by, say, twenty per cent, they would come out of the shadows of cultural life in England and break through into general acceptance.'[27] The problem perceived by both Nettel and Snell was largely the result of a legacy from the nineteenth century.

When the outstanding bands of their day – Besses o' th' Barn, St Hilda, Irwell Springs and Black Dyke – began consistently to achieve top places at Belle Vue and elsewhere, not only their performance standards but also their repertoire were responsible, a repertoire totally suited to the needs of the time.

The general public heard 'art' music mainly through piano transcriptions if they were middle class and band arrangements if they were not, unless they happened to be fortunate enough to live in one of the localities which had, or were visited by, professional orchestras or opera companies. Hence the vast numbers of selections from operatic, symphonic or musical comedy pieces in any band's library: one of their functions was to acquaint a wider public with the melodies they contained.

More important from the bandsman's viewpoint was the stimulus of working to perfect performances of works by the great composers. These made particular demands in techniques like the phrasing of lines originally composed for singers or solo string instruments and were emphasized in the arrangers' tradition of preceding a solo instrumental section with a testing cadenza for the soloist. (Control and tone quality were also tested in slow melody contests, while the need for a chamber player's sensitivity was paramount in the many quartet contests: those established in Oxford in 1944 are still held annually.)

Perhaps the most leviathan, truly Victorian arrangements, were those by Besses o' th' Barn's conductor, Alexander Owen, of selections like *Reminiscences of Rossini's Works*. They sometimes lasted over half an hour and made demands on the stamina of player and listener alike, but the days when each band played only its own individual arrangements were seen to be drawing to a close when Richard Smith established *The Champion Band Journal* in Hull in 1857.[28] This may have been the single greatest step towards improving the repertoire of the brass band, for while the term 'orchestra' meant something totally different to Bach and Beethoven, with typically Victorian foresight (concern for the art generated through commercial motives) Smith took a decision to standardize the instrumentation for which his publications were laid out. This rigorous standardization was possible only after Adolphe Sax had established the family of saxhorns which, with the addition of cornets and trombones, constituted the entire band.

While the individuality of leading bands suffered through their deprivation of tailor-made arrangements, the advantages to more modest bands were incalculable and other brass band publishers quickly appeared. They often adopted the 'journal' form of publication: a subscription system which allowed bands to acquire music in a wide range of styles while bringing economies in production through prepayment of much of the cost.

Standardization also allowed the realization of the concept of the compulsory test piece which all bands were to play in a contest, thus giving a much fairer basis of comparison. The adjudicator was still hidden from both performers and audience so he did not know which band was playing. Drums, with their ability to obscure weaknesses elsewhere, were not allowed.

It was the twentieth century before the first major step was taken by a promoter to improve the repertoire of contesting bands. In 1913 Percy Fletcher offered the National Brass Band Championships a new original work. Its title was *Labour and Love* and it was published by R. Smith, the company then owned by John Henry Iles who was also the promoter of the contest, the thirteenth National Brass Band Championship. In 1925, the year he took over Belle Vue, he commissioned the first original test piece for the British Open Championship: Thomas Keighley's *Macbeth*.

Iles conferred an increased respectability on the repertoire and heightened the awareness of the musical establishment when, following the adoption of Holst's *Moorside Suite* as the 1928 National test piece, he commissioned a work from the Master of the King's Music, Sir Edward Elgar, in 1930. The *Severn Suite* was the result. Eminent composers like John Ireland, Arthur Bliss, Herbert Howells and Ralph Vaughan Williams were to follow, although from 1959 there was a reversion to arrangements in some years.

While such major initiatives were accepted and applauded, the ultimate step had to be handled in a much more careful manner. Away from the influence of the contesting movement, the brass band repertoire had begun to develop spectacularly in the 1960s with works by composers like Martin Dalby, Thea Musgrave, Robert Simpson, Thomas Wilson and Elgar Howarth, the last of whom, with Grimethorpe Colliery Band, was responsible for bringing the band repertoire fully into the twentieth century.

In order to cope with the new music, with its (mild) use of contemporary compositional techniques and increased exploitation of available timbres, a decision was made to allow percussion to participate in the National. The championship section adopted it in 1973 and, moving at a suitably deferential pace, by 1976 all bands were allowed to appear complete. This opened the way for composers like Edward Gregson, already well established as a writer for band, whose *Connotations for Brass Band* was the test piece in 1977.

Performance standards

It was a great step forward when, towards the end of the nineteenth century, divisions or classes of different standards were established. These provided opportunities for bands of broadly similar attainments to compete against each other and also the stimulus of a possible move to a higher class.

The consistent prizewinning of certain bands evident in the last quarter of the nineteenth century caused considerable frustration on the part of those not so successful, the more so when it became clear that perhaps their victories were the result not of superior players as much as of superior training.

An Olympian trio of trainer/conductors had emerged. John Gladney (1839–1911) has been called the 'father of the brass band movement'. He was a professional musician, for thirty years a clarinettist in the Hallé Orchestra, and under his direction Meltham Mills Band won the Belle Vue Contest in three consecutive years, 1876–8. Edwin Swift (1842–1904) was a self-taught musician who followed the trade of weaver until the age of thirty-two. In addition to his teaching activities he was a profuse composer and arranger. Alexander Owen

(1851–1920) had been a cornet player of some repute before turning to conducting. From 1884 he was particularly associated with Besses o' th' Barn, which under his guidance in 1892 won all the major British challenge cups.

Looking at the programmes of contests from the late 1870s onwards the extraordinary industry of these three men becomes apparent. The bands they led to success were based in an area extending from Cambridgeshire to Cumbria and on both sides of the Pennines. When it is considered that, in addition to the vast amount of travelling this demanded, they all produced considerable numbers of arrangements their achievements appear all the greater.

These were the first of the new breed of 'professional conductors' or band trainers, their function to bring a final polish to works often prepared by resident bandmasters. They were men of strong character and healthy bank balances: in 1889 their fee for each 'lesson' was £2 or £3 at a time when a Boosey bass cost less than £20. (Thirty years later Fred Mortimer moved south to conduct the Luton Band for a mere £2 a week.) Their activities were facilitated by the comprehensive railway system that had contributed so much to the development of the contest movement. At the Barnoldswick Contest in 1888 there were ten bands but only three conductors: Gladney, Owen and Swift. Between them they conducted all but one of the winning bands at Belle Vue from 1873 to 1904.

Their relationships with the bands they trained were based on one important premise: respect by the players for the conductor. One of the notable things in Taylor's invaluable oral history *Labour and Love* is that interviewees who had played under these great men inevitably refer to them as 'Mister'. There is never any use of the forename, and it becomes apparent that every bandsman knew his place. Sometimes there was no choice: Owen, for example, was said to lock the bandroom door during rehearsals.[29]

In such a situation time could be taken to give the utmost attention to detail of both technical problems and interpretation. While Owen, despite his custodial tendencies, was reputed always to be a gentleman, later outstanding coaches were not always so considerate. They were, however, equally industrious. William Halliwell (1864–1946) would conduct up to eight bands in a single Crystal Palace contest, rehearsing them one after the other from 3 a.m. on the contest day.[30] In 1923 one of six participants under his direction, the Luton Band, became the first from the South of England to win the 1,000 Guinea Trophy.

Another renowned trainer, Fred Mortimer (1879–1953) was responsible for the Foden Motor Works Band's remarkable achievements during the 1930s. He was probably the last of the Victorian-style disciplinarians, matching his musicianship with an attitude towards the players which seems today frankly incredible for its sheer boorishness. (However, Mortimer deserves admiration for his decision to stay away from Belle Vue for some twenty years from 1929 because of the management's refusal to halt noisy fairground rides during the contest.) His conception of a mellower band sound came as something of a shock to those who had been accustomed to the more strident tone of Yorkshire bands like Black Dyke Mills (at one period achieved through rehearsing out of doors even in the bitterest weather).[31] Foden's reputation had been established by the renowned William Rimmer (1862–1936), who as music editor for Wright & Round from about 1900 left a more enduring presence. He retired from contest conducting in 1909 as he felt temperamentally unsuited to the particular strains it imposed. A sometime cornet pupil, Harry Mortimer, son of Fred Mortimer, led the Fairey Aviation Band through a spectacular string of contest successes during the 1940s.

By the 1960s brass bands had won critical acceptance for their technical standards, if not always for their repertoire. Contesting was no longer necessary as the prime method of developing their overall ability. In 1975 it was accepted that Grimethorpe and Black Dyke could perform in a Henry Wood Promenade Concert, in the same series as the world's leading orchestras.

Band contests had not been truly popular entertainment since the beginning of the century. In 1888 there was an audience of 2,000 for a local contest in Pudsey Shed – an empty weaving shed – in Cornholme, Yorkshire. Three thousand attended a contest at Finedon, Northamptonshire, in 1896. With the advent of the gramophone, the wireless, the 'pictures' and jazz, contest audiences increasingly became restricted to experts and supporters.

The movement suffered during and after the Second World War, not least because it was totally male-oriented. The majority of bands suspended operations, and post-war social tendencies were strongly towards passive entertainment. With bands occupying an increasingly peripheral area in the public awareness it also became more difficult for the man in the street to empathize with the determination to win that was necessary on the part of competitors.

The urge to win

In any seriously competitive situation the feelings of the highly motivated contestants and their supporters will be intense and as a result their reactions may sometimes lack rationality.

The ambience of many contests during the later nineteenth century would have been familiar to those attending sporting events a hundred years later. The *Bacup Times*, published in an area as strong in banding as any in the country, printed a damning letter in its issue of 7 August 1869.

> Hundreds in our mills and workshops may be heard betting upon the result of the contest. In addition there is a vast amount of foul language employed . . . But worst of all, perhaps, is the general drinking and drunkenness that is occasioned by these contests . . . No one who happened to be out in the streets of Bacup at the time of the contest needs to be told that hundreds of drunken people might be seen staggering in all directions . . . The evils flowing from brass band contests we believe are far greater than were the evils connected with bull-baiting and other sports, put down long ago.

The same newspaper in 1902 confirmed much of what its correspondent of some thirty years earlier had written in an account by a journalist who had travelled with local supporters to a contest in Manchester.[32] On the journey home he 'arrived at Victoria Station at half past ten. From that time until five minutes to eleven, I wrestled and struggled with a half drunken crowd apparently thousands strong on the platform'. He then describes a nightmare journey in a compartment crammed with 18 people, 'four of whom were drunk, six of whom smoked the vilest pigtail . . . and the remainder passed the time up to Ramsbottom either quarrelling over the judges' decisions or falling asleep and emitting ghoulish nerve-trying snores'.

These were also trying times for adjudicators. Sam Cope announced his retirement from the judge's tent in 1896 until a national association, bringing 'dignity and propriety' to the conduct of contests, had been formed. The prime reason was a volatile audience reaction, including 'abominable language', to one of his decisions. He blamed 'the betting mania [which] has reached the crowd who chiefly patronise brass band contests'. Lieutenant Charles Godfrey had adjudicated at Belle Vue from 1871 to 1888 but abruptly severed this long-standing connexion as the result of rough treatment at the hands of the audience. In the same year Dr William Spark also ceased his judging activities following pursuit by those disagreeing with his decision. At Lincoln in 1892 spectators gave chase to George Asch who had to run across country to avoid being thrown in a nearby lake. He had been careless enough to read out the names of the winning bands in the wrong order. More seriously, perhaps, reactions of some players on the announcement of the results of the inaugural National championships led to censure in the band press.

On the first page of its first issue, the *Brass Band News* had printed this paragraph:[33]

> There has always been a prejudice against brass bands. Musicians and connoisseurs have been too ready to form their opinions from hearing indifferent badly trained bands belch out a common-place quick march in the streets; nothing can be more unjust than such conclusions. To form a correct judgment, one must hear a Brass Band contest.

In 1893, a mere twelve years later, it was bewailing the decline of band contests, now 'little more than sporting assemblies'.[34]

It is probably not unjustified to read into these accounts a developing situation where contests were ceasing to fulfil the function of family entertainment and becoming events to which a husband and father would choose not to take his wife and children. There are present-day equivalents.

The pressures, though, were intense: more important things than musical perfection might be at stake – in some cases the very existence of the band. The prize-money to be earned by top-class bands was not inconsiderable. Between 1871 and 1883 Meltham Mills won nearly £4,000 under Gladney's direction, a sum that would have bought twenty full sets of new instruments. In one year, 1892, Besses o' th' Barn won a total of £742.6s.0d. Purchase of music, replacement of instruments and uniforms, rental of rehearsal premises and fees for professional conductors all depended to a greater or lesser extent on a band's income from contesting. Earnings from engagements have often been negligible (save in very particular cases with a limited number of bands) and players have frequently tended to subsidize band activities – as would be expected in any pastime.[35] The enhanced income of a band successful in contests could be a significant factor in a band's development.

Conclusions

While contesting led to a spectacular rise in performing standards by brass bands, at a pace unequalled at any other time in any other type of music-making, it led also to an equally unique obsession with contesting and contest results.

With contesting a popular spectator sport and money changing hands, this state of affairs was to be expected. Yet it is significant that every one of the steps taken during the twentieth century to revive the popularity of bands has been based on the contest format. It is equally significant that all of these attempts have had some degree of success.

Contesting relates to the status of a band as it is perceived by others. There has been no case of a band reaching general esteem without contest success. Possibly Black Dyke has been the most regular winner over the longest period, and it has built its unique reputation on that fact.

Looking ahead to the future, the question that has to be asked is whether players will seek to focus more on the achievement of standards for the sake of the music performed – as in the case of other media of musical performance, be they solo or ensemble – than on the winning of prizes as proof of that musicianship: in other words, a general consensus as opposed to the opinion of a particular adjudicator on a specific day. This individual's opinion is considered virtually divine, the purity of the decision maintained by the adjudicator's being prevented from seeing the contestants and thus forming an opinion based on attitude as well as end-product. Hence, perhaps, the extreme reactions of dissenting spectators: it is hard to accept imperfections in the deity.

The contents of the band press, much of which even today reflects the interests of its readers by assuming more of the character of the sporting paper than that of the music journal, indicate that attitudes are unlikely to change in the foreseeable future.

Notes

1 In 1835 Wieprecht invented the tuba, the first instrument to be conceived as a valve-operated brass instrument.
2 E. P. Thompson, *The Making of the English Working Class* (revised edn), Harmondsworth, 1968, p. 123.
3 Ibid., p. 493.
4 S. Bamford, *Passages in the Life of a Radical, 1884–1967*, Oxford, 1984, pp. 146–51.
5 E. Jackson, 'Origin and promotion of brass band contests', *Musical Opinion* (March 1896), p. 393.
6 B. Rainbow, *The Land Without Music*, London, 1967, p. 119.
7 Quoted in Ibid., p. 118.
8 R. Johnston, *Bell-Ringing*, Harmondsworth, 1986, p. 283.
9 *The Musical World*, 24 March 1837, p. 17.

10 Jackson, 'Origin and promotion of brass band contests', *Musical Opinion* (October 1896), pp. 101–2.

11 *Hail, Smiling Morn*, composed by Reginald Spofforth (1770–1827) and published in 1799 as one of a 'Set of Six Glees' retained its popularity as a contest piece up to the end of the nineteenth century.

12 A. R. Taylor, *Brass Bands*, London, 1979, p. 9.

13 H. Hind, *The Brass Band*, London, 1934, p. 89.

14 Ibid.

15 The cooperation of the railway companies was essential to the viability of a contest. A bandmaster at the Redhill contest in 1896, which did not have this support, was quoted in the *British Musician*, August 1896, as saying: 'If my boys take first prize it will barely cover their expenses.'

16 James Melling (1829–70) led the resident brass band at the rival Pomona Palace Gardens, Manchester. He was conductor of Besses o' th' Barn for the last ten years of his life.

17 Tallis Trimnell was one of the few brass band trainers and adjudicators of the time to possess a Mus. Bac.

18 Jackson, 'Origin and promotion', p. 392.

19 Thomas Wright and Harry Round founded the music publishing firm of Wright & Round in Liverpool in 1875.

20 *British Bandsman*, February 1893.

21 See A. E. Musson, *The Typographical Association*, Oxford, 1954, p. 27, for the administration of a typical early nineteenth-century craft union. During the latter part of the century there was some interest in utilizing working men's club regulations for the structure of brass bands. Besses o' th' Barn became a limited company during the 1880s.

22 See V. Brand and G. Brand, *Brass Bands in the Twentieth Century*, Letchworth, 1979, p. 201, for a diagram of the 1977 Display Marching Contest of the Australian National Brass Band Championships.

23 A 'borrowed player' is one who plays in a contest for a band of which he is not a regular member.

24 Notably the National League of Bands' Associations (one of whose objectives was 'the promotion . . . [of] the musical and cultural education of its members').

25 See Taylor, *Brass Bands*; and A. R. Taylor, *Labour and Love*, London, 1983.

26 R. Nettel, 'The Influence of the Industrial Revolution on English music', *Proceedings of the Royal Musical Association*, vol. XVII (1946), p. 32.

27 Quoted in Taylor, *Labour and Love*, p. 265.

28 The first journal of military music to be published in Britain was initiated by Carl Boosé in 1845–6.

29 Quoted in Taylor, *Labour and Love*, p. 10.

30 Ibid., p. 76.

31 Ibid., p. 30.

32 *Bacup Times*, 6 September 1902.

33 *Brass Band News*, 1 October 1881.

34 Reported in the *British Musician*, October 1897.

35 In 1900 Manchester Corporation's fee for a park performance was £2 for the entire band.

4   From 'Repeat and Twiddle' to 'Precision and Snap': The Musical Revolution of the Mid-Nineteenth Century

VIC AND SHEILA GAMMON

In 1928 Gustav Holst composed *A Moorside Suite* for brass band. This work was important as the first composition expressly written for brass band by a 'major' English composer and it is significant that it was the test piece at the National championship at Crystal Palace that year. Subsequently the inter-war years saw brass band works by Elgar, Bantock, Howells, Bliss and others. At last art music composers were taking the brass band seriously as a medium for composition.

Holst's suite was significant in that it drew, in idiom, on the work of recovery undertaken by folk music collectors and composers particularly in the years 1903–14. His daughter commented on the suite: 'it is a fitting acknowledgement of a twenty years' debt of gratitude for the solid and companionable help that folk song had brought him'.[1]

A Moorside Suite brought together the brass band – an institution Dave Russell has described as 'one of the most remarkable working class cultural achievements in European history'[2] – with an idiom which was thought by many to be the musical expression of the spirit of the English people. We might well ask why and how such an institution and an idiom ever lost contact; did they ever have any active relationship in the past?

Writers interested in the musical activities of the working people of England[3] have something of a problem when such questions are raised. Folk music collectors, who ranged areas of the country in the late nineteenth and early twentieth centuries, discovered a residual musical culture that, at least in some of its aspects, was unlike the mainstream of Western art music or the commercial popular musics of the nineteenth century. It was a stratum of music and musical activity that had a life and being of its own.

In recent years the work of these collectors has been subject to a strong and necessary re-examination.[4] Not surprisingly the collectors have been found to be people of their own time who through their work articulated their own artistic and cultural concerns and prejudices. Their wish was to find a basis for popular musical and cultural regeneration and a musical language suitable for the self-consciously English composer. This led them to emphasize in their selection and publication some of those elements in the music they discovered which they interpreted as archaic and deeply meaningful.

The folk music collectors undoubtedly rescued a great deal of music that would otherwise have perished. We value their work greatly. They also bequeathed succeeding generations a great many still widely accepted yet ultimately very misleading ideas about folk music. Put briefly, the collectors indulged in mythology rather than engaging in historical enquiry. They erected a set of notions about music and music making among the lower orders of the eighteenth and nineteenth centuries which we feel have been very damaging.

There is a great difficulty in trying to study popular music, mostly oral and aural music, from a period before sound recording.[5] It is very difficult to reconstruct or imagine what a town band or church band sounded like in 1830. We have to rely on scanty and indirect information, often from hostile witnesses, in an attempt to extend our understanding. Nevertheless, there is an accumulating weight of evidence which affirms that the stylistic basis of popular musical performance was both different and coherent. The institutions in which this older type of music making flourished included church bands, town, village and friendly-society bands, festivals such as friendly-society feast days and harvest homes, the home, the pub and the street.

We now know something, at least, of the repertory and styles of performance of singers and instrumentalists in the century before 1850. Two striking features emerge from this work. First is the eclecticism of lower-class musical culture. This culture drew its repertory from a wide range of available sources, including oral tradition, ballads, psalms, popular songs, popular church music, military music, and popular dance tunes. It certainly included those items which late Victorian and Edwardian collectors were to describe as 'folk song' and 'folk music', but these by no means constituted the whole repertory.

Second, the musical performances of singers and instrumentalists articulated a pervasive musical style which, although at times it might have been influenced by aspects of art music, was in essence its own thing, following its own conventions and idioms. For economy and ease of reference we have described this formation of institutions, repertories and performance style as the 'plebeian musical tradition'.[6]

Some writers have obviously found it difficult to understand such ideas. It is worth pausing for a moment to explore why this is. The point is best illustrated by examples. Golby and Purdue, in their 'populist' reading of cultural history choose Mr Punch as 'the indomitable spirit of English popular culture'. They see a double theme in this history. One aspect is the domestication and taming of popular culture, the other is the continuity of its almost anarchic dimension, including its refusal to be serious or rational.[7] There certainly are aspects of the old popular culture that could be described as anarchic, that refused to be serious, but it was not all like that. To imply that it was is a gross caricature. One process clearly evident here is homogenization, popular culture perceived as a unity and not as constituted by different and often conflicting elements. If Mr Punch is a figure of English popular culture so are Bunyan's pilgrim, Robin Hood and the heroic men and women who inhabit popular ballads. Many of the songs widely current in the eighteenth and nineteenth centuries attest to a level of seriousness rarely attained by modern popular songs, and many popular instrumentalists showed enormous devotion to their music. According to Golby and Purdue, the popular culture of today broadly expresses 'the aspirations and desires of most men as most men are'.[8] Many feminists would probably agree, but what our authors are expressing is really a naive belief in an inherent and eternal human nature.

Given this unpromising start, it is hardly surprising that, citing Vic Gammon's work on the expulsion of the old church bands and the suppression of the old-style popular church music,[9] the authors can conclude that by the late 1850s, 'No doubt the quality of music was improved, but to the impoverishment of the labouring classes whose active participation in church services was greatly reduced'.[10]

If we ignore the fact that great pains were taken in Gammon's work to show that the main performers in church bands were village artisans not labourers, we must ask the question why there is 'no doubt the quality of music was improved'. On whose terms can such a statement be made? Whose music, whose quality? Thus we find the opinions of middle-class reformers transmuted into a statement of historical fact. Many of the old church musicians did not think the changes an improvement and articulated their opinions. What we find here is a transcendent and universal notion of what constitutes music, the perfect complement to the ahistorical and acultural notion of 'men as most men are' that informs the work of these two writers. Populism deserves better!

Dave Russell also, we feel, misunderstands some crucial points. His *Popular Music In England, 1840–1914* is an extremely rewarding and very interesting book, yet there are aspects of his work with which we would like to take issue. Russell argues that while other forms of popular recreation came under attack in the period 1780–1850,

> the pattern of popular music making was left altered but substantially unscathed. Firmly rooted in evangelical culture and carrying strong overtones of moral health, it was allowed to continue and indeed actually encouraged. While upper-class acceptance was essential to survival, however the resilience of the working population was arguably the most crucial factor.[11]

We would not wish to take issue with the idea of resilience ('the act of rebounding or springing back' or 'the power of resuming the original shape or position after compression, bending etc.'[12]) but we think such an account grossly underestimates the alteration that took place in popular music making in the mid-nineteenth century. The phrase 'altered but substantially unscathed' is unclear to us. Russell is right in seeing upper-class (or, more usually, middle-class) acceptance as a significant part of the process and there are some elements of continuity. Nevertheless, we hope to show that he underrates the significance of the change that took place within lower-class music making in the period.

There is obviously a need to explore further a point about musical perception if confusion and misunderstanding are to be avoided. There exist what we would term one-dimensional and two-dimensional views of music. A one-dimensional view of music sees it as a unitary phenomenon. In such a view assessment of a performance, a piece or a style of music (often all three at once) takes place on what we can visualize as a straight line:

Bad ←——————————————————————→ Good

If, however, we take a two-dimensional view of music – a view that the world contains multiple musics not a singular music – then we have to disentangle judgements of quality from judgements of musical style. Let us take the example of jazz and symphonic music:

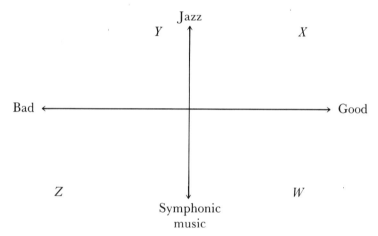

On such a diagram an excellent performance of a Beethoven symphony would be placed in the bottom right hand corner (*W*), an excellent jazz performance in the top right hand corner (*X*), an indifferent jazz performance might be placed at point *Y*, an utterly terrible symphonic performance at point *Z*.

A unitary or one-dimensional view of music is unable to make such basic distinctions. Judging all music by one set of criteria derived from one type of music means that any that does not meet those criteria is categorized as inferior or bad music. All musical styles have practitioners of more and less ability, more and less competence or mastery of the idiom. Judgements about the competence of performers can only be made within the established boundaries of a musical style. The crucial misrecognition takes place when competent performance in a particular musical style is judged as incompetence because of the application of criteria from another musical style.

It is not simply a matter of liking one type of music and not liking another. Judged by the standards of bebop the *Eroica Symphony* is a dismal failure. As a piece of sustained improvisation *The Rite of Spring* is a non-starter. These examples verge on the ridiculous but we think they illustrate our point. For convenience (borrowing a concept from Bourdieu) we will term this judging of one musical style by the criteria of another musical *misrecognition*. It is historically significant; linked to social power it can have very material outcomes in shaping musical activity.

In an artistically liberal and avowedly multicultural society, when 'serious' composers are experimenting with new sounds and forms of music and when jazz gets Arts Council subsidy and can be studied at the Royal College of Music, it is easy but rather facile to discount the historical importance of one-dimensional views of music and musical misrecognition. We would venture to say that a non-pluralist view of music has constituted the dominant outlook of most people for most of human history. Many people still see Western art music as the summit of a musical pinnacle.

The thesis we propose is that the plebeian musical tradition and that of the brass band were quite different and therefore could be visualized on a two-dimensional diagram like that above.

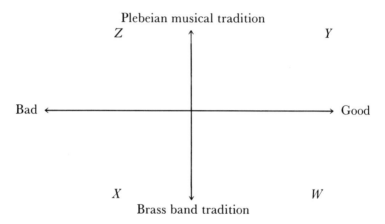

In this diagram W would represent a 'crack' championship winning band, X a poor band bemoaned of by the advocates of banding. Once we accept that we are dealing with different musical styles with different conventions and criteria then we have to admit the possibilities of point Y, a band playing superbly within the conventions of the plebeian musical tradition; and of point Z, a band playing within the conventions of the plebeian musical style but doing so incompetently.

The historian wishing to enquire into the history of types of music that pre-date sound recording is often forced to make use of evidence from the pens of hostile witnesses, witnesses who judge a type of music by alien criteria, be it Indian music, Arabic music, black American music, the music of Gaelic Scotland or the plebeian musical tradition of eighteenth- and nineteenth-century England. By looking for consistencies within hostile accounts one can distil both elements of outlook common to the observers and consistent elements of style in the music being commented on. One can also bring in comparative evidence from societies with dominantly aural musical traditions as well as the evidence of what has been recorded from traditional musicians in England over the past ninety years, to provide comparisons, generate questions, and assist in the formation of interpretations. It is surprising that some historians seem willing to take on trust the testimony of hostile observers without subjecting it to the full rigour of historical criticism.

No music is good or bad until specific and often unconscious criteria are applied to that music. In this sense beauty is in the ear, or rather the brain, of the listener. The brain is no naive organ. Musical perception is the result of a complex process of musical enculturation: the assimilation of the norms and conventions of a particular style or of styles. The degree to which individuals 'master' these norms and conventions conditions the degree to which we respond to and are able to understand differences within a particular musical style.

Having mastered one set of musical norms and conventions, one style, individuals have historically tended to judge all other types of music by the internalized criteria of the assimilated style. The fact that this is an intellectually invalid procedure has not stopped it being a potent historical force; nor do we feel society is free of this force today even though there is more real 'polymusicality', more real response to and valuing of different musical styles, more ability to play in different musical styles than probably at any time in the past.

Between about 1830 and 1860 a great deal of what was distinctive about the music making of artisans and the labouring poor was destroyed or went underground. A different and, in many ways (at least initially), alien set of musical values, elite and middle-class in origin, was promulgated and gained ascendency. That working-class music making flourished under the new conditions is testimony to a sort of resilience, but this should not lead us to think that lower-class music making resumed its original shape or position. The most public aspects of working-class music making were metamorphosed in the period, the less public aspects retained something of the old musical culture but were increasingly marginalized. The most important agent of this profound change, although it was not the only one, was the brass band.

Not to see the enormity of this change is a failure of both assessment and imagination. Given the degree of misunderstanding and misinterpretation of these issues there is obviously a need to spell out in detail the nature of this musical revolution. We will try to do this by a series of comparisons of before and after, briefly illustrating the points we make.

Musical literacy was not unknown within the plebeian musical tradition. Manuscript music books for church band and country dance musicians survive in considerable quantities and we have good evidence that town and village bands made use of lovingly copied manuscripts. Sheet music was very expensive in the eighteenth and early nineteenth centuries and hand copying provided one of the only practical ways of getting hold of unknown music.

The use of musical notation is significant and is evidence against the damaging notion of a purely oral/aural folk tradition. Yet we should not protest too much. It seems certain, from the evidence we have considered, that the majority of instrumentalists active in the first third of the nineteenth century were ear-players, who learned their playing without reading the notes. No doubt within bands there was quite a lot of direct teaching of melodies and parts. The importance of memory and/or the ability to recreate melody parts is crucial within a dominantly aural musical tradition. It is precisely that sort of tradition which encourages such abilities.

Brass bands used copied-out manuscripts, but with the development of cheaper printed music, produced specially to supply the need, print took over from manuscript. Performance increasingly became print-based. No doubt there were (and still are) good ear-players whose grasp of musical notation was not well developed but who, if performing with good readers, would grasp their parts well enough. Yet as the pressure for excellence grew the pressure to read well must also have grown.

The great advantage of the existence of a score and of parts is that the co-ordination of large groups of musicians playing prearranged music becomes a practical possibility. This is no small advantage.

Ethnomusicologists have noticed that the introduction of notation has often accompanied and has probably been causal in fundamentally changing musical practice.[13] Musical notation gives a system of classification which has the potential for structuring the way we think about and conceive musical sound. Once we have acquired it we tend to try to fit all musical experience into its framework, and it becomes incorporated into our sense of reality. (In Bourdieu's terms it becomes *doxic*, a self-evident part of the mental equipment with which we interpret and cope with the world.) 'Every established order tends to produce (to very different degrees and with very different means) the naturalization of its own arbitrariness'.[14]

Anyone who has tried to transcribe traditional music into Western musical notation knows how hard it is to get timings and pitch variations down accurately. Bartók's system for doing this produces a score which is monstrously complicated. Such music is not made for Western notation and Western notation is not made for it. Yet once the mental habit of perceiving music through Western notation is acquired that which will not fit within the regularities of the notational system (e.g. crotchet beats and exact subdivisions and semi-tone pitch divisions) is considered anomalous, offensive, dangerous, incompetent or wrong.[15] Alternatively it is not perceived at all – because no mental equipment exists for its perception the element or item is simply not noticed. Most usually, it is interpreted (misrecognized) as a failure within a system of which it is not even a part. In his support, Bartók realized that he was dealing with a coherent musical system and struggled to understand and appreciate it. Brass band teachers of the nineteenth century simply wrote off expressions of the older popular style as ignorance and incompetence.

We are not suggesting that an aural musical culture is somehow more tolerant than a literate one. Both operate on a basis of a system of classification and both tend to intolerance, but we think the mechanism of response and the reasons for that intolerance are very different. The former is deeply traditional, absorbing acceptable change often without noticing it but rejecting that which is too alien to be absorbed; the latter, in operating from a notational base, projects that which is learned from notation (in origin a descriptive system) onto all musical experience (thus making it prescriptive).

Nor are we arguing that an aural musical culture is inherently superior to a literate one. We can see positive aspects to both. What we would want to oppose is a notion that an aural musical culture is necessarily or inherently inferior to a literate one. What we are trying to understand in this essay is something of the nature of the change from the one to the other. Given the profound significance of this change it is worth taking some space to explore the implications of a shift from a dominantly aural to a dominantly literate musical tradition.

Written down, the musical piece gains a permanence it never had in a world dominated by memory and re-creation. The existence of a score encourages people to treat that score as a source of authority, a final arbiter in case of dispute. Notation is not music but, in the case of dispute, appeal is not to what sounds best to the performers but to a notion of authorial correctness. 'Permanently available and amenable to rationalistic verbal explication, the score rapidly usurps the sound experience of music as the focus of verbal attention and becomes the key stone of an eminently verbalisable conception of what "music is".'[16]

In a dominantly aural but partly literate musical culture, written music can have the effect of stabilizing a repertory, of transmitting music from past to present *without* stopping processes of elaboration, decoration and variation which are usual features of aural tradition. It has been argued that oral/aural cultures live in a world of the permanent present where even if innovation takes place it is absorbed without fuss and often without recognition. The past is often adjusted to suit the present.[17]

Musical notation probably originated as a mnemonic device. Within a dominantly aural culture, such as early nineteenth-century England, it probably retained much of that function, but it has the potential to grow to dominate musical practice. It is difficult for us to grasp the profound changes in the conceptualization of music that the coming of musical literacy implies. In the main this is due to our ignorance of and our lack of empathy for the aural/oral mind within a dominantly aural/oral culture.[18] To a band instructor of the 1880s (and to many of his contemporaries and successors) knowledge of music was equated with knowledge of musical notation:

> Supposing, now, the case of a band is taken which starts without any knowledge of music. The first thing necessary is to get the rudimental part well into the minds of the pupils.

His method was to drill his students 'after the manner of an ordinary school-lesson'.

> By the end of that time most of the members could read the notes, and also count the time tolerably well. One of the best results of this method was it got rid of those who were not in earnest about the thing – in a word the drones.[19]

It is a commonplace of the study of oral poetry that literacy disables the oral poet. He or she is no longer able to combine motifs, to improvise, to rhapsodize once written language has entered his or her consciousness.[20] Although there is a great deal of evidence of musical literacy and oral tradition coexisting and interacting in nineteenth-century England (and in many other periods and places), it is equally clear that widespread musical literacy is destructive to aural methods of musical creation and re-creation.

In aural musical cultures it is often the case that the mental skills of memorization and re-creation using formulas are often highly developed; in literate musical cultures these mental skills tend not to be developed and are in a sense replaced by sight-reading and musical reproduction.

If musical notation is combined with an outlook on the world that posits, within strict limits, correct and incorrect ways of doing things, the result, given the possibility of an appeal to authorial correctness, is to change the musician from a musical speaker to a musical reproducer.[21] As Nettl puts it: 'a Western concert is to a large extent an exercise in mental and dexterous ability'.[22] George J. Bowles, advising aspiring band contestants in 1888, wrote:

> The special points to work for are: accurate rendering in a mechanical sense, that is, as to notes and time; expression of light and shade, correct phrasing, etc., playing in time and quality of intonation.
> The extra and unusual efforts put forth by the individual members of a band to gain the above points in preparing for a contest must necessarily raise the status of that band, for these are the essential points which go to make up the best quality of performance.[23]

The musical score reduces sound to graphic representation, the aural to the visual. Its material form presents us with a reification of music. It promotes an elision of thought which transforms lived aural experience existing in time into lines and dots existing on a flat page. The process is complete when we describe such a representation as music. (A fascinating contrast to this is offered by the fact that country musicians in southern England use the noun *music* to mean a musical instrument.) Print suggests to us that what is represented has a reality apart from musical performance. As Wishart argues, permanence and scrutability of the text fundamentally challenged the immediate dialectic of musical action and musical experience.[24]

No notational system can exactly prescribe what a piece should sound like. Western notation is moderately good at prescribing pitch and timing, less good at prescribing dynamics, hopeless at prescribing timbre. At any time, within a defined context there exist practical conventions which regulate how a score is to be interpreted. These change over time and the musicians may be largely unaware of their existence. Thus even within a musical system strongly reliant on notation there exists a residual aural tradition in which conductors, musical directors and adjudicators play a central role. Needless to say, its criteria may be totally at variance with the musical conventions of an earlier aural tradition.

All performance is re-creation, but a performance from the exact memorization of a score is profoundly different from a performance in which an aural musician reassembles and remakes even a piece he or she has played hundreds of times before. We are therefore making a conceptual distinction between playing from memory ('aural') and memorization ('literate'). In a predominantly aural musical culture the instrumentalist absorbs the music he or she knows, makes it part of his or her being in a way that makes possible the re-creation of a piece from schemata and fragments stored in memory, in a literal sense a combination of recollection and improvisation within known conventions. In a dominantly literate musical culture, memorization, where it occurs, tends to be by rote. It is interesting that an 1887 contributor to the *British Bandsman* stressed the importance of memorization of all aspects of a part – 'all marks, *rallentandos*, pauses, etc.' – to a soloist.[25] This suggests (as does a great deal of other evidence) that musical literacy induces score dependence and diminishes the ability to play from memory.

This tendency to make the musically literate score-dependent has been widely observed. Although there are exceptions, given a high degree of musical training it seems common that only some musicians, notably those who reach a high state of proficiency, ever really seem to break this dependency, usually through a process of memorization, not through musical speaking in the aural sense.

In some circumstances literate musicians with less training do seem to be able to break away from score dependency. World musics give us many examples of types of music that have a notational base but which loosen their ties and their dependence. Examples would be New Orleans street music and jazz, Bohemian polka music as performed in Texas, and Jewish *klezma* music.

Musical reading did not simply take over from aural transmission as the dominant form of access to a musical repertory; taking the society as a whole, it is probable that aural forms of musical communication remained numerically greater in nineteenth-century England, but the significance of the brass band movement is that musical literacy gained the prestige associated with what we might call the leading sector of popular music making. Henceforth 'real' musicians were perceived as literate musicians and aural musicians relegated to a secondary status.[26]

Specialist musicians appear in many different societies. A purely aural musical culture will produce differing musical competences, but a society in which literate and aural modes of transmission are current inevitably produces a greater degree of musical, social and cultural fragmentation. In nineteenth-century England, the huge culture shock and social revolution of industrialization and urbanization increased these tendencies.

Music literacy can be a 'mystery', a means of integrating initiates into a craft and excluding others. For a complex of reasons, not least of which was the middle-class belief in the social utility of music for the working class, the mystery of music literacy was extended in nineteenth-century England as thousands learned to read staff and sol-fa notation. Nevertheless, the increase in musical literacy had the effect of increasing the significance of the division between musical literates and illiterates.

The role of Western musical notation might usefully be compared in some ways to that of Latin within medieval society – a *lingua franca* which cut across linguistic barriers, allowing the communication of ideas and material among those initiated into its use. The effect of musical literacy on significant sections of the nineteenth-century working class was to make them feel a connection with the prestigious art music of Europe, however modified and adapted were the forms in which they encountered it (for example, selections of themes from 'great' composers).

It is possible to view an aural musical culture as a kind of 'restricted code', performances being limited by a traditional repertory, traditional conventions, known ways of performing and a limited vocabulary of musical reference. It is reasonable to argue that musical literacy extends the range of music that can be performed. Both systems of musical production are, however, limiting in their different ways. Both leave the musician without the ability to grasp music radically different from what is familiar through that particular mode of communication.

Freed from dependence on memory and encounter, literacy means that written-down music from the past becomes available and composed and notated music becomes communicable over great distances. Musical notation liberates music from the tyranny of the present but it does not open up all music from the past – only that tiny fraction which has been developed through the use of musical notation.[27] Only sound recording can accomplish this final act and this only for musics recorded during the twentieth century.

It might be thought that musical literacy would encourage critical attitudes and a relativist approach to music by showing the music of the past to be different from that of the present. Instead, musical writers of the period proposed a developmental and later evolutionary model of musical progress in order to justify the present in relation to the past, thus dealing with this unsettling by-product of music literacy. They also developed the 'great man' or 'genius' theory of musical creation, a concept in tune with nineteenth-century individualism.[28]

The change from a dominantly aural to a dominantly literate musical practice underlay significant change in performance style. The elements of the older plebeian musical style we will detail here are derived both from a reading of contemporary source material and detailed listening to English traditional performers, the inheritors of the plebeian musical tradition, who have been recorded over the last eighty years.

Church bands, village and town bands and musicians performed their music in a style which drew its conventions from traditional practice. There is good evidence for believing that the major elements of their way of playing included an emphasis on volume with relatively little use of dynamics (although these are sometimes indicated in manuscript books). When, in 1859, a band was employed to play for a celebration of the Mid-Sussex and Southwater Benefit Association, an observer noted: 'the band of music engaged was certainly very superior to the noisy apology for music which is generally heard at annual festivals of this kind'.[29] A use of embellishment, decoration and elaboration in the different lines played seems to have been common. In 1831, J. A. Latrobe accused the country church musicians of 'throwing in, according to their notions of beauty, shakes, turns, cadences, and other frivolous ornaments'.[30] Sometimes the music would make use of a controlled flexibility of tempo, playing slightly before or behind the beat, emphasizing the off-beat in dance music. The musical conventions of these early bands were known and used by the musicians themselves in their playing, and although we have no doubt that elements of elite musical practice were sometimes imitated and absorbed, the configuration of elements that made up the plebeian musical style was in many ways quite different from professional and elite amateur musical practice.[31]

Sometimes we catch a critical echo of the older plebeian style of playing in the brass band literature. In an appreciation of Richard Smith, *The Illustrated News of the World* in 1861 compared him to other performers:

> As a cornet player he is one of the best in the kingdom, both as to tone and true musicianlike feeling. Not like some quack performers we could point out, who get themselves paroted [*sic*] in some spluttering cornet solo, in the shape of a polka, with stupid variations, and who could not read correctly, under any circumstances, a simple melody, as far as regards time or phrasing.[32]

The consonance between Latrobe's 'frivolous ornaments' of 1831 and this writer's 'stupid variations' thirty years later is notable. Other writers report in a critical vein on what may reasonably be interpreted as examples of a popular semi-improvisational style of playing. George Bernard Shaw noticed musicians 'busking' (improvising inner parts, Shaw called it 'vamping') on more than one occasion.[33]

By the last third of the century, the dominance of the score, coupled with professional interest and direction, contesting and adjudication, led to an emphasis on playing the music exactly as written, on precise time-keeping, on the 'correct' interpretation of dynamics and on the production of a good and even tone. A writer of 1887 informs us that a good player:

> must know how to express and how to shape tune particles by the process called phrasing. Again, he must learn to recognise the composer's purpose and mode of thought, as revealed in the various forms of musical design. Then he must have a trained perception of proportion in combining sounds, and in the exact adjustment of time measurements and rhythmical formations.[34]

George Bernard Shaw, writing appreciatively on the Salvation Army in 1906, articulated a favourite theme which was strikingly in tune with his political views – the need for strong direction from the musically able before much could be achieved. 'But mere enthusiasm could not have produced the remarkable precision and snap in their execution. They must have worked hard and been well-coached by their conductors.'[35] Because the brass band movement saw itself as partaking in the great tradition of European art music, the musical theory underlying the practice was established, elaborated and widely published. It is notable that an important conductor like Edwin Swift was able to teach himself transposition, harmony and arranging from published works.[36]

No doubt there were differences in performance style within the plebeian musical tradition. Even within living memory and the age of sound-recording, traditional instrumentalists from Sussex, East Anglia and Northumberland demonstrate marked regional variations, musical accents if you like, in the way they play, although they work within the broad outlines of the plebeian musical tradition. The significant point is that, whereas the musical standards of the plebeian musical tradition were generated within that tradition, the musical standards of the brass band movement were absorbed from music professionals and members of the middle class. The most important agency for cultural standardization and the setting of musical models was the brass band contest.

Repertory changed along with style. Early nineteenth-century bands played a repertory which consisted of what we would call traditional dance tunes, marches (often these two were interchangeable) some popular song airs (such as 'Rule, Britannia!' and 'God Save the King') and if they were church musicians they played the old-style church music which included the so-called fuguing tunes. Interestingly, a considerable proportion of this repertory got onto contemporary barrel organs and part of it survives as regimental marches. Having listened to early recordings of military bands playing such pieces, it is clear that their style of performance had little in common with the way traditional musicians play the same pieces.

The brass bands in the second half of the century played a very different repertory. In some ways it was very modern and included recently composed quadrille sets and other dance music such as polkas, popular song and hymn arrangements, but most noticeably selections from operas and strung-together themes from 'great' composers with titles like 'The Works of Beethoven'. In 1869 the *Sussex Agricultural Express* reported a harvest home in West Hoathly.

> The proceedings were enlivened during the afternoon by the excellent performance of the Ockenden Band, which attended by permission of W. W. Burrell, Esq. The following programme was gone through in masterly style:

Pas Redouble – 'Kadner'	Gurtner.
Selection – 'Faust'	Gounod.
Valse – 'Corn Flower'	Coote.
Galop – 'Belgravia'	C. R. Bloe.
Glee – 'Chough and Crow'	Bishop.
Quadrille – 'Winters night'	Marriott.
Polka – 'Levy-A'-than'	J. Levy.
Valse – 'Blanche'	H. Farmer.
Quadrille – 'Sicily'	D'Albert.
March – 'Come where my love lies dreaming'	Christy's Minstrels.
Pas Redouble – 'Monte Christo'	J. Rivers.
Selection – 'Orphee Ansi Enfers'	Offenbach.
Galop – 'Impetuous'	Pironelle.
March – 'Lucia di Lammermoor'	Donizetti.
Valse – 'Juliet'	C. Coote jun.
Glee – 'Red Cross Knight'	Callcott.
Quadrille – 'Donnybrook'	R. Smith.
Galop – 'Cupid's Arrows'	C. Barthman.
Polka – 'Rataplan'	H. Koenig.
March – 'Toll the Bell'	Christy's Minstrels.
God save the Queen.[37]	

Sir Walter W. Burrell, Bart, MP, local landowner of Cuckfield and West Grinstead Park in Sussex was patron and financier of the Ockenden Band, which was named after his house in Cuckfield. The *Sussex Agricultural Express* of 7 January 1879 has the description 'Sir W. W. Burrell's own private Band'.

In the older bands, as in the military band tradition, the emphasis was on ensemble work. The adoption, particularly of operatic selections, including arias, created the conditions for the emergence of the star soloist.

The instrumentation of the early bands was very variable. In churches there might be almost any combination of fiddles, cellos, flutes, clarinets, bassoons ranging in number from two or three to a dozen or more. Occasionally brass instruments crept into church bands, and there are cases of double basses and serpents being used. Town bands had combinations of wind and generally rather primitive brass instruments. In Lewes Town Hall there is a painting dating from 1830 by A. Archer entitled *Arrival of William IV and Queen Adelaide at 'The Friars' Lewes*. The Lewes Town Band is shown in one corner and there is a list of the band members attached to the picture. The instrumentation of the band was:

three clarionets
two clarionets or oboes
two french horns
two bugles
one flute
two bassoons
one trombone
one bass drum

Henry Burstow listed the Horsham Town Band of around 1835 or 1840 as:

one flute/fife
three clarionets
two keyed bugles
one trumpet
two trombones
one french horn
one serpent
one drum[38]

Source material provides many variations on these types of combinations.

It must be said that while some of the instruments that have come down to us from the period are obviously well made, the quality of others must have been variable. Some church band musicians made their own instruments, as did James Nye who lived near Lewes in Sussex.[39] Metal fiddles and cellos have been reported from different parts of the country, one assumes mostly the work of local smiths.

It would be good to think that industrial progress in the second half of the century brought with it a reduction in price of instruments and a general improvement in quality. The standardization of instruments certainly helped bands perform together without the difficulty of ill-matched instruments, although many non-standard combinations, making use of old instruments and playing skills, existed throughout the century. Also many instrument makers in the nineteenth century produced cheap and shoddy goods. No doubt those manufacturers who struck up good working relationships with bands and attended contests in order to do business were reputable and made reasonable-quality instruments. Nevertheless, if the positive aspects of Victorian musical instrument making were craftsmanship combined with industrial production, the negative aspect was the widespread distribution of shoddy goods. Interestingly, the production of relatively cheap instruments also influenced the remnant of the ear-playing musicians: cheap concertinas, melodeons, mouth organs, penny whistles and banjos – all in their way nineteenth century inventions or adaptations – provided the classic instruments for traditional pub music in the later nineteenth and early twentieth century.

The size of the earlier bands tended to be smaller than the later brass bands. Church bands had anything from two or three to a dozen players, occasionally – as in the case of West Tarring, Sussex – as many as fourteen. Town bands usually counted their members in double figures, but rarely more than twenty. Not that all brass bands achieved the approved numbers and balance of instruments of the 'classic contesting bands',[40] as many old photographs show.

The development of what has been termed a music service industry in the second half of the nineteenth century no doubt improved retail services for musicians. The increasing availability of cheap music was a luxury undreamed of by musicians earlier in the century. The development of hire-purchase no doubt facilitated instrument purchase.

Yet we think there is a significant difference between early and later bands in terms of control and ownership of instruments. Although there are examples in church wardens' accounts of parish funds being used for the purchase of strings, reeds and particularly the more expensive lower instruments, cellos and bassoons, the general impression is of individual ownership of instruments. Different patterns existed later in the century but corporate ownership and control of instruments was by no means uncommon. Collectively and institutionally owned sets of instruments can be found in a number of museums or mouldering away in cupboards and under stages of village halls.

If we consider the events at which bands played we find some continuity but significantly some radical change. The early bands tended to play for social events in which the music was simply an adjunct to the event, be it a church service, a parade, a celebration such as a benefit club feast day, or a dance. Even the *ad hoc* ensembles that played in pubs did so as an accompaniment to drinking and socializing.

Clearly much of this pattern continued into the era of the brass bands, although the 1840s and 1850s saw the wholesale expulsion of the church bands from religious services. As well as undertaking many of these older customary functions, brass bands increasingly played in contests and concerts, events at which the music was the central if not the only reason for the performance. This change of emphasis was highly significant in popular perceptions of music – for the first time the music itself became a central focus of attention, not just a necessary component of an event the main function of which was non-musical.

We have no doubt that the enthusiasm of particular individuals was vital in inspiring and holding together a band in the early nineteenth century.[41] The family tradition was also very important. The Horsham town band, observed for posterity by the young Henry Burstow, had no less than seven Potters in a band of twelve players.[42] There is some evidence of itinerant teachers of music training choirs for a short period and then moving on but we do not believe these shadowy people had a very widespread influence. In the main, amateur enthusiasm kept the church bands going.

Enthusiastic individuals were obviously of vital importance in the success of brass bands and the significance of particular families remains to the present day. Many bands selected their own trainer from among their ranks but increasingly there was a trend towards the use of professional and semi-professional trainers and conductors. The influence on the movement of such legendary figures as John Gladney, Edwin Swift and Alexander Owen is well documented. The movement also provided professional or semi-professional work for a large number of other people.[43]

Consideration of the role of trainers and conductors leads on to a consideration of educational styles within bands. Within the earlier tradition there seemed to exist a great deal of autonomy in learning style, a great deal of the sort of learning-by-doing which has been widely observed by ethnomusicologists. Keith Swanwick makes the following observations and reflections on John Blacking's work on the Venda people of South Africa:

> Reading Blacking's description of the way in which the Venda learn music, I am reminded of my own experience as a boy in a Midlands village brass band. Music was to some extent learned in the context of other social activities; we knew that we would be playing at Remembrance Day services or garden parties or on parade at other village events. I mastered the technique of the E flat tenor horn informally, without instruction – the band master never quite got round to *instruction*. Most of the playing was of whole pieces or long sections with very little fragmentation into part-learning or analysis of particular difficulties. In fact, Blacking's description of the Venda fits perfectly: 'The main technique of learning was by observation and listening, trial and error, and then frequent rehearsal'. It was also considered vital to be playing with others. Few members of the band seemed to practise at home very often or for long and most technical progress seemed to be achieved when playing together. I suspect that this pattern of learning is still prevalent today in church choirs, amateur orchestras, rock bands, folk groups, the Salvation Army, steel bands and many other variations of our rich musical culture.[44]

It would seem reasonable, therefore, to assume that such a learning process was as common in brass bands as it had been in earlier ensembles. We should, however, notice a growing emphasis on training, instruction and discipline and some of the sources suggest that fragmentation into part-learning and the analysis of particular difficulties was a favoured nineteenth-century practice within the brass band movement. The method of the brass band teacher previously quoted was 'to devote one night in each week, for a period of two months, to exercises written upon a blackboard to be learnt and repeated by the pupils, sometimes singly, and sometimes together'. He practised fragmentation into parts and made a great use of scales and exercises. He emphasized the need for home practice and stressed that teaching should be, 'systematic, progressive and persevering'. One senses little feeling of joy in this approach.[45]

Sets of rules are not unknown for early bands but the most common ethos one encounters is that of a voluntary association. Early bands were renowned for an independence of attitude, pride and confidence in what they did, and what we would describe as an exuberant hedonism, which was often expressed in quite extravagant actions.[46]

Acts of 'masculine gaiety', the expression of disgust at contest decisions, and unruliness were features of the brass band movement, yet such actions are always contrasted with a normative idea of what behaviour should be. In some respects the 'sporting' ethos of the brass band movement is inherited directly from an aspect of the old popular culture of the eighteenth and nineteenth centuries. The interplay of the ethos of rational recreation, aggressive competitiveness and what Golby and Purdue describe as an 'appetite for beer and sensation'[47] forms one of the most fascinating dynamics within the brass band movement. Temperance sponsorship of bands with subsequent lapsing or defection of members is a recurring motif but good anecdotes of this type should not lead us to think that temperance did not have a solid base in the working class and among many bandsmen. The use of uniforms is significant in this context. A uniform implies subservience of the individual will to disciplined behaviour – uniforms were rare among early bands outside the military.

Discussion of behaviour leads us on to a discussion of patronage and questions of control. The church bands flourished in a particular set of ecclesiastical conditions where clerical authority was weak and musicians exercised considerable autonomy and gained a significant control over the music of the parish church. Certainly church and chapel provided a basis for musical activity but it is misleading to describe what the church generally did for the church bands as patronage. It was the reimposition of clerical authority which led to the expulsion and suppression of church bands. Both church and early town bands drew most of their membership from artisans, a traditionally independent group who had sufficient income to finance an interest in music, as well as flexible 'pre-industrial' work patterns which ensured blocks of time in which to practice.[48]

The 'classic' brass band is very different. In the case of subscription bands something of the old independence could be retained but even here support from wealthy members of the community could be of crucial importance and could exercise decisive influence. An account of the formation of a town band at Ashford in Kent in 1859 gives fascinating insight into the attitudes and values in play:

Ashford Town Band – A meeting was held on Monday evening in the lower Public Room, for the purpose of taking steps to establish a town band. Mr. Wills was chairman. Mr. Farley said he had sketched a few resolutions, which he would read seriatim:- 1st, – That a good band is required in this town, to contribute to the recreation and amusement of the inhabitants more especially of those engaged in daily toil, and also to assist in cultivating a musical taste.

2nd,- That a committee be appointed, and requested to solicit donations, and make necessary arrangements with a proper band master and band.

3rd,- That two evenings in every week be set apart for the band to play in public.

4th,- That by the kind permission of Mr. J. Lewis, the band play in the field adjoining Mr Epps' garden once each week: and, in case the S. E. R. Company with their officers and servants approve and support the project it shall play in the triangle of the New Town the other evening in each week; otherwise it shall play both evenings in Mr. Lewis's field.

These resolutions were put by the chairman and unanimously adopted. The Rev. J. P. Alcock then proposed an additional resolution, to the effect – that as the object of this meeting is to promote innocent recreation, and to cultivate a taste for music, the band shall not meet for practice at any inn or public house. This met with some opposition, but was eventually carried.[49]

In the case of works bands the situation is much clearer. The owners could exercise a control and direction over band policy unknown to earlier bands. They could also finance the professional instruction of the band if they felt inclined, as was the case with the previously cited Ockenden Band of Cuckfield financed by Sir Walter W. Burrell, and numerous industrial examples. In the case of volunteer bands a layer of military-style discipline could be added.

In all cases enhanced status within a community and the resultant self-esteem were important motivations for participation in music making. In the case of competing brass bands the additional confirmation of competition success was a possibility. A significant number of bands incorporated references to their contest-winning prowess in their titles.

In the case of both earlier and later bands, taking part could lead to supplementary income for the bandsmen. This could be in money or in kind, often in the form of beer and food. This aspect of banding forms a continuity although in the brass band period the additional possibility of prize money existed.[50]

The image of the brass band as a product of the industrial regions, a land of mills and pit villages, is an overdrawn stereotype. Certainly the industrial heartland of Yorkshire and Lancashire was the cradle of the movement and produced most of the champion 'crack' bands. Nevertheless, the movement was much more widespread and its influence went far beyond the manufacturing counties of the North. Bands from the South of England existed in their hundreds and probably thousands, although they seldom achieved much at the national contests.

In social terms the brass band movement was essentially working class, even in the South. The decline of the small workshop and the independent artisan, the co-option of hand workshops into the industrial process which altered 'pre-industrial' work patterns even if it intensified manual production, all worked against the continuation of the leisure patterns of the past. Mobility and enforced migration also had a negative influence on old ways.

Russell has noticed that the strength of the band movement was in the relatively small industrial villages of Yorkshire and Lancashire.[51] This is a very important point. The Industrial Revolution transformed old and created new industrial villages, which provided new and different social conditions. Initial dislocation was followed by relatively stable settlement in a close environment and this sort of pattern seems to have been a very suitable seedbed for band development, but it was not the only one. The 'forest' communities of north Sussex, Horsham, Crawley, Horsted Keynes, Nutley, Fairwarp, Turners Hill, West Hoathly and East Grinstead were veritable hothouses of band activity in the later nineteenth century.[52] These were market towns and villages partially enmeshed in what some observers have seen as an archaic type of economy.[53] Brass bands seem to have flourished in small-scale communities, but it does not seem possible to generalize beyond this observation.

We have tried to show that while there were some continuities in the activities of amateur bands that performed in the nineteenth century the major discontinuities are far more significant. The middle decades of the nineteenth century witnessed a remaking of the musical activities of working people. A new style of music emerged, new instrumentations, new forms of organization and institution – most significantly the brass band contest. This amounts to significantly more than a pattern of popular music making 'left altered but unscathed'.[54]

On the negative side the middle decades of the nineteenth century witnessed the destruction of church bands, a purposeful and deliberate act. The 1850s also witnessed the reform of military music – one wonders how much because of its neglected state and how much because the style of playing of military musicians was out of step with elite musical tastes.

On the positive side we believe that the nineteenth century increased opportunities for participation in active music making. It would be quite wrong to see the changes of the mid-nineteenth century as simply a defeat for indigenous working-class musical culture – as wrong as to see the changes as the manifestation of the ever forward march of progress. In trying to sort out the gains and losses the result would probably depend as much on each individual's approach and attitude to music as on the evidence produced.

The plebeian musical tradition was not so much destroyed by the advent of the brass band and the related changes of the mid-nineteenth century, rather it lost its place as the basis of much working-class music making and went underground. It was there in the activities of numerous urban and rural amateur musicians; it is still audible in some aspects of the music hall. Significantly, the fast-developing musical instrument industry found there were profits to be made in catering for its needs.

The example of the concertina neatly illustrates the point. To most people a concertina is a concertina but actually there are three distinct types, really three distinct instruments, all developed in the nineteenth century and each of them serving different needs.

The English concertina is a fully chromatic instrument and has the same bottom note and roughly the range of the violin, for which it was often substituted. The notes of the scale of C are placed on alternate sides of the instrument. The English concertina lends itself to solo line playing and although it is possible to play in thirds and to play chords it is not easy to provide melody *and* substantial accompaniment on the instrument. It was marketed as a drawing-room instrument, and also came in various sizes from treble to bass to be played in ensembles and concertina bands. These concertina bands modelled themselves on brass bands, dressed in uniforms, played a standard brass band repertory from brass band scores, and had contests organized at Belle Vue and Crystal Palace. A number of concertina bands were active until the inter-war period.

The duet concertina is also fully chromatic but has a much wider range than the English, covering most of the notes on a piano keyboard. The left hand plays the lower notes, the right hand the higher; there is a substantial overlap of notes on the two sides, allowing considerable flexibility. It seems to have been a somewhat later development than the other two types. There are different systems of note layout, ergonomically designed, all apparently quite illogical on the surface, but all allowing the playing of complex music with full self-accompaniment. The duet concertina was the instrument of the musically ambitious player and was much used by professionals, as well as by aspiring amateurs.

The Anglo (or more properly Anglo-German) concertina offers a very different note arrangement from the other two. The duet and English both play the same note on the push as on the pull; this is not so on the Anglo. Its notes are arranged in rows so that if one pushes on, say, a C row one gets the notes of the tonic chord CEGC', and if one pulls one gets the other diatonic notes DFAB. Usually there are two diatonic rows, most often in G and C. Better instruments have a third row consisting of chromatic notes not available on the two diatonic rows. Its note arrangement make it very similar to those other highly popular instruments, the melodeon and the mouth organ. The push/pull arrangement of the notes make it hard to play in a legato style, but when playing diatonic dance music the instrument itself fairly dances, producing a lively, forceful and jumpy sound.

Needless to say, the Anglo was the instrument most favoured by working-class ear-players in the nineteenth century. The three types of concertina neatly demonstrate the differentiation of the nineteenth-century instrument-buying public. In a sense they also graphically illustrate the fragmentation of working-class musical culture in the nineteenth century. Professionals and high-flyers played the duet; middle-class people and musically literate, respectable working-class members of concertina bands played the English; ear-players and the musically disrespectable played the Anglo. Prices were stratified according to the complexity of the instrument and the market.

In a wider perspective we have seen how two musical value systems could operate within one class. This raises the question how did people experience and cope with this clash of values? Could people move between different types of music making?

The evidence is contradictory but interesting. On the one hand, the adoption by significant portions of the working class of a value system derived from Western art music, which categorized music as good or bad according to particular criteria, must have had the effect of devaluing much self-made working-class music. On the other hand, there is significant evidence of many musicians being able to play different types of music, able to move between sight-reading in a band and playing by ear and from memory. 'Trombone Billy', a friend and musical associate of Scan Tester, the Sussex Anglo concertina player, was both a trained bandsman and an able pub musician who could play hornpipes for stepdancing on his trombone.[55] The phenomenon we might term 'polymusicality' has been raised into an educational goal by recent writers.[56] On the other hand, ear-playing musicians, able musicians who greatly enjoyed their music, must often have been rejected from ensembles where reading musical notation was seen as an absolute necessity. This happened to Scan Tester himself – one of the few English traditional musicians to have been extensively recorded. In the 1960s he told Reg Hall:

the bandmaster wanted me to join the band. Well, he wanted me to join like the others to learn music . . . Well, the man what was the bandmaster of the band, he used to be a shoemaker and used to go down there, and he used to be pointing this music out to me trying to learn me. He was a cornet player and, 'course, I couldn't learn that music, you know. I wasn't no good. I tried! I tried hard enough to learn it, but I couldn't, and they all thought I was going to learn music, because I was good on any music [musical instrument]. I was playing a music, but as for to learn the music to read it off, I couldn't, and I never did, and that was the reason why that I come out of the band . . .[57]

Yet even when instrumentalists were able to move between different styles of playing the effect of the existence of different musical value systems operating within working-class culture must have been to devalue the older and now less esteemed way of playing. The fragmentation of working-class culture, one section upwardly aspirant, willing to accept and absorb middle-class values, in the process disowning that which they had owned, the other section clinging, at times defensively, to what they had known and valued, must have led to a great loss of cultural class cohesion.

It is worth considering the wider implications of this analysis in terms of debates about popular culture and class relations in nineteenth-century England. Historians have rightly become sceptical about the efforts and achievements of middle-class reformers, rational recreationists and moral crusaders. Whatever feelings of self-satisfaction their efforts brought them, they often did not bring the results desired. No doubt some rational recreationists deluded themselves about the success of their efforts. It would be totally naive of us to think that any attempt at reformation would be successful in a simple or linear way. In a dynamic and contested social field the end result of such efforts would inevitably be different from the aims and aspirations of the reformers. Yet it would be equally naive to believe that such efforts were without effect in changing and modifying working-class culture in profound and significant ways.

By marginalizing, dismissing and devaluing positive elements of the old plebeian musical tradition, the mid-nineteenth-century encounter between auto-nomous lower-class culture and middle-class taste and reforming zeal created the conditions for both the incorporated, patronized and denigrated culture of brass bands (albeit a culture in which a new and in many ways positive identity could be forged) and, ironically, in the cultural partial vacuum created, the conditions for the success of commercial provision of popular music.

The older musical culture did not die, although a fairly systematic attempt was made to destroy it. Nor did it simply fade away. What survived of it tended to go underground to become part of the defensive and insular culture that characterized the later nineteenth-century working class. In part the old tradition was replaced by music and musical activities approved by the middle class, although as in the case of the brass band, these were sometimes transformed in non-approved ways by working-class practitioners, a process Russell has described as the 'working class capacity to extract the maximum benefit from rational recreation while ignoring or deflecting its ideology'.[58] In part something of the idiom and style of the old tradition found its way into music hall and thence into more general commercial provision of popular music, perhaps to be 're-absorbed' by the public house singing tradition. Something of the old spirit was retained in the populist evangelical music of the Salvation Army – brass instruments, Anglo concertinas and all. Aspects of the old tradition survived to be picked up in selected places by Edwardian folk music collectors and later enthusiasts.

There is even some evidence that after training and drilling in the rigours of music literacy some ensembles seemed to revert to something like older aural styles of playing. Mention has been made above of bands of literate musicians who have taken their ensemble playing away from strict reproduction of exact pitches and time values. Playing for dancing seems to promote among brass musicians that specific quality jazz musicians call 'swing'. Recordings of brass players playing for the Britannia Coconut Dancers from Bacup and the Helston Furry Dance testify to this. Adapting Ong's phrase, we must consider this phenomenon 'secondary aurality', a state where musical literacy has had and retains a marked influence.[59]

When all this is considered the marginalization and residualization of the old, dominantly aural, plebeian musical culture is an inescapable fact, as is the dominance of a musical ideal derived, if somewhat adapted, from Western art music. We think this can justifiably be described as the incorporation of working-class music making into the musical-aesthetic world of elite and bourgeois taste. This was achieved, though never totally and never in an uncontested way, centrally through the brass band.

This acceptance by a significant portion of the working class of what were initially alien musical conventions meant a rejection of the plebeian musical tradition as a basis for musical development, represented a denial of self-worth and led to a further fragmentation of working-class culture. Simultaneously and crucially, it ensured a subordinate and contemned place for working-class music making within bourgeois culture. 'Our aims', stated the *British Bandsman* in its prospectus of 1887, 'are to stimulate, and, where it is non-existent, to create and foster in bandsmen a desire for and a love of good and high-class music . . . and lastly to urge a claim for a higher status in the musical world for band professors'.

The low esteem of band professors is but one aspect of the low status of brass bands in the musical world. The acceptance of some central and vital aspects of middle-class musical taste meant that the working-class musical culture could easily be judged by prevailing musical standards and by those standards be judged wanting:

> Plenty of instances could be found in which wealthy amateurs, often large employers of labour, have promoted the establishment of brass or reed bands, by aiding in the purchase of instruments, and the engagement of teachers. It is, of course, a matter of opinion whether a brass-band is very much of a musical blessing, but that does not interfere with the motive of the person who aids it with his money.[60]

When considering musicians to accompany a choral society, Fisher felt that a local teacher might be thankful to get mediocre woodwind players but 'might consider himself fortunate if no member of the local brass band offered his services on the trombone'.[61] H. E. Adkins, writing in the 1920s, commented:

> The Military Bands of our towns and villages were nondescript organizations, being, more often than not, the manifestation of goodwill towards music on the part of certain members of the community, but just as frequently they were exhibitions of the inefficacy of goodwill without proper direction.[62]

Such disparaging remarks about amateur bands are common.

One way to deal with such judgement was to assail the heights of excellence as a contest-winning 'crack' band. Yet even this did not ensure respect and value from social and musical 'superiors'. No doubt many working men derived enormous pleasure and satisfaction from playing in a brass band, but perhaps we should seriously question whether the loss of a socially independent stylistic basis for the development of working-class music making was worth what was gained. What happened is what happened. From our position in the late twentieth century it is hard to see that the basis for a very different musical and social development existed. That does not mean we should not make the effort.

Our aim in this chapter has not been to say that the brass band movement was a bad thing – clearly tens of thousands of people obtained enormous pleasure and satisfaction from playing in brass bands. Rather, our desire has been to approach positively the aural musical world of the early nineteenth century and before;[63] to challenge Whiggish interpretations of musical history which base themselves on an uncritical notion of progress; to point out that all changes in musical practice are the product of contestation within cultural fields and inevitably involve losses as well as gains.[64] Frederick Jones, veteran of the Falmer and Stanmer church bands, lived through the changes in musical style and regretted the loss of the older music. 'Alas they were indeed happy meetings, notwithstanding the disdain, shall I say contempt with which a more educated public regarded our old compositions with their repeat and twiddle.'[65] Ultimately we favour aesthetic tolerance; or at least a form of musical relativism which accepts and does not deny real (objective) and experienced (lived and felt) differences in styles and in responses. Intolerance which does not recognize itself as such (a common fault of much liberalism) is still intolerance. Musical taste as a social and cultural marker has for centuries been and will continue to be used in social and cultural conflict whether we favour tolerance or not.

The routes that led to our starting point, Holst's *A Moorside Suite* of 1928, are complex. In the mid-nineteenth century, working-class music making took a great step towards European art music. In the early twentieth century, English art music found a new basis for itself in some of the previously despised and rejected music of the English working class. *A Moorside Suite*, the work of a socialist composer who had played the trombone in a theatre band, represents the coming together of these two highly significant musical impulses.[66] We find the irony compelling.

Acknowledgements

This essay is respectfully and affectionately dedicated to Reg Hall, musician, writer, enthusiast and friend, whose ideas on traditional and popular music have been a constant source of stimulation and challenge.

Notes

1 C. Bainbridge, *Brass Triumphant*, London, 1980, pp. 69–70; I. Holst, *The Music of Gustav Holst*, (2nd edn), London, 1968, p. 100.
2 D. Russell, *Popular Music in England, 1840–1914*, Manchester, 1987, p. 162.
3 We write self-consciously about England and English music in this chapter, not through any narrow-minded nationalism but because it is the country we have studied. Moreover, the social, historical and musical processes which took place in Wales, Scotland and Ireland were so entirely different from those in England that it is impossible to propose an account which fits them all.
4 See particularly V. Gammon, 'Folk song collecting in Sussex and Surrey 1843–1914', *History Workshop*, vol. 10 (1980); D. Harker, *Fakesong*, Milton Keynes, 1985; M. Pickering, *Village Song and Culture*, London, 1982.
5 See V. Gammon, 'Problems of method in the historical study of popular music' in *Popular Music Perspectives*, Exeter, 1982.
6 Following E. P. Thompson in 'Patrician Society: Plebian Culture', *Journal of Social History*, vol. VII (1974).
7 J. M. Golby and A. W. Purdue, *The Civilisation of the Crowd*, London, 1984, pp. 14 –15.
8 Ibid., p. 13.
9 V. Gammon, '"Babylonian performances": the rise and suppression of popular church music, 1660–1870' in E. Yeo and S. Yeo, *Popular Culture and Class Conflict 1590–1914*, Brighton, 1981.
10 Golby and Purdue, *Civilisation*, p. 106.
11 Russell, *Popular Music*, p. 160.
12 *The Shorter Oxford English Dictionary*, p. 1807.
13 B. Nettl, *The Study of Ethnomusicology*, Chicago, 1983, p. 329.
14 P. Bourdieu, *Outline of a Theory of Practice*, Cambridge, 1977, p. 164.
15 See M. Douglas, *Purity and Danger*, Harmondsworth, 1970, generally.
16 T. Wishart, 'Musical writing, musical speaking' in J. Shepherd, P. Virden, G. Vulliamy, T. Wishart, *Whose Music?*, London, 1977, p. 136.
17 J. Goody, *Literacy in Traditional Societies*, Cambridge, 1968, pp. 30–4.
18 W. J. Ong, *Orality and Literacy*, London, 1982, *passim*.
19 *British Bandsman*, March 1888, p. 106.
20 A. B. Lord, *The Singer of Tales*, New York, 1965; Ong, *Orality*.
21 Wishart, 'Musical writing', *passim*.
22 Nettl, *Ethnomusicology*, p. 328.
23 *British Bandsman*, April 1888, p. 131.
24 Wishart, 'Musical Writing', p. 136.
25 *British Bandsman*, October 1887, p. 22.
26 Goody, *Literacy*, p. 68.
27 Ibid., p. 53.
28 See, for example, H. Parry, *The Art of Music*, London, 1893, passim.
29 *Sussex Agricultural Express*, 16 July 1859.
30 J. A. La Trobe, *The Music of the Church Considered in Its Various Branches, Congregational and Choral*, Thames Ditton, 1831, p. 138.

31 V. Gammon, 'Popular music in rural society: Sussex 1815–1914', unpublished DPhil. thesis, University of Sussex, 1985, *passim*.
32 Quoted in the *British Bandsman*, June 1888, p. 166.
33 G. B. Shaw, *London Music in 1888–89 as Heard by Corno Di Bassetto*, London, 1937, p. 203.
34 E. H. Turpin, 'A Preamble', the *British Bandsman*, September 1887.
35 G. B. Shaw, *Shaw's Music*, vol. 3, London, 1981, p. 589.
36 A. Taylor, *Brass Bands*, London, 1979, p. 74.
37 *Sussex Agricultural Express*, 11 September 1869.
38 H. Burstow, *Reminiscences of Horsham*, Norwood, PA, 1975, p. 50.
39 J. Nye (ed. V. Gammon), *A Small Account of my Travels through the Wilderness*, Brighton, 1982.
40 Taylor, *Brass Bands*, pp. 72–3.
41 Gammon, 'Popular music', p. 34.
42 Burstow, *Reminiscences*, p. 50.
43 Gammon, 'Popular music', pp. 127 and 289–90.
44 K. Swanwick, *Music, Mind and Education*, London, 1988, p. 128.
45 *British Bandsman*, March 1988, p. 106. For an interesting comparison, see B. Jackson, *Working Class Community*, London, 1968, pp. 21–22.
46 Gammon, 'Popular music', p. 31.
47 Golby and Purdue, *Civilisation*, p. 14.
48 Gammon, 'Popular music', pp. 32 and 121.
49 *Sussex Agricultural Express*, 21 June 1859, p. 2.
50 Burstow, *Reminiscences*, p. 50; Shaw, *Shaw's Music*, vol. 2, p. 122.
51 Russell, *Popular Music*, pp. 165–7.
52 Gammon, 'Popular music', p. 129; R. Hall, *I Never Played to Many Posh Dances . . . Scan Tester, Sussex Musician, 1887–1972*, Essex 1990, pp. 91–5 and 105.
53 M. Reed, 'The peasantry of nineteenth-century England: a neglected class?', *History Workshop*, vol. 18 (1984), *passim*.
54 Russell, *Popular Music*, p. 160.
55 Hall, *I Never Played*, p. 31.
56 Swanwick, *Music*, pp. 115–17 and *passim*.
57 Hall, *I Never Played*, p. 103.
58 Russell, *Popular Music*, p. 170.
59 Ong, *Orality*, p. 137.
60 H. Fisher, *The Musical Profession*, London, n.d. (1888), p. 113.
61 Ibid., p. 101.
62 H. E. Adkins, *Treatise on the Military Band* (revised edn), London, 1958, p. 8.
63 Ong, *Orality*, p. 175.
64 P. Bourdieu, *Distinction*, London, 1984, *passim*; P. Bourdieu, 'Intellectual Field and Creative Project', in M. F. D. Young (ed.), *Knowledge and Control*, London, 1971, pp. 161ff.
65 K. H. MacDermott's MS, I, 54 (letter of 25 May 1917), in the library of the Sussex Archaeological Society, Lewes.
66 Holst, *Gustav Holst*, pp. 100 and 140; I Holst, *Gustav Holst* (2nd edn), London, 1969, *passim*.

5   *The Brass Band in Australia: The Transplantation of British Popular Culture, 1850–1950*

DUNCAN BYTHELL

I

That brass bands were a prominent and ubiquitous feature of Australia's musical and cultural life in the late nineteenth and early twentieth centuries is evident from the magnificent rotundas which still adorn her public parks and gardens from the major cities down to the smallest country towns. That such bands, although by no means defunct, no longer play so important a part is suggested by the fact that these fine structures – whether elegant, ponderous, or merely bizarre – are nowadays more commonly used as picturesque and convenient settings for wedding ceremonies than for musical performances. However, to capture a real sense of the brass band's place in Australian history, we need to go beyond these evocative, if decaying, artefacts to the close-printed pages of local newspapers of fifty to a hundred years ago. Even a cursory glance will show that few occasions in public life – whether one-off events like laying a foundation stone, or annual rituals such as the trade unions' celebrations of Eight Hours Day – were complete without at least one band in attendance to add solemnity, dignity, or a festive air to the proceedings, as appropriate. Nor were brass bands on hand simply when pomp and circumstance were the order of the day. They entertained the crowds at sporting fixtures; gave their services free for worthy causes – fifty-two bands were said to have played at various Melbourne venues for 'hospital Sunday' in 1929;[1] added to the jollity of trade union picnics and Sunday School outings; and provided a relaxing background to such outdoor routines as late-night shopping on a Friday and post-prandial perambulation on a Sunday afternoon. And, whilst secular bands – with municipal permission, of course – made their distinctive contribution to sabbath ritual, their religious counterparts in the Salvation Army were also active in harnessing this popular form of music making to the stern task of accomplishing the Lord's work.

A few moments' reflection will make it clear that in an age when gramophone, radio and other electronic means of storing and reproducing music were lacking and when all music was necessarily 'live', the brass band must have played a major part in the musical education of both performers and audiences in Australia, as elsewhere in the Western world. Until the advent of radio in the 1920s, bands provided most Australians with their only real opportunity to hear concerted instrumental music, and with their first (and often their only) acquaintance with the popular classics. Similarly, it was only by learning a brass instrument that many young men could have been introduced to the pleasures of developing their own musicianship. In fact, an interesting list could be compiled of Australians, later prominent in many walks of life, who were bandsmen in their youth: it would include John Brownlee, the opera singer (1900–69); Frederick Curwen, sportsman, lawyer, and president of the Young Australia League (1894–1964); and Gordon Chalk, the Queensland politician.[2] In addition, it should be noted that a handful of men who began their musical careers in brass bands moved successfully into the 'serious' profession as orchestral players: the Partington family, from Tasmania, provided brass players for several Australian symphony orchestras for a considerable part of the twentieth century;[3] most impressive of all, the cornet player, Percy Code (1888–1953) – whose bandmaster father had groomed him to be the Alex Owen of the Antipodes – ended his life rather as the Adrian Boult, being chief conductor of the Australian Broadcasting Commission's orchestras in the 1930s and 1940s.[4]

Finally, in recalling the former role of brass bands in Australian life, it must be remembered that they also offered a new type of team game and spectator sport to a society which takes such things seriously. Brass band contests – at local, state, and even national level – were frequent and widespread from the 1890s to the 1930s; and the state-wide Band Associations which grew up to regulate contesting served to create the sense that there was indeed a brass band *movement* in Australia. From 1900 until it went into abeyance in 1924, the annual South Street contest at Ballarat was regarded as 'the Mecca of Australian bandsmen', and crowds of 20,000 and more would gather to watch the marching, listen respectfully to the playing, and cheer on their favourites.[5] Sometimes, partisan spirits boiled over with unseemly consequences. There were notoriously ugly scenes at the final of the New South Wales contest in Sydney in 1931, when a large part of the crowd disputed the verdict of the British adjudicator, Cyril Jenkins. The judge's tent was besieged, instruments were 'played in a derisory fashion', and the luckless man suffered the terrifying indignity of being 'counted out'. Order was only restored when the police had been called and the conductor of the losing band had personally escorted Jenkins to the safety of an awaiting motor car.[6]

Yet despite their contribution to so many different aspects of Australian life, brass bands have so far escaped the attention of historians both of Australian music and of Australian leisure and popular culture. Not that band histories are completely non-existent: the brass band press everywhere has always been fond of filling odd corners with potted histories and old photographs of individual bands; and if Australian bands have been neglected, those of New Zealand have found a champion in Stanley Newcombe.[7] For the most part, however, band histories have been written by band enthusiasts rather than by professional historians. Their style tends to be narrative and anecdotal, their chronology vague, and their content dominated by tales of heroic individuals and their achievements on the contest field. Why, then, have scholars overlooked them?

It is easy to demonstrate the extent of their neglect in the standard histories of Australian music. For example, W. A. Orchard's classic account, published in the early 1950s, while devoting some space to amateur choral societies, contains a bare handful of brief and scattered references which testify to the mere existence of brass bands. Only in an appendix, entitled 'New South Wales Provincial Towns' and written not by Orchard but by a series of local correspondents, is the place of brass bands in Australia's musical history taken seriously; and not until literally the last page of the book, in a brief section on Bathurst, is a brass band actually described as 'the City's greatest and most honoured musical institution'.[8] This refusal to admit the brass band to a place in orthodox musical history is, of course, nothing new. It parallels British experience, and can presumably be explained in the same way. To those brought up in the bourgeois tradition of European classical music, brass bands were amateur bodies, and amateurism could easily be equated with low standards of technique and musicianship; at best, they played only unauthentic arrangements of 'great' music, while at worst they played trash; and finally, to the serious musician, the vulgarity and the false motives associated with band contests must have been more reminiscent of the football stadium than of the concert hall.

But if musical – and social – snobbery, together with that deference to all things British which some have called 'cultural cringe', easily explain why brass bands have been written out of Australia's musical history, it is less easy to understand why the new generation of social historians have so far overlooked them, given their strong interest in the history of other leisure pursuits. Yet bands go unmentioned, for example, in Spearritt and Walker's 1979 collection of essays on *Australian Popular Culture*, and are commemorated pictorially in that splendid bicentennial extravaganza, the ten-volume *Australians: A Historical Library*, only by one photograph of a Salvation Army band and one of the rotunda at Stawell, Victoria.[9] The only extended treatment of their place in community life by an academic social historian known to me is in J. McEwen's 1979 Sydney PhD thesis on 'The Newcastle coalmining district of New South Wales, 1860–1900'. It may be, of course, that this neglect is unconscious: even so, one cannot avoid the suspicion that the brass band has been ignored because it does not fit easily into any of the currently fashionable approaches which characterize much recent work by Australian social historians. For instance, historians interested in the distinctively 'Australian' aspects of their society would, understandably, have had little time for an institution which was self-evidently an import from Britain and a prime example of the derivative and colonial character of Australian culture at the time. Nor is it surprising that the brass band has failed to excite the enthusiasm of left-inclined historians, who might easily have interpreted its development as an obvious example of bourgeois cultural hegemony and a sinister form of 'social control', designed to take the workers' minds off more serious matters. Finally, since the brass band was, until recently, an exclusively male preserve, one cannot blame Australia's feminist historians for failing to see anything interesting in it.

If these are indeed the reasons for the neglect it must be admitted that they have some validity. Nevertheless, it would be unwise to put too much emphasis on arguments about 'social control' until we know more about how, when and where bands were set up, who joined them, how they operated, and how they related to their local communities. It would be even less sensible to dismiss the brass band as a British cultural export until we have examined the ways in which it was subtly modified over the years as it took root and developed in its new environment. A proper understanding of the history of Australian society and culture depends not so much on emphasizing the uniquely 'Australian' as on striking the right balance between the similarities and differences which came to exist between the colonies and the 'Old Country', especially in the period of recurrent mass migration from the gold rushes of the 1850s to the depression of the 1930s.

It must be stressed at the outset that this chapter is introductory, and its conclusions are often speculative and tentative. If it can stake a modest claim to being the first word on the subject, it cannot pretend to be the last. Indeed, there are many issues, particularly with regard to quantification, which it cannot consider at all. How many Australians actually played in brass bands? Were Australian bandsmen more numerous than British bandsmen in proportion to population? How did the number who joined bands compare with, say, the number who regularly played cricket on an organized (but amateur) basis? Knowing how many bands existed at a given time would not, of course, solve the central problem, which is how many Australians played in a band *at some time in their lives?* Life-long bandsmen, who gravitated gracefully down the ranks from solo cornet to E♭ bass as lips got slack and breath got short, were, almost certainly, greatly outnumbered by young men whose band careers took up a mere part of that brief interlude between leaving school and getting married. Un-answered questions such as these will require detailed work on local sources which only a historian based permanently in Australia could hope to undertake. It is important, therefore, to give a clear indication of the materials which have gone into the production of this preliminary sketch.

Being small, informal, and voluntary organizations, individual brass bands tend to generate relatively little paper in their ordinary course of business (although they often leave behind plenty of photographs). Given that they were often also ephemeral bodies, little of even this meagre documentation is likely to survive a band's demise. Certainly, very few band archives have yet found their way into Australia's major academic libraries and record offices, though some material must surely still remain locally and in private hands. One particularly well-documented band is that which existed at Tooth's Brewery, Sydney, between 1927 and 1932, since its records are preserved with the firm's archives at the Australian National University; but, for reasons which will become apparent, Tooth's Band was hardly a typical outfit.[10] In the absence of this basic material, what follows has had to be built up as a mosaic from fragments collected from a wide range of sources, many of which are only indirectly concerned with brass bands and their activities. Among printed materials, undoubtedly the most important for tracing the activities of individual bands and assessing their role in community life are the local newspapers which proliferated throughout Australia at precisely the same time as the bands themselves; and it is certain that Australian historians wishing to examine the rise and decline of brass bands in detail in particular localities will find these, overall, the most valuable source of information. In addition, as bands become more common, a specialist brass band press developed to cater for enthusiasts and provide a mouthpiece for 'the movement'. Like its British counterpart, its editors relied heavily on local correspondents and band secretaries for information about the activities and achievements of individual bands up and down the country. The New South Wales-based *Australasian Bandsman* and the Victoria-based *Australian Band News* both seem to have started life around 1900, but it is not until just before they merged in 1926 to form the monthly *Australian Band and Orchestra News* that I have been able to locate a file of these publications, in Sydney's Mitchell Library. Among other specialist publications, it should be noted that the Salvation Army in Australia ran a monthly paper for its own bandsmen and songsters entitled *The Musician*, but unfortunately this only began publication in 1947. Other ephemeral periodicals may have existed locally but, like the Ballarat-based *Australian Band Leader* (1971–2), probably lasted only a short time before expiring for lack of readers and advertisers.

Apart from the specialist and general newspaper press, the activities of brass bands can also be studied – intermittently, but sometimes in revealing detail – in the surviving records of the Australian labour movement, with which they had many links. They can also be followed in the archives of local municipal bodies, with which they were often associated on civic occasions, and to which they generally looked for funding. A partial survey of trade union, trades hall, and Eight Hours committee records in the ANU's Archives of Business and Labour and the Melbourne University Archives, together with a somewhat cursory sampling of the wide variety of local material available in the Newcastle (New South Wales) City Library, proved particularly fruitful in illuminating the ways in which records of this kind can cast light on Australia's neglected brass band history.

II

By the end of the 1890s, the British brass band – that is, the specific combination of cornets, saxhorns and trombones which had become standardized in Britain, thanks to the growth of contesting and the activities of the music publishers and instrument makers – had become established as the normal type of wind band operating in Australia. As in Britain there had, of course, been earlier, informal groupings of brass and woodwind instruments which served as forerunners of the 'movement'. Military bands accompanied the troops sent to police Britain's new penal colony from the very beginning, and subsequently the development of colonial militias and volunteer forces in the 1860s and 1870s extended the links between wind bands and the armed forces. It is possible, too, that civilian banding in South Australia owed something to German immigrants of an earlier generation, as well as to the British prototype of the late nineteenth century. Nevertheless, during the great proliferation of civilian bands which accompanied the tenfold increase in Australian population between 1850 and the outbreak of the First World War, it is clear, both from photographic evidence and from the growth of contesting, that the standard instrumentation of the classic British band was quickly accepted in Australia, and largely displaced other less rigid formations. There is no reason for us to be surprised at this, in view of the massive role played by ordinary, wage-earning emigrants from Britain in building-up Australia's population and developing its communities and institutions. Their mass migration occurred at exactly the time when the brass band was establishing itself as a key element in popular music making back home, and it was only natural for the migrants to carry it with them as part of their cultural baggage. The contribution of British-born bandsmen to Australian banding is particularly noticeable in mining areas whose counterparts in 'the Old Country' were major centres of the movement. Thus McEwen has attributed the popularity of bands in the Newcastle coalfield district of New South Wales to the concentration there of migrants from the colliery villages of North-East England; while Philip Payton has drawn attention to the vigorous band tradition which Cornish miners created in South Australia's 'Little Cornwall'.[11] In terms of named individuals, approximately one-third of the thirty or so men noticed in *The Biographical Register* of the *Australian Dictionary of Biography* as having brass band connexions were British-born;[12] while in New Zealand it has been observed that the first known trio of slide trombones in a brass band (1885) included Messrs Hepplestone and Charlesworth, respectively from Batley and Linthwaite, in Yorkshire.[13] Finally, Australian banding received a further boost from Britain when the Salvation Army began its operations. The establishment of the first Salvationist band followed the arrival in Adelaide in 1881 of Captain Thomas Sutherland ('Glory Tom') who, we are told, led his musical forces through the streets playing his pocket-cornet, and 'marching backwards in the approved Christian Mission style'.[14]

Not only was the link between British and Australian bands established and sustained by the continued flow of migrant bandsmen to the colonies. In the early twentieth century, colonial standards were maintained, and the purity of the transplanted traditions preserved, by the frequent appearance of adjudicators from Britain at major Australian band contests, such as South Street, Ballarat. James Ord Hume – a prolific composer and arranger of band music – visited Australia and New Zealand in 1903 and again in 1924, and is credited with having persuaded New Zealand bands to give up the valve-trombone in favour of the authentic slide-version preferred in Britain.[15] More important still, Australian bands relied heavily on importing – via such establishments as Palings in Sydney – both their instruments and their sheet music from Britain. Virtually all advertisements for brass instruments in the Australian specialist press in the 1920s were for the popular Besson and Boosey models made in England; and, although the major instrument suppliers in the Australian cities undertook repairs, I have found no significant evidence of the actual manufacture of brass instruments in Australia itself. Likewise with music: when Sydney's Professional Musicians' Band wished to add the overture 'Morning, Noon, and Night' to its repertoire in 1931, it was unable to do so, because Palings did not have the parts in stock, and it would have taken too long, and cost too much, to import them from Britain.[16] Not surprisingly, Australian banding produced its own composers, some of whom had their work and arrangements published locally. Outstanding among them was Alexander Lithgow (1870–1929) – the 'Sousa of the Antipodes' – who dominated Tasmanian banding from the 1890s to the 1920s, and who has been accorded the distinction, unique for a bandsman, of a full-scale entry in the *Australian Dictionary of Biography*.[17]

The traffic between 'home' and 'colonies' was, in fact, two-way. If Britain's famous Besses o' th' Barn Band toured Australasia to great acclaim in 1907, it must be remembered that the Newcastle Steelworks Band returned the compliment, with equal success, in 1924, and that Melbourne's Malvern Tramways Band – widely regarded as the best in Australia in the 1920s – nurtured ambitious plans to follow in its footsteps.[18] Prominent Australian bandsmen also visited Britain on an individual basis: Percy Code and Percy Jones (1885–1948) both completed their musical training in the United Kingdom; Harry Shugg (1891–1968), Malvern's bandmaster in the 1920s, managed a vigorous conducting and adjudicating tour of Britain even if his band did not; while Frank Wright (1901–71), Australia's leading cornet player in the generation after Code, emigrated permanently to Britain in the 1930s, was quickly appointed organizer of concerts in London's parks for the London County Council, and established himself as a leading figure in the British brass band world.[19]

Given the original links and continuing connexions between British and Australian bands, it is not surprising that their role in both the musical and the social life of their respective countries showed many essential and enduring similarities. As our discussion of Orchard's history has indicated, Australian bands, like their British counterparts, were a distinct and largely separate stratum of the musical world, ignored and despised by an establishment which saw opera, chamber recitals, choral festivals, and symphony concerts as the only legitimate forms of serious music. Their detachment from the educational system seems equally complete. School bands were not unknown in Australia – indeed the St Vincent Boys' Band (Melbourne) and the St Augustine's Band (Geelong) achieved very high standards, and a number of other residential educational establishments seem to have maintained bands at various times both for their current pupils and their alumni.[20] But in a scathing editorial in 1929, the *Australian Band and Orchestra News* lamented the apparent lack of interest in fostering bands in state day schools, despite the beneficial effects which an early introduction to banding was alleged to have in promoting the physical and moral health of young men.[21] The result was that, as in Britain, youngsters had to learn brass instruments outside the context of formal schooling, and thus one possible channel for maintaining a steady flow of recruits into 'the movement' was blocked, at least, until recent years.

Socially, it is clear that Australian bands fulfilled a similar function for bandsmen and their families to that in Britain. Men joined and stayed with their bands because of the mixtures of conviviality and cameraderie, of music making and money making, which membership brought. In lean times, the band could provide a network of emotional and material assistance, and there are several examples in the 1930s of bands using the proceeds of the collecting tin specifically to support their unemployed members.[22] Similarly, although women players seem not to have been accepted in brass bands until after the Second World War, there were various opportunities for wives and girlfriends to support their menfolk. Few bands appear to have been without a ladies' committee which, characteristically, would run dances, euchre parties (the Australian equivalent of whist drives) and other social events to help raise funds. Quite possibly, this may actually have *extended* involvement in brass bands to a larger proportion and a wider cross-section of the local community than was the case with some of the more restricted, male-dominated 'participation' sports. Organizationally, too, Australian brass bands closely resembled their British equivalents. Although it is proper to talk of a brass band *movement*, the fact remains that each band was an independent, voluntary, and self-governing organization, owning its own property, determining its own business, and disciplining its own members. Each band came into being through some exercise of local initiative, and survival depended on its current membership having both the will and the means – in terms of both human and material resources – to carry on.

Because of the essential independence of each individual band, it is difficult to generalize with any precision about the rise and decline of 'the movement' in Australia, or to make exact comparisons with Britain as regards chronology. However, it seems likely that, as in many other areas, there was something of a time-lag between British and colonial experience. Dave Russell's work on brass bands in Yorkshire suggests that, numerically speaking, they reached their peak in the first decade of the twentieth century, and found it increasingly difficult to keep up their appeal, both to players and to audiences, in the face of an ever growing range of alternative attractions thereafter.[23] In the long run, of course, the same cultural and social processes which slowly made brass bands unpopular and unfashionable in Britain – particularly in the inter-war period – also operated in Australia. My general impression is that contesting only really caught on in Australia in the 1890s and early 1900s, and that the heyday of the movement lasted into the 1920s: certainly, contesting seems to have remained popular, despite the unhappy demise of the Ballarat competition in 1924, and there is evidence of new bands being formed (although there are also signs of defunct bands in some smaller county towns) down to the end of the decade.[24] What seems quite clear, on the other hand, is that the depression of the early 1930s had a sudden, severe and lasting effect on Australian bands, and greatly accelerated the decline of the movement. Tooth's Brewery Band folded in 1932 as a result of a loss of members through unemployment, a decline in financial support from the brewery, and a lack of paid engagements.[25] Palings stopped importing musical instruments from Britain between 1930 and 1933 in the face of declining demand.[26] Most revealing of all, the *Australian Band and Orchestra News* changed its name in 1937 to the *Australian Dance and Brass Band News* – an obvious sign that it was seeking to appeal to a new market of amateur musicians. Even in

Newcastle – which generally disputed Ballarat's claim to be the centre of Australia banding – there is the very strong sense of a movement in decay in the late 1930s. Despite a successful contesting record, Hamilton Citizens' Band, in a desperate plea for help to the local municipal council, claimed in 1937 that it had 'nowhere to practice, nowhere to meet, and no money to pay for a meeting place. Their debts amounted to over £100, principally due to the bandmaster'.[27]

III

Differences in the chronology of expansion and contraction of the brass band movement in Australia are only one of the ways in which it diverged from the British model. Another contrast can be found in the geographical distribution of bands. As in Britain, there were clearly areas within Australia which, in proportion to their populations, were 'over-banded', and others which were correspondingly 'under-banded'. It is impossible at present to express these differences in a quantitative fashion, but my general impression is that banding was particularly strong in the Newcastle and Queensland coalfields, in the Victorian and Western Australian goldfields, and in the copper-mining district of South Australia, in the early twentieth century – which suggests that the traditional British association between brass bands and mining communities also applied in Australia. Similarly, it is likely that the importance of the band in community life was greater in small, up-country towns than in the major cities: the towns of northern Tasmania, for example, seem to have been enthusiastic centres. Nevertheless, there seems to be a striking difference in the active and central role of the Australian state capitals in the movement, as compared with London's relatively modest place back home. According to its headed notepaper, of the New South Wales Band Association's 50 affiliated bands in 1930, 26 were 'metropolitan' and 24 'country'; while a graded listing of the 60 competing bands registered with the Victorian Band Association in 1925 indicates that about half of those in the top three grades – and a majority of those in Grades A and B – were Melbourne-based.[28] These figures refer, of course, only to affiliated bands which were likely to be interested in contesting, and it is probable that many country bands, with little prospect of taking part in state contests, were unregistered. Nevertheless, the apparent strength of the movement's *metropolitan* bases, compared with Britain, is remarkable.

Also noticeable are several differences in the typology of Australian brass bands. Again, current knowledge permits only an impressionistic picture to be painted: but the relative insignificance of *workplace*-based (and company-subsidized) bands is striking, and was the subject of a lengthy editorial in the *Australasian Band and Orchestra News* in December 1929, which reckoned that there were 'not more than ten in the whole of Australia'.[29] Even some of the so-called 'works bands' received only minimal support from the company with which they were associated. The Newcastle Steelworks Band of the mid-1920s went to some pains to stress its financial independence of the Broken Hill Proprietary Company;[30] while the Queenstown (Tasmania) Band, on appealing to the local Mount Lyell Mining Company for a grant in 1905, was brusquely informed by the company secretary that 'music does not come within the scope of the company's operations'.[31] It looks as if the short-lived Tooth's Brewery Band was indeed exceptional in having its instruments and uniforms entirely paid for by the company – at a cost of £1000 – when it started up in 1927.[32]

Increasingly, individual Australian bands seem in many cases to have become identified with particular localities and municipalities, and their names suggest that they were seen, at least in part, as essentially civic organizations enjoying a special association with the public and community life of their own town or city. This town-band association ultimately reflected the marked dependence of Australian bands on municipal subsidies, which is discussed later. However, some of the leading bands in the movement's early days, in the 1890s and early 1900s, carried the name not of their town but of their leader and founder. Thus Melbourne had Code's and Riley's bands, Ballarat had Prout's and Bulch's, and Newcastle had Barkel's. Some of these bands were subsequently adopted by a local municipality and acquired official town-band status.[33] The origins of most Australian bands will remain obscure until more local research has been done, but the implication is that, although reliance on municipal patronage came to be a feature of banding in Australia, it was not necessarily the case that municipal initiative had established bands in the first instance – although many may have been originally set-up as 'subscription' bands with the patronage of an *ad hoc* committee of leading citizens.[34] The relationship between brass bands and other voluntary organizations – such as churches or social clubs – also calls for further investigation before any definitive statements can be made. Is it, for example, of any significance that 'temperance' bands appear to have been almost non-existent in Australia? Perhaps not, in view of the fact that the word 'temperance' ought not to be taken literally when used in the titles of British bands. Again, how important was the Salvation Army's input into the development of Australian banding? The impression is that the Army's bands were less isolated from, and better integrated with, the ordinary 'civilian' bands than was the case in Britain, but detailed local testing is needed before we can be certain.[35]

When we consider the movement as a whole, rather than the individual bands which made it up, it is probable that contesting was of greater importance in Australia than it was in Britain. This is partly because the commercial interests – the music publishers, instrument makers, and so on – who stood to gain financially by actively promoting the expansion of the movement on the 'supply' side in Britain, did not exist in Australia. In particular, the absence of major local publishers gave the brass band press in Australia a significantly different character from that in Britain, where the specialist journals were essentially promoted by the music publishers. Nevertheless, if contesting was vital in creating and sustaining the sense of 'a movement', it would appear that Australian contesting practice came to diverge from the British pattern at several points. For obvious reasons of time, cost, and distance, nation-wide and inter-state contests were difficult to organize, as few bands could afford to travel far outside their own localities. It cost Hamilton Citizens' Band (from Newcastle) £200 to take part in the 1925 Brisbane contest;[36] and only a handful of eastern bands were able to make it to the 1929 West Australian contest held to celebrate that colony's centenary, despite the organizers' offer of £150 'appearance money' to each band.[37] Even the prospect of useful inter-state advertising was not enough to persuade Sydney's Tooth's Brewery to fund visits by its band to Perth, Maryborough (Queensland) or even Ballarat.[38] In order to encourage 'outside' bands to the 1938 New South Wales state contest at Newcastle, the organizers had to make elaborate provision for meals and accommodation for visiting bandsmen, and set up a special camp site for them.[39] The difficulty of organizing an effective national structure for contesting may be one reason why the brass band movement in Australia failed to throw up an entrepreneurial figure like John Henry Iles, who dominated the British contest scene for most of the first half of the twentieth century through his control of the Crystal Palace, Belle Vue, and the *British Bandsman*.

But if the scope of Australian contesting remained essentially regional in banding's heyday, there can be no doubt that contests had an enormous appeal, both to bandsmen and to audiences. By contrast with Britain, the emphasis was on visual spectacle as well as on efficient playing, and quick-step march competitions, with the bands executing elaborate manoeuvres while playing on the march, remained a major feature of most contests. For sheer entertainment value there can have been little to match a good brass band contest in the smaller towns, as the two-day programme for the 1935 Cessnock (near Newcastle) competition – in which five Grade B bands took part – indicates. The contest began with the bands marching from the railway station to the sports ground on Saturday afternoon, and ended with the adjudication and presentation of prizes at 10.30 p.m. on Sunday evening. In between times, the audience were treated to two demonstrations of massed band marching and two of massed band playing, together with four rounds of competition: quick-step march; waltz; own-choice light opera selection; and test piece.[40] It is thus not surprising that keen Victorian bandsmen in the late 1920s lamented the demise of the South Street contest, and blamed the alleged backwardness of the movement in their own state on this untimely (and perhaps unseemly) event.[41]

Among the other differences which emerged, it is also possible that, for a variety of reasons, Australian brass bands were more fragile and ephemeral than their British counterparts. The frequent and bewildering changes of name among Hobart bands, for example, suggests that they were constantly forming, going defunct, and re-forming.[42] The relative lack of a sense of community identity and loyalty, the rootlessness and migratory tendencies of Australian workers compared with their stay-at-home cousins in Britain, together with the vagaries of unemployment and the lack of public welfare provision, may all have contributed to instability and a rapid turnover in band membership. Once again, detailed local research will be needed to verify this hypothesis, but the problems which particularly affected bands in small country towns are well indicated in the following account from the secretary of the Ararat Citizens' Band (Victoria) in 1925:

> We are experiencing the usual luck of country bands, good players leaving: cannot be helped, as players must seek employment where it is to be found. We were fortunate in obtaining work for a good cornettist . . . but we will soon lose a good boy cornettist

whose family are removing to the city. We have only one eupho [*sic*] player, and badly require another, and have no baritones. Want of balance in band, but we cannot help it at present.[43]

These sentiments were echoed five years later in the comment of the bandmaster of Hughenden Town Band (north-west Queensland) that 'it is a very hard uphill fight to keep the band going in a town like Hughenden'. Part of the trouble was the low motivation of some of the players, who 'played only when there was free admittance to a show or races', but the real difficulty was that 'Hughenden having no industry in the town, it is very hard to secure jobs for bandsmen, so there is nothing left but to teach the boys'.[44] Nor was this problem necessarily peculiar to country bands. One of the major reasons why Tooth's Brewery Band established itself so quickly and successfully in the late 1920s was that the company was initially persuaded to give priority in employment to experienced players from outside who would strengthen the band; but, for understandable reasons, this policy could not be continued once depression struck hard in 1930, and by February 1931 the band's secretary was lamenting the loss of key players as a result of the Brewery's retrenchment of its workforce: 'our bass section is practically wiped out, our fine euphonium player lost to us, and our trombone trio split'.[45]

If local and cyclical unemployment made it difficult for Australian bands to hold on to their players, it is also possible that they could not offer the other financial inducements which made long-term loyalty attractive in Britain. We have already noted that bands could try to help their members in material ways in hard times; but what happened in good times? Published and unpublished band accounts suggest that it was common practice in Australia to pay the bandmaster an annual retainer and to cover players' travelling expenses; but how widespread was the British custom of an annual 'dividend', whereby the year's operating profit, often derived from Christmas playing, was shared out among the players? The elaborate rules of Tooth's Brewery Band provided for such a share-out, but band finances only permitted one dividend during its five-year existence: the sum involved (£5 a head) was roughly equivalent to a week's wages.[46]

In raising this issue, we are forced to explore the entire financial basis on which Australian bands operated; and it is here that some of the biggest contrasts with Britain seem to emerge. In general, of course, brass bands tend to live from hand to mouth and from year to year, and when extraordinary expenditure is called for – on instruments, uniforms, or contest expenses – extra efforts will be made to raise extra income. It is also true that the published balance sheets of many brass bands do not necessarily reflect the real extent of their annual turnover, since, with so many small cash transactions, it is easy to dip into the collecting tin at the end of a day's playing in order to defray some immediate expense. Apart from occasional windfalls – and few bands can have been so fortunate as Singleton Town Band (New South Wales), which won a major prize in the State Lottery in 1935[47] – most band income was derived either from the fees charged when the band was hired for an engagement, or from collections and admission charges when the band sponsored its own public appearances. Unfortunately, paid engagements, though greatly prized, are generally only obtained by competitive tendering; while the proceeds of public collections are entirely unpredictable. At the same time, it must be remembered that bands were often expected to give their services gratis on public occasions and for charitable causes. What all this could mean over a year's activities is indicated by the following account of the Bendigo (Victoria) Municipal Band in 1929: 'During the year, the band has assembled together on 124 occasions, as follows: 88 rehearsals, 7 paid engagements, 21 free concerts (for charity and other public functions), 8 recitals for band funds.'[48]

Given that many band activities would not generate income, and that many others yielded variable and unpredictable amounts, it was obviously desirable to have other more reliable sources of revenue. Regular, voluntary fund-raising, through social events organized by band members and ladies' committees, was one method; but it was altogether less troublesome to try and discover a sympathetic sponsor. Although, as we have seen, genuine works bands were uncommon in Australia, individual bands may well have benefited from the private benevolence of local worthies: for example, it can surely have been of no disadvantage to the Collingwood Citizens' Band that its president for many years was that enigmatic entrepreneur and *eminence grise* of the Labor Party, John Wren! Similarly, the Wallsend Band was probably not unique in the Newcastle coalfield in being supported by a monthly levy of 3*d*. per member raised by the local Miners' Lodge.[49] But for the most part – and in recognition of their public and civic role – many Australian bands came to rely on a regular annual grant from their local municipal council.

Quite why, or when, this happened is difficult to say: and the generosity of city fathers was, in any case, very variable. During the 1920s, Brunswick Council (Melbourne) gave its band £200 a year, Kogorah (Sydney) and Hobart £150, but Brisbane only £39.[50] In small country towns, the grant could be no more than a token gesture: Forbes Town Band had to be content with £15, and the Leeton District Band received only £5.[51] Direct cash grants were not the only form of municipal support, however. Sometimes, the local band would be given shared use of a council-owned building as a rent-free bandroom: on occasions, this might be the sports pavilion on the town playing fields, although in Coburg (Melbourne) the band was given the use of the local maternity clinic in the evenings![52] The provision of a rotunda (or bandstand) in the local park or on the beach was also a civic responsibility, and the weekly roster of bands engaged to play there could, in Sydney or Newcastle, give councils another form of patronage to be shared around the local bands. Nevertheless, municipal funding was often criticized by bandsmen for being unreliable and parsimonious. Band subsidy – which seems often to have been earmarked for paying the bandmaster's stipend – was an obvious target for economy when public finances were under strain, as in Newcastle during the 1930s depression; while the reorganization of local government in the same area in 1938 served only to eliminate some of the smaller councils which had formerly supported 'their' band. More seriously, it seems that relying on local authority grants could even be counter-productive: in the first place, it carried with it the obligation to turn out gratis for civic events and charitable causes; and second, it may have discouraged private donations, even on those occasions when the collecting box could be passed round, on the grounds that the band didn't 'need' more money, because it already enjoyed a council subsidy.

Finally, it is worth examining the links between Australian brass bands and the local labour movement in order to suggest some further divergences from the British pattern. To deal with this question adequately, it would of course be necessary to know more about the social composition of Australian bands: just how working-class were they? This would raise the further problem of whether the class structures of Britain and Australia were indeed identical in the late nineteenth and early twentieth centuries. Neither of these important issues can be pursued in a preliminary sketch of this kind, and we must be content to note that the links between Australian brass bands and organized labour were many and complex. We have already commented on the popularity of brass bands in mining districts, and it is easy to demonstrate, from both local newspapers and union archives, how extensively trade unions used bands for processions, demonstrations and social occasions. Indeed, some specifically trade union bands existed. The Victorian Boot Trade Band, established literally to drum up support when the union was at a low ebb in the depression of 1896, is a notable example: subsidized by the union to the extent of £26 a year (which paid the bandmaster's salary), the band was much in evidence at Labour functions in Melbourne until 1909, when it was formally taken over by the Trades Hall Council and renamed the Trades Hall Band.[53] Although the Sydney Boot Trade Unions failed in their attempts to set up a similar band in 1905, there seem to have been 'Labour' and Trades Hall bands elsewhere;[54] and, even when there were not, there was certainly an assumption among union officials that local bands would and should lend their support – preferably gratis – at labour rituals. Yet such assumptions were not entirely justified, as the experience of the Ballarat Eight Hours committee suggests. In the late 1880s, the organizers of the annual commemoration regularly hired up to eight local bands for the procession, for a donation of two guineas each. But in the early years of the twentieth century, the minute books suggest a growing reluctance on the part of the bands to appear for this nominal payment, especially if it meant loss of wages to their members. Matters came to a head in 1911, when the City Band put in a tender of ten guineas, and Prout's Band one of five guineas: the committee felt obliged to appoint a deputation 'to wait upon [the] bands urging upon each the claims of [the] 8 Hours Day Movement to sympathetic consideration from a working-class standpoint with respect to [the] attitude of the bands'.[55]

In fact, trade union and Trades Hall records in Sydney and Melbourne indicate that, regardless of whether bandsmen were workers or trade unionists, it was normally assumed that those who wanted the services of a band must expect to hire it at the going rate: and the consideration of tenders from rival bands was normally an agenda item when a metropolitan union was planning its annual picnic or its contribution to Eight Hours Day. However, a different link between bandsmen and unionists was highlighted in the early twentieth century in both of Australia's leading cities by the unseemly disputes which broke out when the

Professional Musicians' Union sought a monopoly of trade union playing for its members and protested at the unfraternal behaviour of 'amateur' bands who took jobs at less than the union rate.

In Sydney, the problem surfaced soon after the Professional Musicians' Union affiliated to the Trades and Labour Council in 1900. The union – whose membership, mainly employed in the orchestra pits of theatres and cinemas, included a particularly large number of cornet players – tried from time to time to organize a military band from its own ranks. From an early date, it sought to impress upon the Trades and Labour Council and its constituent members that, on good union principles, it had 'a right to supply all musical wants to all the trade unions'.[56] In practice, the union could not raise enough professional wind players to meet all the requirements of a major event such as Eight Hours Day; and it had to be content with securing priority of employment, at official union rates, rather than a monopoly. For its part, the Trades and Labour Council tried at least to ensure that the amateur bands engaged privately by individual unions included only men who were members of their own appropriate union, and it was regarded as improper that notorious anti-unionists should be employed on trade union occasions. As a result of this compromise, the 1904 Eight Hours procession was headed by a sixty-strong band of professional musicians while fifteen other 'first class bands' also took part.[54] The union's secretary believed he had provided 'a combination that not only will be a credit to our association but a credit to Australia. I want to show the people of Sydney', he went on, 'that we have a band here equal to any in any part of the world'.[58]

Brass bands and the Musicians' Union also clashed on the question of engagements being taken by amateurs (with paid jobs elsewhere) which would otherwise have gone to professionals. The Musicians' Union was especially suspicious of bands composed of secure, well-paid employees from the railways, tramways, police, or post office, and tried on several occasions to persuade the managers of these public bodies to stop their men taking engagements, even when they gave their services free, if 'there was any probability of the engagement of professional musicians'.[59] Likewise, the Musicians' Union protested vigorously when Sydney's municipal authorities engaged amateur bands for the parks at cheap rates. These issues became particularly contentious in the late 1920s and early 1930s, when professional musicians suffered both from the effects of the general recession and from diminishing employment prospects as silent films gave way to 'talkies'. Once again, in the interests of its unemployed members, the union reasserted its claims for priority in Eight Hours Day playing and park engagements, and reactivated the Professional Musicians' Band. Brass band enthusiasts, in turn, ridiculed the inflated pretensions of the professionals who, in any case, were quite incapable of raising an all-brass ensemble, given their particular membership. As one disgruntled observer of the 1929 Eight Hours parade wrote:

> What a difference there is now in the playing of the bands from that of some years back when the amateur bands held sway. At that time bands could be heard some distance off, but not today . . . The professional musicians had six bands present, and none of them except the last one in the procession could be heard until almost on top

of you. The amateur bands that took part made all the difference . . . One could easily pick out the bands which compete in marching competitions.[60]

Nor was the difference simply one of the loudness of the playing or the smartness of the turnout. As the Professional Musicians' Band committee itself admitted, it was also a matter of musical quality, because there was clearly a conflict of priorities between fielding the best band possible, and fielding one which gave employment to otherwise out-of-work musicians. In January 1931, the committee agreed that 'things musically in the band were not up to standard at some important engagements' and that 'the best men for the best jobs was advisable at all times'. One telling argument advanced in the discussion on this occasion was that 'within the next few weeks a monster band contest will be held, and a great number of visiting bandsmen from different states would be in Sydney and would no doubt be present at the band's performances'.[61] Although rather oblique, there could surely be no finer compliment to the high standard of musicianship attained by the leading Australian brass bands in the heyday of the movement.

IV

When we speak of an international popular culture today, especially in music, we are likely to think of an American-dominated world whose origins lie in the gramophone record and whose current symbols are the transistor and the Walkman. But at the beginning of this century, there was a rather different European-derived musical popular culture, whose essence lay in *making* music rather than merely listening to it. Amateur bands playing popular works by contemporary European composers on various combinations of cheap, mass-produced wind instruments were a major element in this culture, which was carried round the world not by the airwaves or in electronic devices, but in the heads, hearts, and hands of tens of thousands of ordinary European emigrants who took their home-grown customs, institutions, and pastimes with them when they put down new roots in strange places. The *British* strand within this transplanted popular culture was particularly important, and it was best able to thrive unchecked and little-changed in those small and distant communities where immigration from places other than the United Kingdom was negligible, and where, in the fullest sense, cultural links with the 'Old Country' were kept strong by being continuously renewed. Not surprisingly, Australia, New Zealand, and Canada met these conditions perfectly in the late nineteenth and early twentieth centuries.

The diffusion throughout the Empire (and especially the White Dominions) of the British brass band in this period is a prime example of this process at work; in the musical world, other examples could be found in the proliferation of choral societies and competitive music festivals, while in the wider sphere, the process is evident in the games people played and the literature they read. Whether any other European society exported so much of its popular culture undiluted in the late nineteenth century is doubtful, although one is reminded, for example, of the way in which Italian immigrants to South America carried their love of opera with them to São Paulo and Buenos Aires. Still, we must never forget that there were probably no other societies in the world so obviously 'colonial' in 1900 as Britain's antipodean outposts.

But if there was nowhere in the late Victorian world quite like Australia, it was also the case that Australia was never simply a clone of Britain, in popular culture or in anything else. And this comparative case study of the brass band suggests one important difference, with considerable implications for our historical understanding of the two societies. The popular culture which flourished in late Victorian Britain was essentially *provincial*. Like the trade unions, friendly societies, co-ops and other voluntary institutions which grew 'from below' and gradually coalesced to form the labour movement, the complex of leisure activities and interests – from pigeon-fancying to brass-banding – by which working men created a cultural world of their own, developed earliest, and remained entrenched longest, in the industrial towns and villages of outer Britain, rather than in the capital. 'Provincialism' in this deep-rooted sense did not exist in Australia and, in the case of the brass band, it is striking that Melbourne and Sydney were major centres of interest and activity in our period in a way that, back home, London was *not*. Indeed, it is not much of an exaggeration to say that *metropolitan* influence on the history of both the British working class and the British labour movement was of minor importance in the nineteenth century (although the position has changed significantly during the twentieth). In this sense, much of British labour history can be best summed up as 'scenes from provincial life': whereas, gold-diggers and sheep-shearers notwithstanding, most of Australian labour history can be more aptly described as 'a tale of two cities'.

Acknowledgements

The fieldwork for this study could not have been undertaken without a Visiting Fellowship at the Research School of Social Sciences, Australian National University, in 1987. I am especially grateful to the staffs of the Archives of Business and Labour at the ANU and of Newcastle (NSW) Public Library Local History Collection for enabling me to use records in their care. Early drafts of the paper benefited from comments by Mark Bailey and by participants in research seminars at Durham University and at the Australian Studies Centre, London University.

Notes

1 *Australasian Band and Orchestra News* (Melbourne), vol. 25 (October 1929), p. 5.
2 On J. Brownlee, see *Australian Dictionary of Biography* (hereafter *ADB*), vol. 7, pp. 450–1. On F. Curwen, see *A Biographical Register: Notes from the Name-index of the ADB*, Canberra, 1987 (hereafter *Biographical Register*), vol. 1, p. 154. On G. Chalk, I am indebted to Dr Cameron Hazlehurst for private information.
3 On the Partington family, see D. Madden, *A History of Hobart's Brass Bands*, Davenport, Tas., no date, unpaginated.
4 *ADB*, vol. 8, p. 48.
5 On the early history of the South Street contest, see *Australian Musical News*, vol. 1, no. 1

(1911), p. 10; vol. 3, no. 12 (1914), p. 357; *Australian Band Leader* (Ballarat), vol. 1, no. 1 (1971), p. 13.

6 *Sydney Morning Herald*, 27 January 1931.

7 S. P. Newcombe, *The Music of the People: The Story of the Band Movement in New Zealand 1845–1963*, Christchurch, 1963.

8 W. A. Orchard, *Music in Australia*, Melbourne, 1952; the references to Bathurst are on pp. 221–2.

9 P. Spearritt and D. Walker (eds), *Australian Popular Culture*, Sydney, 1979. F. Crowley, A. D. Gilbert, K. S. Inglis and P. Spearritt (eds), *Australians: A Historical Library*, Sydney, 1987, vol. III, p. 444 and vol. VIII, p. 386.

10 The records of Tooth's Brewery are deposited at the Australian National University, Canberra, in the Archives of Business and Labour (hereafter ANU/ABL). The papers relating to the Brewery Band are classified at N20/4016–4038.

11 J. McEwen, 'The Newcastle coalmining district of New South Wales, 1860–1900', PhD thesis, University of Sydney, 1979, especially Chapter 6; P. Payton, *The Cornish Miner in Australia*, Redruth, 1984.

12 I am grateful to Ann Smith, of the staff of the Australian Dictionary of Biography, ANU, for her assistance in analysing the name-index prior to the publication of the *Biographical Register*.

13 Newcombe, *Music of the People*, p. 36.

14 *The Musician* (Melbourne), vol. 1, no. 7 (March 1948), p. 111.

15 Newcombe, *Music of the People*, pp. 65–6.

16 ANU/ABL Records of the Musicians Union of Australia. T7/6/1 Minutes of the Professional Musicians Band, 3 March 1931.

17 *ADB*, vol. 10, pp. 119–20.

18 *Australian Band News* (Avoca, Vic.), vol. 20 (May 1925), p. 12; vol. 25 (July 1929), p. 6; *Australian Band and Orchestra News*, vol. 21 (April 1926), p. 15.

19 On P. Code, see *ADB*, vol. 8, p. 48. On P. Jones and H. Shugg, see *Biographical Register*, vol. 1, p. 378; vol. 2, p. 257. There is an obituary of Frank Wright, discussing his early career in Australia, in *Australian Band Leader*, vol. 1, no. 1 (October 1971), p. 10.

20 The Newcastle district may have been exceptional in fostering school bands: there were said to be six in existence in 1902 (*Newcastle Morning Herald*, 7 July 1962).

21 *Australasian Band and Orchestra News*, vol. 25 (October 1929), p. 1.

22 For example, in the winter of 1931, Hamilton Citizens' Band was giving the major part of the profits derived from concerts and engagements to twelve of its players who were out of work (Newcastle Public Library, Local Collection, A 2519, Hamilton Municipal Council, Correspondence, Box 2. File 6/170. Letter from Band Secretary to Town Clerk, 30 June 1931). South Melbourne Band used the proceeds of collections in a similar way (*Australasian Band and Orchestra News*, vol. 25 (September 1929), p. 16; and vol. 25 (December 1929), p. 14).

23 D. Russell, 'The popular musical societies of the Yorkshire textile district, 1850–1914', DPhil. thesis, University of York, 1979, pp. 104–6.

24 For example, during the course of 1925, the *Australian Band News* reported the establishment of new bands at Tongala (near Echuca), Red Cliffs (near Mildura), the Glen Iris brickworks, St Mark's Church Fitzroy, and among Melbourne's Seventh Day Adventists. On the other hand, the *Australasian Band and Orchestra News*, vol. 25 (December 1929), pp. 17–21, in a lengthy survey of the country bands of New South Wales, reported that the bands at Gundagai, Braidwood and Nowra were defunct.

25 For a fuller account of Tooth's Brewery Band, see D. Bythell, 'Brewers and Bandsmen', *ABLative* (the Newsletter of the ANU Archives of Business and Labour), no. 8 (1988) pp. 3–5.

26 E. Keane, *Music for a Hundred Years: The Story of the House of Paling*, Sydney, 1954, p. 64.

27 Minutes of a joint meeting of band committee and council sub-committee, 1937,

Newcastle, Local Collection. A 2519. Hamilton Municipal Council – Correspondence. Box 2. File 6/170.

28 Various letterheads of the Band Association of New South Wales for the late 1920s were found in the correspondence files of Tooth's Brewery Band (ANU/ABL N 20/4021). A graded list of Victorian bands appeared in *Australian Band News*, vol. 20 (August 1925), p. 11.

29 *Australasian Band and Orchestra News*, vol. 25 (December 1929), p. 1.

30 The Steelworks Band received a grant of £50 from the Broken Hill Proprietary Company in its foundation year, 1916 (*Newcastle Morning Herald*, 2 February 1917). However, in 1924 the band's secretary maintained that the band 'does not receive any subsidy from the B.H.P. Co. or any other source whatever'. (V. Beacroft to Town Clerk of Hamilton, 8 February 1924, Newcastle, Local Collection. A 2519. Hamilton Municipal Council – Correspondence, Box 2. File 2/15.)

31 G. Blainey, *The Peaks of Lyell* (4th edn), Melbourne, 1978, p. 234. The Company became more generous in its support of local bands in the 1920s.

32 By the end of 1927, Tooth's Brewery had spent £796 on instruments and stands, and £225 on uniforms and medallions (ANU/ABL N 20/4016, memo from R. C. Middleton to General Manager, 22 December 1927).

33 For example, Turner's Brunswick Band (Melbourne) was officially adopted as the Fitzroy Municipal Band in 1925, although only after some acrimonious debate in the Council Chamber (*Australian Band News*, vol. 20 (July 1925), p. 15). Similarly, in 1918, Merewether Council recognized and subsidized the Band of Park Street Methodist Church Young Men's Club, which had been founded two years earlier, as its municipal band (*The History of Merewether*, Newcastle, 1935, pp. 63–64, an anonymous official history, commemorating the fiftieth anniversary of the Municipality, copy in Newcastle Local Collection).

34 Interestingly – in the light of its later importance as a centre of Australian banding – Newcastle was only 'relieved from the odium of being the only city in the Southern Hemisphere without a town band' in 1879 by a zealous citizens' committee, which set about raising a public subscription in order to transform the existing Volunteer Artillery Band into the City Band (*Newcastle Morning Herald*, 14 October 1879).

35 For example, some Salvation Army bands seem to have enjoyed municipal subsidies (*The Musician*, vol. 1, no. 6, February 1948, p. 1).

36 Balance sheets of the Hamilton Citizens' Band, Newcastle, Local Collection. A 2519 Hamilton Municipal Council – Correspondence, Box 2. File 6/170.

37 *Australian Band and Orchestra News*, vol. 25 (September 1929).

38 ANU/ABL. The estimated cost of sending Tooth's Band to Perth was £1200 (N 20/4018, memo from R. C. Middleton, 8 March 1929). More modestly, an appearance at Ballarat was estimated to cost £275 (N 20/4019, letter from Band Secretary to Managing Director, 16 May 1932).

39 See the introductory *Brochure* for the 1938 New South Wales Championship at Newcastle. (Copy in Newcastle, Local Collection, Cuttings File 'Bands').

40 A copy of the 'Souvenir Programme' is in the pamphlet collection, Newcastle, Local Collection.

41 The Ballarat contest went into abeyance after 1924 because of disputes between the management of the South Street Society (which organized the whole eisteddfod) and the Victorian Bands Association (under whose rules the all-important competition for bands was conducted). See *Australian Band News*, vol. 20 (January–February 1925). Attempts by the Ballarat-based Victorian Bands Association to establish a contest independent of South Street in the later 1920s proved unsuccessful, and in the following decade the Association was replaced as the governing body of Victorian banding by the Melbourne-based Victorian Band League. See *Australian Band Leader*, vol. 1, no. 3 (1971), p. 10.

42 See Madden, *Hobart's Brass Bands, passim.*

43 *Australian Band News*, vol. 20 (June 1925), p. 3.

44 *Australasian Band and Orchestra News*, vol. 25 (January 1930), p. 17.

45 ANU/ABL N 20/4023, letter from Band Secretary to Managing Director, 10 February 1931.

46 ANU/ABL N 20/4019, band accounts for the year ending 15 May 1930.

47 *Australian Band Leader*, vol. 1, no. 4, (1972), pp. 6 and 8.

48 *Australasian Band and Orchestra News*, vol. 25 (November 1929), p. 11.

49 *Official Souvenir* of the 'Back to Wallsend Week', Wallsend, 1935. Copy in Newcastle, Local Collection, Cuttings File 'Wallsend'.

50 *Australian Band News*, vol. 20 (January 1925); *Australasian Band and Orchestra News*, vol. 25 (September 1929), p. 24; vol. 25 (October 1929), p. 10; and vol. 26 (February 1930), p. 23.

51 *Australasian Band and Orchestra News*, vol. 25 (October 1929), p. 9; vol. 25 (December 1929), p. 15.

52 Report to the Minister of Public Health on the Welfare of Women and Children (*Parliamentary Papers of Victoria*, vol. 2, no. 9 (1926), p. 550). I am grateful to Philippa Mein Smith for this reference.

53 The history of the Victorian Bootmakers' Band can be traced in the minute books of union's general and committee meetings between 1896 and 1908 (ANU/ABL T5/1 and T5/2).

54 Attempts to establish a Bootmakers' Band in Sydney are referred to in the Boot Trade Council Minutes of 18 October 1905 and 14 August 1906 (ANU/ABL T4/9 and T4/1/2).

55 The Minutes of the Ballarat Eight Hours Anniversary Committee are in ANU/ABL. For 1911, see the meeting of 23 March in E97/4/2.

56 The Minutes of the Professional Musicians' Union, Sydney branch, are in ANU/ABL. See meeting of 13 June 1901, T7/1/2.

57 *Sydney Morning Herald*, 3 October 1904.

58 Secretary's report to the A.G.M. of the Professional Musicians' Union, 15 August 1904 (ANU/ABL T7/1/4).

59 See, for example, minutes of the meetings of 28 March 1901 (ANU/ABL T7/1/2); 16, 23 and 30 January 1906 (T7/1/4); and 27 October 1913 (T7/1/5).

60 *Australasian Band and Orchestra News*, vol. 25 (October 1929), p. 11.

61 Musicians' Union of Australia, Sydney Branch. Minutes of the Professional Musicians Band (ANU/ABL T7/6/1, meeting of 5 January 1931).

6   *Postscript*

TREVOR HERBERT

One of the more effective invasions into post-war British consciousness by brass bands occurred in the late 1970s when an advertising agency, acquitting its contract to Hovis, a long-established manufacturer of brown wholemeal bread, used brass band music as background for a successful television commercial. The scene looks like a small nineteenth-century northern mill town – in fact the film was shot in the Dorset town of Shaftesbury. In thirty seconds it portrayed an idealized vision of Victorian, working-class boyhood as the baker's lad pushed his bike up the cobbled streets to be rewarded with a generous slice of the warm, buttered product. The voice-over had a rich and brittle edge that was neither Yorkshire nor Lancashire but miscellaneously 'northern'. The music track was the homogeneous tones of a brass band playing the famous third movement theme from Dvorak's *Ninth Symphony*. The music (typically) drew all of the strands of the commercial together and gave the whole a potency which it would otherwise have lacked. The images were, of course, almost entirely false, but the use of music in this commercial illustrated the manner by and in which a certain stereotype of brass bands is ingrained into the general pattern of stereotypes that image-makers manipulate and utilize. The successful running of this commercial was almost exactly concurrent with the promotion of *The Cornish Floral Dance* which I alluded to in the Introduction of this book. The Hovis advertisement was followed up by more Hovis advertisements using the same formula. More recently, the British United Pharmaceutical Association (BUPA), a private medical organization, has used band music for its television commercials. Here the ad-man's task was not to get business – at least not mainly or exclusively – but to improve the image of BUPA so that it would be seen not as an elitist haven for the sick-but-wealthy, but as a caring, compassionate service for all. Again, the band music, slow and flowing, stated something that could not be rendered in words or pictures with adequate subtlety. Orchestral music can, of course, be slow and flowing, but brass bands can, with a remarkable lack of ambiguity, create, even today, assumptions about 'class'.

The sound of brass bands is, it seems, a commodity that is capable of stimulating immediate thoughts of class, history and geography. To most people, brass bands are 'historically' and geographically fixed in a period when railway transport was new and warm brown bread was the staple diet of good folk, and in a place between Derby and Carlisle. Even the practitioners of brass band music have substituted anecdote for history, and have drawn between themselves as they are now and bands as they once were no clear link. The perceived crisis of the modern brass band movement is, in part, a consequence of the failure of bands to have a clear and true idea of the origins and development of banding which puts the present into perspective. The failure of the subject matter of brass bands to figure in serious study or to be absorbed into active debates in musicology, social history, cultural theory and other relevant areas of traditional and progressive scholarship emanates from the absence of a body of literature from which intellectual hypotheses can be drawn. This, too, is a self-perpetuating syndrome.

The contributions to this volume contain many pointers to the relevance of the *study* of the phenomena of the brass band movement to defined areas of scholarship and to the brass band movement itself. It may seem ridiculous to suggest that band enthusiasts, who simply and correctly perceive the brass band as an absorbing hobby, should be concerned about the 'cultural identity' of the activity to which they have such uninhibited attachment. But the most cursory association with band people and their channels of communication demonstrates that questions of 'respectability' and 'being taken seriously' are seldom far below the surface.

Much of what has been written in the preceding chapters illustrates how these concerns have come about. Also, as any perceptive reader will have observed, a number of questions are revealed that are not fully addressed. It has been outside the scope of this book to deal with several issues, but the questions raised serve to indicate the extent to which investigation of brass brands is new. There is an enormous amount of primary source material that is worthy of examination and has hardly been researched. Also, assuming that a greater amount of primary source investigation takes place, there is still a need for the fruits of that investigation to be integrated and synthesized into theoretical study.

It is easy to define several areas for future research. The first is the central issue of brass band repertoire. A cursory examination of the repertoire reveals certain watersheds. One such watershed was the advent of printed journal music, another is the point in the 1880s or 1890s when publishers achieved a consensus on the instrumentation of brass bands. Others include the introduction of more weighty 'test pieces', the establishment of a currency of test pieces according to the technical demands they impose on players, and so on. But these areas contain subtleties and subsets. What, for example, are the legacies of the organizational and administrative pressures of the movement on the repertoire and consequently on musical style? What is the legacy of there *not* being a standard instrumentation until banding was almost at the peak of its popularity? To what extent did the overwhelming dominance in the nineteenth century of operatic transcriptions infuse a style and taste in brass band music that was sustained in the 'original' repertoire.

In Chapter 1, I alluded several times to the 'musical idiom' of brass bands. Few would deny that this idiom exists and has many facets. At a purely technical level, it is possible to point to features like tone quality, articulation, pitch, the occurrence in band music of certain phrases and figurations that fit the finger and tongue movements involved in brass playing, the notion of homogeneity – the idea of the 'organ-like' quality of brass bands, and so on. It is, after all, these elements that provide the material for promoters of brown bread and medical insurance. Though it may be true, as Vic and Sheila Gammon have argued, that brass bands represent a departure from the plebian tradition to a more formal text-based, conductor-led activity, it remains the case that, from the nineteenth century, brass bands represent a domain of music making which was different to the mainstream of professional instrumental music and the various alternative forms of elitist instrumental music culture. This domain is characterized not just by the social condition in which the music was and is made but in the identity of the music product itself. If one accepts that the experience of playing in a brass band conditions the musical instincts of the practitioners, and if one accepts – as one must – that brass band and Salvationist band players have been the majority of brass players in Britain since the mid-nineteenth century and have probably provided the majority of *professional* brass players in the twentieth century, then it seems extraordinarily unlikely that brass bands have not exerted an influence on the mainstream of British music. The brass parts in the music of twentieth-century composers, such as Elgar, Holst and Walton, whatever other influences they have absorbed, surely contain a debt to the origins of the players that they were written for. But it is not just in art music that one should look for this legacy. Dave Russell has drawn attention to the involvement of brass band players in dance and jazz bands. If the style of those bands owes something to American influence but is, in other respects, different from American bands, where do those differences come from? The study of musical style in this respect requires not just contemplation but also experiment. Locked into the description of the development of brass band instruments which Arnold Myers gives in his technical appendix is a stylistic and idiomatic history that is gradually becoming lost. The true understanding of the earlier styles of brass bands, particularly in the nineteenth century, is only realized if attempts are made to reconstruct the performances of early bands using the original texts and instruments. Fortunately, examples of all the necessary material have survived. The so-called 'early music' movement has shown how attempts to reconstruct performance styles and idioms have cast light on and enriched entire areas of the repertoire. The technique, ethic and purpose of this movement is not confined, as it once was, to pre-Baroque music, but now encompasses the nineteenth- and early twentieth-century repertoire. Neither is it confined to high art music. The recent work of musicians like John McGlin on 1920s Broadway musicals shows that even music with which we are supposed to have a high familiarity and for which there are extant original recordings is capable of revealing hidden secrets.

While the significance of bands in British music history – both art and popular – requires clarification, it is to be hoped that some of the material in this book will also stimulate interest among social historians. All historical material is a primary source for something, but the true significance of brass bands is only revealed if the social historian is cognizant of the special type of phenomena that brass bands are. Brass banding is often lumped together with sport and other activities and discussed as a conglomerate called 'leisure'. The whole point about banding is that, within its own terms, it has a special, unique social-historical importance; it is important to appreciate banding as a *musical* activity. For example, there may have been a sector of the brass band community in the nineteenth century who were illiterate but who were perfectly literate and deft in music. In the twentieth century, brass bands have been a primary means of communication between people from different parts of the country. The greatest part of that communication was through musical performances and these performances articulated an array of tastes through a clearly understood (if not defined) set of denominators. One denominator, for example, was technical virtuosity but, as I have explained earlier, this was a particular type of virtuosity. Another denominator may be lyricism. Lyricism in brass playing does not demand the sort of virtuosity to which band enthusiasts award such high regard. But the subtlety of phrasing, the beauty of tone, that many band players have is a means of expression that is equally important. If films, poems, indeed creative works in total, form a source for social historians, then the manner in which musical communication manifests itself should also have some significance.

There is little in this book that overtly ties the historical material that makes its bulk with established arguments of cultural theory. This may be a shortcoming; if it is, it is mine, because the book is my design. There are two reasons why cultural theory is not in the foreground. The first is that I – and, I feel, most of the other contributors, too – do not regard cultural theory as a helpful starting point for discourse. Secondly, the subject of brass bands is so under-researched that it would take not just this book but a couple more like it before the cultural theorists would have something substantial to bite on. The other area that I am aware of as a possible gap in this book is the question of class analysis. Terms like 'working class', 'middle class', 'art music' and 'popular music' have been used freely and frequently. No doubt the authors' assumptions show through. For example, 'working classes' and 'middle classes' often appear, rather than the more monolithic 'working class' and 'middle class' or 'bourgeoisie', implying – accurately, I think – a pragmatic view of class as having to do with broad categories containing interlinked status groups, as against the economically determined sectors of standard Marxist theory. Similarly, we have tended to treat 'art' unproblematically as referring to elite cultural forms of high social status, and 'popular', equally straightforwardly, as related to the vernacular practices of ordinary people. The fact that these terms are not carefully defined in the book should not detract from its main purpose. There is, after all, no shortage of writings on these subjects and the inclusion of a lengthy discussion of definitions here, at this stage of band research, would have added to the density but probably cast little light. It is for others now to take up the necessary task of showing what the historical material can tell us about the intricate relationships between class and musical culture in nineteenth- and twentieth-century Britain.

Appendix 1: Instruments and Instrumentation in British Brass Bands

ARNOLD MYERS

Instruments of the earliest brass bands

The first all-brass bands of the 1830s departed from the centuries-old tradition in bands of accompanying melody played on woodwind with harmony played on brass. The common wind-band instrumentation of clarinets with horns and other brass instruments was varied to produce the brass band: cornets as principal melody instruments accompanied by a variety of brass instruments of middle and low tessituras. The widespread adoption of the new instrumentation would seem to have been a matter of taste: a preference for the sound of concerted brass instruments made possible by the inventions of the early years of the nineteenth century. The price lists of D'Almaine (Table 2) and Jordan (Table 3) show that the expense of equipping a band with cornets would have been slightly more than for providing the same number of clarinets.

The rise of the all-brass band seems to have followed hard on the heels of the invention of the cornet in the late 1820s and its introduction to Britain shortly after. All-brass groups would have been possible earlier: the keyed bugle was a popular melody instrument and horns, trombones and ophicleides were already used in military and civilian wind bands. There is no evidence that any brass bands were formed with all the upper parts played by keyed bugles.

The surviving evidence is not plentiful. Listings of the instrumentation of early brass bands, usefully assembled by J. L. Scott,[1] show a wide variety of groupings used in the period up to 1845. Cornets and keyed bugles were variously accompanied by French horns and trumpets (probably mostly valved horns and trumpets), trombones, ophicleides, bass horns and serpents. The bass drum and side drum were as in other bands which performed outdoors and on the march.

Often clarinets were used in what were otherwise all-brass groups – a usage which continued throughout the nineteenth century and into the twentieth, though since the 1870s not in major contests. The presence of clarinets did not alter the essential nature of brass bands: they replaced one or more Bb cornets or were used to provide brightness in the upper register in the role usually played by the soprano cornet. Later, in the 1890s and again in the 1970s, some bands sought to improve the effect of this topmost voice by using high Eb trumpets in place of the difficult Eb soprano cornet. The principal melodic line was always taken by the Bb cornet (often crooked into Ab in the 1840s, 1850s and 1860s).

Table 2 Price list of instruments: D'Almaine & Co, London, 1839

Clarionet	
with five keys	£1–1–0 to £3–3–0
with thirteen keys	£3–0–0 to £5–10–0
Cornopean or cornet a piston	
with two valves	£4–4–0 to £7–7–0
with three valves	£5–12–6 to £8–8–0
Bugle	
with six keys	£1–15–0 to £2–5–0
with eight roller keys	£5–10–0 to £6–10–0
French horn	
with four crooks	£4–5–0
with ten crooks	£9–0–0
Alto slide trombone	£2–5–0 to £4–15–0
Tenor slide trombone	£2–10–0 to £4–18–0
Bass slide trombone	£3–0–0 to £5–17–6
Valve trombone	£12–12–0 to £15–15–0
Ophicleide	
with nine keys	£7–10–0 to £15–15–0
with eleven keys	£9–9–0 to £16–16–0
with patent valve stops	£18–0–0 to £21–0–0
Serpent	
with three keys	£5–15–0 to £7–0–0
with five keys	£6–12–0 to £7–17–6
Bass horn with four keys	£6–6–0 to £7–10–0
Side drum	
wood	£2–12–6 upwards
brass	£4–10–0 upwards
Bass drum	
24 inch	£5–17–6 upwards
30 inch	£8–5–0 upwards

The cheaper bugles and bass horns are in brass, the more expensive in copper.

Source: H. Edmund Poole, 'A Catalogue of Musical Instruments offered for sale in 1839 by D'Almaine & Co., 20 Soho Square', *Galpin Society Journal*, vol. XXV (1982), pp. 2–36.

The trombones
Of the instruments used by brass bands in the 1830s, the trombone, (invented by the early sixteenth century) was the oldest.[2] Its concept was so simple, and its early form so satisfactory, that its subsequent development has been in matters of detail such as bore size and the interior profile of the mouthpiece. The tuning slide was added in the middle of the nineteenth century: even as late at 1889, Joseph Higham's cheaper models lacked this useful feature. Although the tenor size (mostly pitched in eight-foot C or nine-foot Bb) has been the most widely used, the standard complement was a set of alto, tenor and bass – disposed either in F, C and G or in Eb, Bb and F. The trombone had virtually disappeared in Britain for most of the eighteenth century,[3] but in the first quarter of the nineteenth century it returned to fashion, frequently with a forceful style of playing which gave it associations only now being thrown off, but no doubt appealing to many bandsmen and bandmasters. The alto, capable of less volume than the tenor and bass, and not as full in tone as valved horns, was less popular in the early brass bands, and does not appear to have

been much used at all after the 1860s. The bass in G, more manageable than the F bass (but with the outer slide still controlled by means of a handle), had a particular appeal to players in Britain; they were as numerous in early bands as tenor trombones and also became the standard bass trombone in the orchestra.

Some trombones were made with valves (usually three) instead of a slide. Valve trombones are arguably easier to learn to play, especially for those who already play a valved instrument, and are more robust – but they have never equalled the slide trombone in quality of tone. They were used by some brass bands, but became less common towards the end of the nineteenth century.

The French horn and the trumpet
These instruments were used by military and other wind bands at the time of the formation of the first all-brass bands, and naturally many of the early brass bands used them. At that time valved and natural horns[4] and trumpets [5] were in use, but it appears that the valved

Table 3   Price list for James Jordan, Liverpool, 1851

	Good quality	*Best quality*
Clarionet, B, C, Eb or F		
6 key'd	£1–1–0	£2–0–0
13 key'd	£2–2–0	£5–5–0
Cornopean with transposing slide	£3–0–0	£6–0–0
Cornopean with crooks	£4–0–0	£7–0–0
Cornopean, best german silver	£10–0–0	£20–0–0
Valve trumpet	£3–3–0	£8–8–0
Valve horns	£6–6–0	£12–12–0
Soprano Sax horn in Eb, D & Db	£3–0–0	£6–0–0
Treble Sax horn in Bb & Ab	£3–10–0	£6–10–0
Alto Sax horn in F	£4–0–0	£7–0–0
Tenor Sax horn in Eb, D or Db	£4–10–0	£7–10–0
Barytone Sax horn in C or B	£5–10–0	£9–0–0
Clavicor	£4–14–6	£10–0–0
Alto slide trombone	£1–5–0	£2–10–0
Tenor slide trombone	£1–10–0	£4–4–0
Bass slide trombone	£2–0–0	£5–5–0
Alto valve trombone in F	£3–3–0	£7–7–0
Tenor valve trombone in C or Bb	£4–4–0	£8–8–0
Bass valve trombone in G or F	£4–14–6	£9–9–0
Bassetto Sax horn in Db or C	£6–0–0	£10–0–0
Basso Sax horn in Bb or A	£7–0–0	£12–0–0
Contrabass saxhorn in F, Eb or C	£10–0–0	£16–0–0
Bombardone	£10–10–0	£16–16–0
Key'd ophicleide	£5–5–0	£10–10–0
Key'd serpent	£7–7–0	£14–14–0
Side drum		
wood shell	£1–10–0	£3–3–0
brass shell	£2–10–0	£4–4–0
Bass drum	£4–4–0	£9–9–0

Source: Peter Mactaggart and Ann Mactaggart (eds), *Musical Instruments in the 1851 Exhibition*, Welwyn, 1986, pp. 107–8.

instruments were preferred for bands. Both were used more to fill out the harmony and add their different voices to the tone colour of the band rather than as leading melodic instruments. Both were pitched most commonly in F (the horn with a twelve-foot tube length, the trumpet six feet) but provided with crooks for Eb, D, C, etc. It was not until later that orchestral players ceased to use crooks and play music in all keys entirely with the valves, so it would be reasonable to assume that horn and trumpet players in brass bands made some use of crooks, even though in any one band the music was probably arranged using a relatively small range of keys signatures. As clavicors and saxhorns were adopted in bands in the late 1840s and the 1850s, the use of French horns and trumpets fell away.

The serpent and bass horn

The serpent,[6] being a popular bass instrument, was adopted by some of the earliest brass bands. It was nearly always made of wood (often walnut) with leather binding; the crook and sometimes the mouthpiece were of brass. It is usual to class it as a 'brass' instrument on account of its being played with a mouthpiece, comparable in size to that of a euphonium, but with a cup shape approximating to a hemisphere.

It was most commonly built in C, with an eight-foot tube length. The compass extends down to C_2, not very low, but the serpent in a group of instruments can give the impression of an instrument an octave lower. It is not a loud instrument, but can add a telling effect of depth. As with other brass instruments, there is no upper limit to its range, but above G_4 the tone looses character.

With its adoption as a band instrument, the serpent became more widely played in its old age than in its youth. Several modified versions were made and favoured in different countries, generally easier to carry around and of a narrower bore than the serpent. The bass horn enjoyed a certain popularity in Britain alongside the serpent. It was invented by a Frenchman exiled in London, Louis Alexander Frichot, in the 1790s, and is of brass or copper in the form of a V with a large curving crook.[7] It had three or four keys, retaining the serpent's six fingerholes in widely spaced groups of three and rather unfocused tone colour. Bass horns were usually pitched in C. Few were made after 1835.

The keyed bugle

The keyed bugle was invented and patented in 1810 by a militia bandmaster living in Ireland, Joseph Haliday (born in Baildon, Yorkshire in 1774)[8] and gained immediate acceptance. It was a flexible and versatile instrument, the only soprano brass instrument of agility that was fully chromatic. Although the keyed trumpet was already in use in continental Europe, the keyed bugle appears to have been an independent (and more successful) invention. The conical bore and the large, well-spaced tone holes (see Plate 7) proved satisfactory acoustically: the disparity in tone quality between notes with the keys closed and those with the keys open can be reduced with practice to be as negligible as on woodwind instruments. The most widely used size was the four-foot C or Bb – in Britain bugles were generally built in C but more frequently played with a short looped crook to give a Bb instrument. The smaller Eb bugle (similarly playable in Db) seems to have been used less frequently in the early brass bands. The original maker of the keyed bugle was probably Matthew Pace: his move to London from Dublin in 1816 no doubt furthered the popularity of the bugle in England. Although used alongside cornets, its popularity waned after 1840 and bugle tone colour was later supplied in bands by the flugel horn.

Ophicleide

The keyed bugle's popularity was matched – and outlived – by that of the ophicleide, invented by 1817 in Paris by the maker Halari and patented by him in 1821.[9] The ophicleide was conceived as the bass member of a family of three sizes. The alto ophicleide, falling between the bass and the keyed bugle, had less success, and was replaced by valved

Plate 7   Keyed bugles in Eb (Pace) and C with Bb crook (Greenhill) both circa 1840. (*Source: Cyfarthfa Castle Museum and John Webb, Padbrook, Wiltshire, respectively.*)

instruments. Halari deserves credit not only for developing the ophicleide (*ophis* = serpent, *kleis* = cover or stopper) but also for producing it in a form which required little modification in its fifty or more years of popularity.

The distinguishing features of the ophicleide are its almost perfectly conical bore and its relatively large tone holes, all of which are covered by keys. Ophicleides are pitched in eight-foot C or nine-foot Bb. Unlike later valved basses, they make regular use of all the fundamentals: their compass is three octaves and more, from B_1 and A_1 respectively. The sound is firm and clear – not with the full mellowness of the euphonium or the reediness of the saxophone, but somewhere between the two.

The cornet

The valve, invented in 1814 by Heinrich Stölzel and Friedrich Blühmel in Prussia, was first applied to the horn and the trumpet.[10] Within a few years, however, Stölzel and others were making valved brass instruments in a variety of sizes and shapes – in essence the present kinds of brass band instrument. The names given to them (*Bass-Trompete, chromatisches Basshorn*) we would now find misleading. Although the initial development of these instruments was in Germany and Austria, it was largely the French remodelling of these instruments which was imported and copied in Britain.

The cornet, a valved version of the then popular post-horn, was invented circa 1828. It is not known who made the first cornet (it may well have been Halari in Paris) but its popularity was immediate, especially in France and Britain. In Britain, it was made by Pace and others: in addition, large numbers were imported from France and Germany by the end of the 1830s. It was first known as the *cornet-à-piston* in France and the cornopean in Britain, though this latter term is now reserved for the early form with Stölzel valves and a single 'clapper' key for trills (see Plate 8) that was a feature of instruments made for the British market.

Like the keyed bugle, the two principal sizes were the three-foot Eb and the four-foot Bb, the latter size being far more numerous and providing the leading voice of the band. Like French horns of the time, cornets were supplied with crooks. The Eb soprano cornet was frequently played crooked into Db in the 1850s and 1860s. The Bb (more rarely C) contralto was usually supplied with shanks for Bb and A, crooks for Ab and G, sometimes for F and low Eb also. Shanks (straight lengths of tubing up to eight inches long) and crooks (longer lengths with one or more loops) are inserted between the mouthpiece and the body of the instrument to lower the entire pitch range. Shanks and crooks were generally used to put the instrument in a different key to facilitate reading music parts; other advantages were a more mellow sound and a downwards extension of the compass. The mouthpiece for the early cornet was deeper and more funnel-shaped than that used towards the end of the nineteenth century.

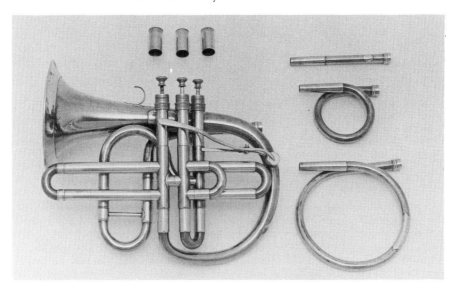

Plate 8 Cornopean (Pace) with clapper key, crooks and touchpiece protectors, *c.*1845. (*Source: Edinburgh University Collection of Historic Musical Instruments.*)

The clavicor

Among the derivatives of the German early experimental valved brass instruments of the 1820s developed in France were Guichard's valved ophicleide (1832) and 'Clavicor' (1838).[11] The latter could take the role of the alto ophicleide, filling the middle of the harmony of the band, offering a horn-like instrument of alto or tenor tessitura more suited to marching bands than valved French horns.

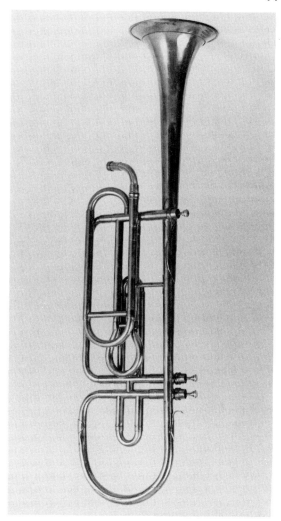

Plate 9   Clavicor in D♭ (Pace, *c*.1840). (*Source: Frank Tomes Esq., Merton Park.*)

The clavicor (or 'alt-horn') was latterly made in Britain also (see Plate 9) and was used by a significant number of brass bands in the 1840s and 1850s.

Instrumentation

These, then, were the brass instruments available in the movement's first decade. Some of the earliest surviving published music for brass band consists of parts of Wessel & Co.'s *Journal for Brass Band*, the arrangements being by William Childe, dating from the early 1840s.[12] We must presume that the instrumentation is fairly typical of the better bands of the time, although the bandmaster of a band buying the publication would have been expected to make adaptations for the forces at his disposal. The instrumentation, showing how far brass bands had developed by the time Sax's instruments were introduced, is, in no. 15 (*A Fantasia on Scotch Airs*):

one cornet à pistons in Eb and Db
two cornets in Ab
one cornet in Ab and Bb
two French horns in Eb
one valve trumpet in Eb
one alto trombone
one tenor trombone
one bass trombone
one ophicleide
tympani

Other music in the same series calls for similar instruments, but standing in different keys: in no. 12 (*Gems from the Opera*) the soprano cornet (in D) is optional, the solo cornet is in A, the other two cornets are in G, the horns are in Eb/D and C/E, two trumpets (in C and D) are called for, and there are optional parts for two more horns in G.

The instrumentation of the successful and well-equipped Cyfarthfa Band has been described elsewhere.[13] In both the Childe arrangements and the Cyfarthfa part books, the ophicleide part is far from being a simple bass line: it is wide ranging and often rapidly moving, similar to the solo euphonium part in later brass band music.

Inventions, hopeful and fruitful

The valve, as we have seen, was invented in 1814. Within a few years the horn, trumpet and trombone were equipped with valves, and new instruments, such as the clavicor, were developed. The importance of the invention was that it gave freedom to construct instruments with any desired bore profile, and consequently a variety of tone qualities. Previous chromatic brass instruments had been limited to those of largely cylindrical bore with slides (trombone and slide trumpet), those of conical bore with tone holes (serpent and keyed bugle families) and the French horn when played in the upper part of its compass with the difficult technique of hand-stopping. With valves, medium- and wide-bore instruments could be built with intermediate profiles, partly cylindrical and partly conical. The cornets, horns, euphoniums and basses of the modern brass band are just such intermediate bore profile instruments.

The original form of valve, the Stölzel valve, was a piston valve in which the piston casing itself was continued into the main tubing of the instrument at the lower end, the windway following right-angled bends inside the pistons. Since the piston diameter was that of the bore of the instruments, the bends inside the pistons were necessarily abrupt. This form of valve was used on the early cornets (cornopeans) and clavicors in British brass bands until the late 1840s and early 1850s (see Plates 8 and 9). It continued to be used on some cheaper imported cornets for a further thirty or forty years.

The rotary valve also seems to have been conceived by Stölzel and Blühmel in 1814, but was not developed until 1828 (when Blühmel patented a form with three windways in the rotor) and 1835, when Joseph Riedl in Vienna patented the form which has continued to the present day with two windways in the rotor. The bends inside the rotor are also right-angled, but less abrupt than in the Stölzel valve. Although widely used in Germany, Austria and Italy, the rotary valve has been less popular in Britain. A small number of brass bands have used instruments imported from Germany and Austria; Joseph Higham in Manchester made some rather elegant rotary valve instruments. With the recent adoption of Bb + F trombones, however, most brass bands now boast one or two instruments with one (occasionally two) rotary valves (see Plate 10).

The Berlin valve was also a piston valve, developed in 1835 by Wilhelm Wieprecht and Carl Wilhelm Moritz, with a wide-diameter piston. The windway goes straight through

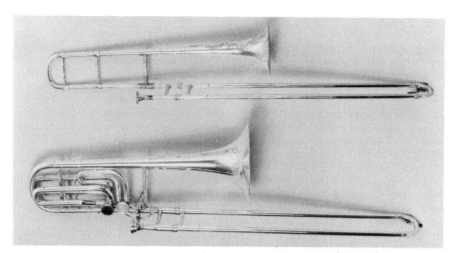

Plate 10 Narrow bore trombone in B♭ (Pace, *c.*1895) and wide bore trombone in B♭ with valves for F and G (Boosey & Hawkes, *c.*1980) as currently used for bass trombone parts. (*Source: Edinburgh University Collection of Historic Musical Instruments.*)

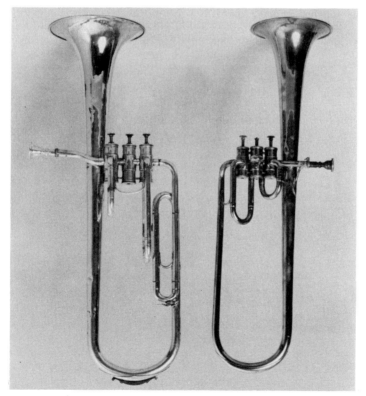

Plate 11 Tenor saxhorn in F and contralto saxhorn in B♭ (both Sax, imported by Distin, *c.*1845). (*Source: Edinburgh Collection of Historic Musical Instruments and Christopher Baines Esq., Burford, respectively.*)

the piston when the piston is not depressed, but takes two right-angled turns when the valve is operated. The use of this valve in Britain only extended to some early instruments by Adolphe Sax in the late 1840s (see Plate 11).

The design of piston valve now used universally is that of the Parisian maker Étienne François Périnet (1839). The piston diameter is wider than that of the Stölzel valve, but narrower than that of the Berlin; the windways are compactly arranged with gentle curves in three dimensions minimizing the disparity in resistance between natural and valved notes. The fine cornets by Courtois imported from Paris in the mid-1850s had Périnet valves; since then the vast majority of valved brass band instruments made at home or imported from abroad have used them (see Plate 12).

The other continental valve designs, such as the Vienna valve, saw little service in Britain; the ingenious valves being developed in America at the same time were unknown. There were, however, some native inventions. In England, John Shaw patented 'swivel valves' in 1838.[14] The idea was modified and marketed by the maker Köhler of London in his 'Patent Lever' instruments, which were shown at the 1851 Great Exhibition.[15] Difficulty in maintaining airtightness is usually given as the reason for the discontinuation of these valves.

Later, in 1862, George Samson patented his 'Finger-Slide' valves,[16] which showed some similarity to the earliest British trumpet valves of Pace in that the casing in which the piston moved was extended into a windway at both ends, the touchpiece connecting with the piston through a slot in the side of the casing. Instruments with Samson valves, made by Rudall, Rose, Carte & Co., show a very high standard of workmanship, but the complexity must have led to both high initial expense and difficulty of maintenance.

Plate 12 Cornet in B♭ (Besson) presented to Alexander Owen as a prize at the 'First Sight' contest at Mossley in 1874. A typical cornet of the British brass band. (*Source: Stalybridge Band.*)

These must be regarded as the only commercially successful valve designs to have originated in Britain, and even this success was short-lived. Several 'Patent Lever' instruments, mostly cornets, and a handful of 'Finger-Slide' instruments survive.

The basses

Stölzel, extending the application of the valve from existing to completely new instruments, developed twelve-foot F bass valved instruments in the 1820s.[17] Parallel developments took place elsewhere: in Paris, for example, the maker Guichard patented a valved ophicleide in 1832. The name *Bombardon* was given in Austria to relatively wide-bore valved basses from 1829. In Berlin, the enterprising bandmaster Wilhelm Wieprecht had already introduced valved instruments into Prussian military bands when, in 1835, he developed a wide-bore bass in conjunction with the maker, Carl Wilhelm Moritz, with the name *Bass-Tuba*.[18] The wider bore was accompanied by the new design of piston valve, discussed above. Although some Austrian and German instruments were imported into Britain, it was not until the tuba was remodelled by Adolphe Sax as a member of his family of saxhorns in 1843, and subsequently promoted in Britain by the Distin family, that they were widely adopted by brass bands.

The basses are easier to carry on the march when wrapped round the player, the weight resting on the shoulder rather than held or strapped in front. Such 'circular basses' were used by many brass bands in the second half of the nineteenth century. (The term 'helicon' was not widely used in Britain at the time.) The American derivative of the circular bass, the sousaphone, has seen very little use in British brass bands.

Saxhorns

Adolphe Sax, the Belgian-born inventor and maker of wind instruments who from 1842 worked in Paris, met with considerable opposition from rival makers when he patented his 'Saxhorns' in 1843,[19] and became ruinously embroiled in litigation in defending the patent. He can, however, be given credit for producing well-made instruments in a family of consistent design and graded sizes, but the members of the family were not new: comparable instruments had been in use in Germany and elsewhere for years. He initially used the Berlin valves (see Plate 11). Ignoring the extreme sizes, rarely used, the family consisted of a soprano in three-foot F or Eb, a contralto in four-foot C or Bb, a tenor in six-foot F or Eb, a baritone in eight-foot C or nine-foot Bb, a bass in eight-foot C or nine-foot Bb, and contrabasses in twelve-foot F or thirteen-foot Eb (later also in eighteen-foot Bb). The bass was distinguished from the baritone by its larger bore. The tenor and baritone saxhorns differed little from the instruments already known variously as clavicors or althorns, a source of confusion in nomenclature that has persisted to this day. The contralto was somewhere between the relatively narrow-bored cornet and the wider-bore valved bugle (flugel horn).

The fact that British brass bands adopted the saxhorns so readily is largely due to Sax's association with the Distin family, stemming from their meeting in Paris in 1844,[20] and the promotion of Sax's instruments by the Distins in Britain. The Distin family enjoyed a popularity and esteem in Britain in the mid-nineteenth century with which only that of the Mortimer family in the twentieth can be compared, and their agency in London for Sax instruments was highly influential. Saxhorns were marketed by Henry Distin from 1845. When, five years later, he started making similar instruments, Sax replaced Distin as his London agent. The adoption of saxhorns by the brass bands of Britain was remarkable in its rapidity: the prizewinning band at the well-documented Burton Constable contest of 1845[21] was already using several. The Mossley Temperance Band purchased a full set of saxhorns in 1853 and won the first prize at the Belle Vue contest that year. Many bands took names such as 'Hawick Saxhorn Band' even if they retained trombones and ophicleides in addition to the Sax model instruments.

After a time, similar instruments by other makers were frequently called 'saxhorns'. The

Plate 13 Ophicleide (Smith), ten keys (formerly eleven keys), *c*.1840 and contrabass saxhorn in E♭ (Courtois, *c*.1865). (*Source: Edinburgh University Collection of Historic Musical Instruments.*)

tenor horns and baritones of the present-day brass band are tenor and baritone saxhorns. The bass saxhorn was replaced by the very similar euphonium, and the contrabasses, alternatively known as bombardons in bands (and tubas in orchestras) are now, in brass band parlance, merely 'basses', E♭ or BB♭ ('double Bs').

The Euphonium
The fact that the term 'bass saxhorn' or 'B♭ bass' gave way to the Austrian name, *Euphonium*, for virtually the same instrument as developed by F. Sommer in 1843,[22] is probably to some extent due to the attractiveness of the word, and to some extent because the role played by the instrument, like that of the ophicleide latterly, was not to play the bass of the harmony but to provide an independent melodic line at tenor pitch. Like the ophicleide, the euphonium has a wide compass and is capable of virtuoso performance. It contributes much to the characteristic rich sound of the full brass band.

Flugel horn

The keyed bugle was more rapidly replaced by valved bugles in German-speaking countries than in Britain. Even when the keyed bugle was no longer used, it was not always replaced in brass bands except by cornets. The desire for an alternative tone colour at the pitch of the principal melody line led to the adoption of the *Flügelhorn*, the name for the valved bugle prevalent in Austria, rather than the contralto saxhorn. It has never had the importance that it has in Austrian bands, and even if there were two or three in a brass band in the 1870s, they mostly doubled two or three of the cornet parts. The single 'flugel' in a brass band has usually doubled the principal or 'repiano' cornet line in the *tuttis* and contributes its own occasional solo, though in modern scoring it can equally be grouped with the horns or be given an independent part.

The pattern of manufacture and import 1845–73

When all-brass bands arrived, there were a number of British makers who were capable of producing the instruments required. The firms of Pace, Percival, Key, Greenhill, Roe, Smith, Wigglesworth, Metzler, and Sandbach produced high-quality instruments in their workshops. Some of their work has survived in museum collections. The expanding market also absorbed a flood of imported instruments (especially the cornopeans which were needed in large numbers) mostly from France and Germany. Often, British dealers would stamp their own name on these imported instruments.[23] Many of these imports were very cheap compared with the hand-crafted British models, though some high-quality instruments from firms such as Halary and Sax were sold in Britain.

After acting as agent for Sax for five years, Henry Distin decided that he could more profitably make instruments and set up his own workshop in 1850. In 1868 he sold his thriving business to Boosey & Co. for £9,700, though the name Distin was retained for trading purposes for several years. Other makers[24] who commenced manufacture of brass band instruments in mid-century were Köhler & Son (active throughout), William Brown (from 1851), Rudall, Rose, Carte & Co (already making woodwind, adding brass on joining with Key & Co. *c.*1857), F. Besson (from 1857, though a related firm was manufacturing from 1837 in Paris), George Butler (from 1858 as a branch of a Dublin firm), and Rivière & Hawkes, later Hawkes & Son (already repairing, adding manufacture in 1875). All these were in London; the principal provincial makers of brass band instruments were Joseph Higham (from 1842) in Manchester and James Gisborne (from *c.*1839) in Birmingham.

Instrumentation

Very useful evidence of the kinds and numbers of instruments being used by the leading brass bands in the early 1860s has survived. Over eighty forms used by bands entering contests are preserved in the Archive of Enderby Jackson papers now in the care of Raymond Ainscoe.[25] Since only bands reasonably certain of their balance of instruments would enter a contest at the national level, we can assume that the instrumentation of these bands represents the 'state of the art' at that time.

The 34 surviving forms from the 1860 Crystal Palace contest show that the average band (18 players) consisted of:

1–2 sopranos, mostly in Db but some in Eb
5   cornets, mostly in Ab but some in Bb
0–1 alto saxhorns in Ab
2–3 tenor saxhorns or alt horns, mostly in Db but some in Eb
1–2 baritones, mostly in Ab but some in Bb
1   tenor trombone, mostly in C but some in Bb

Table 4 Price list for Boosey & Co. trading as Distin & Co., *c*.1873

	Ordinary	Equisonant pistons
Imported (French) cornet in B♭	£1–5–0	
New model cornet in B♭	£3–3–0	'The cheapest English cornet manufactured'
New model cornet in B♭		£4–4–0
Soprano saxhorn in E♭ and D♭	£2–0–0	
Soprano cornet-a-pistons	£3–5–0	£4–10–0
Alto saxhorn or flugel horn	£3–10–0	£4–10–0
Tenor horn in F or E♭	£4–0–0	£5–0–0
Baritone in C or B♭	£4–10–0	£5–10–0
Alto slide trombone in E♭	£2–0–0	
Tenor slide trombone in C or B♭	£3–0–0	
Bass slide trombone in G or F	£4–0–0	
Euphonion or bass saxhorn		
in C or B♭ three valves	£5–10–0	£7–0–0
in C or B♭ four valves	£6–10–0	£8–10–0
Contrabass saxhorn or Bombardon		
in F or E♭ three valves	£6–10–0	£8–10–0
in F or E♭ four valves	£7–10–0	£9–10–0
in BB♭ three valves	£8–10–0	£10–10–0
Monstre champion circular bass		
in E♭ three valves	£12–0–0	£14–0–0
in BB♭, three valves	£13–0–0	£15–0–0
Side drum, rope and tug, 14 inch		
wood shell	£2–0–0	
brass shell	£2–10–0 to £4–10–0	
Bass drum		
28 inch diameter	£6–15–0	
32 inch diameter	£8–10–0	

Valve trombones priced at £1–0–0 more than the slide trombones (£2–10–0 more for Equisonant pistons)

1   bass trombone, mostly in G
1–2 ophicleides, mostly in C but some in B♭
1   sax bass or euphonium, mostly in B♭ or A♭, some in C
2   contrabass saxhorns or bombardons, mostly in E♭ but some in D♭

There were a scattering of soprano saxhorns, alto trombones, flugel horns, clarinets, trumpets, French horns and BB♭ contrabasses. In each band there was usually a mixture of instruments from the E♭/B♭ and the D♭/A♭ dispositions of valved instruments and the F/C/G and E♭/B♭/F dispositions of trombones, though some maintained a 'purer' instrumentation. One band, the Darlington Temperance Brass Band, consisted entirely of instruments standing in natural keys: soprano in D, six cornets in A, alt horn in E, two alt horns in D, valve tenor trombone in C, baritone in B, euphonium in A, two ophicleides in C and two bombardons in D.

We cannot be certain to what extent the valved instruments were built in keys such as D♭ and A♭. Most of the surviving instruments are in F, E♭, C or B♭, and we can surmise that these instruments were commonly used with crooks, alternative tuning slides or tuning-slide extensions. The fact that it is mostly the smaller instruments which are in the Db/Ab disposition would support this: it could only be a nuisance to deal with a crook or an extended tuning slide for a euphonium or a bombardon. Where crooks or tuning slide extensions were used, we would expect this to be for reasons of tone colour preference in the case of cornets (cornopeans) and in order to extend the range downwards in the case of bass instruments.

Several bands gave the names of a side drummer, bass drummer or both, and sometimes a cymbal player: the form of the Darwen Temperance Band, Lancashire, listed 'Drummer, but will not bring his drum of course'. As was to be the case for over a hundred years, percussion instruments were not allowed to be used in contest playing. However, the 1862 entry form for the South Yorkshire Railway Company's Brass Band included 'Bass drum, of course will be required for street playing', perhaps indicating that the band would march from the railway station to the Crystal Palace.

There are twenty-three surviving entry forms for the 1861 Crystal Palace Contest. The average size of the bands was now slightly smaller (seventeen). There were relatively fewer ophicleides. One band, however, still sported a keyed bugle: the Wakefield Foresters commenced their form with 'Bugle in Db' and went on to include three ophicleides in C. The bombardon player of the Mossley Amateur Brass Band near Stalybridge is cited on the form as being the 'first public player on a four-keyed bombardon': if this was the case, he was the forerunner of many future Eb bass players in bands where either one or both Eb basses were equipped with a fourth valve. The entry form of W. L. Marriner's Band (also the Band of the 35th York Rifle Volunteer Corps), Keighley, listed a unique instrument, the double slide contra bass trombone in Bb which has been described by this author elsewhere.[26] One would dismiss this invention as an aberration were it not for the fact that its player actually won the prize for the best bass player in this contest.

The thirteen surviving forms from the 1862 Crystal Palace Contest show still relatively fewer ophicleides, but half the bands now use flugel horns. W. L. Marriner's Private Brass Band listed two flugel horns (they entered none in 1861) and the Eb bass sonorophone which was their prize for the best bass player the previous year. The sonorophones were a family of bell-forward rotary-valve instruments patented in 1856 by James Waddell and marketed by Metzler & Co.[27] The circular coils of the main tubing are held in front of the player like a steering wheel. They can occasionally be seen in photographs of bands in the late nineteenth century. In terms of sound quality and response to the player they did not differ markedly from the other valved instruments used in brass bands. The Allendale Saxhorn Band boasted valved trombones in Eb, Bb and F. Overall, about one in ten of the trombones were listed in these forms as valve trombones: the actual proportion may have been a little higher since none is listed specifically as a slide trombone.

The five forms surviving from the 1863 Crystal Palace Contest and the seven surviving from the Order of Druids' Brass Band Contest at the Royal Park Garden, Leeds, in the same year show the same trends continuing. There is only one ophicleide mentioned, and trumpets have disappeared altogether.

The business of instrument making

Improvements in the design of valves and refinement of the design of instruments led to the models which have continued to this day: the cornet, the flugel, saxhorns, euphonium and the basses. After the last of Enderby Jackson's Grand National Crystal Palace contests in 1863, the annual contest at Belle Vue, Manchester, was the most prestigious and influential. Following the incident at the 1873 contest in which a Black Dyke euphonium player played trombone solos on a valve trombone, the rules were tightened. Valve trombones were excluded, and the present-day band instrumentation can be said to have crystallized from this date. Of course, it took some time for the rules of other contests to follow, and the instrumentation of non-contesting bands has never been standardized. We can safely assume that some small village bands carried on using valve trombones, clarinets and, no doubt, ophicleides throughout the century.

The brass instruments specified by the major contests have been as follows:[28]

one soprano cornet in E♭
eight cornets in B♭
one flugel horn in B♭
three tenor saxhorns ('tenor horns') in E♭
two baritones in B♭
two tenor trombones in B♭
one bass trombone
two euphoniums in B♭
two basses in E♭
two basses in B♭

with a total of twenty-four players; sometimes one extra player has been allowed who would double one of the parts: a fourth trombone or, more usually, a further cornet. The numbers of each kind of instrument have been determined by the repertoire of test pieces rather than the contest rules. The body of published compositions and arrangements for brass band has both grown more rapidly and been musically more satisfactory as a result of being written for a standard combination.

Although the kinds and numbers of brass instruments in the full contesting band have not changed since the mid-1870s, the instruments themselves have evolved and the sound of a full brass band today is noticeably different from the sound of bands to be heard in early recordings. In general, the modern band is louder and thicker; the late Victorian band brighter, lighter and crisper.[29] In general, the evolution of the instruments of the brass band has followed that of instruments of the British orchestra, and the overall sound quality has changed similarly.

Mass production
In general in the history of musical instruments, the invention of successful new instruments leads to experimentation with ensemble and the formation of new musical groupings. If these in turn are successful, a repertoire is established and makers find that there is no demand for new kinds of instruments, only for improvements in the existing ones. Although instruments basically similar in bore profile to saxhorns (such as Distin's 'Ventil Horns' and 'Tenor Cor', Metzler's 'Sonorophones' and Courtois's 'Koenig Horns') were introduced, none gained wide acceptance in brass bands, though individual bands certainly used them here and there to play tenor horn parts. Besson's 'Cornophones' (a family of instruments similar to saxotrombas or to Wagner tubas) might have made a useful contribution to the instrumentation of the brass band, but their launch in the 1890s was fifty years too late for this.

In the 1870s and 1880s, the number of brass bands was increasing dramatically, and the market for sales better than at any time before or since. Nearly every community seemed to support a band, not necessarily of a particularly high standard, so there was a demand for inexpensive instruments. Also, the proliferation of contests fostered an increase in the number of more competent bands which could and did afford instruments of better tone quality, dynamic range, compass, intonation and response to the player.

In the second half of the nineteenth century, most of the instruments for brass bands were made by the larger firms – those capable of mass production such as Boosey, Hawkes, Besson, and Higham. Imports continued, still mostly of cheap models, but including some fine instruments such as the Viennese instruments used by the Cyfarthfa Band and the Courtois instruments imported from Paris by S. A. Chappell. Makers had a vested interest

Table 5   Price list for P. Robinson, trading as Joseph Higham, 1889

	Cheapest	*Patent clear-bore*
Soprano cornet in E♭	£2–12–0	£6–10–0
Cornet in B♭	£3–0–0	£7–0–0
Flugel horn in B♭	£3–3–0	£7–0–0
Alto or tenor in E♭	£3–12–0	£7–10–0
Baritone in B♭	£4–10–0	£8–0–0
Tenor slide trombone in B♭	£2–2–0	
Bass slide trombone in G	£2–12–0	
Euphonion, bass		
in B♭ three valves	£5–5–0	£9–10–0
in B♭ four valves	£6–10–0	£11–0–0
Bombardon		
in E♭ three valves	£7–10–0	£11–11–0
in E♭ four valves	£8–10–0	£14–0–0
in B♭ three valves	£11–11–0	£15–15–0
Circular bombardon, over shoulder		
in E♭ three valves	£12–12–0	£16–16–0
in B♭, three valves	£14–10–0	£18–18–0
Side drum, brass shell		
with cord and braces	£2–10–0 upwards	
with six tuning screws	£3–10–0	
Bass drum	£6–6–0 upwards	

Silverplating charged extra, ranging from £2–0–0 for a soprano cornet to £12–0–0 for a circular bombardon in B♭.

Source: Howard Higham Robinson, a descendant of Peter Robinson, proprietor of the firm in 1889.

in the brass band movement, and regularly gave presentation instruments to prizewinners in contests.

The advertisements of the leading makers were quick to enumerate the prizewinning bands using their instruments after each major contest. Gisborne & Co of Birmingham claimed in 1905[30] that its instruments were used by Besses o' th' Barn, Black Dike, Kingston Mills, Irwell Springs, Wingates, among others. Besson & Co claimed in 1907[31] that bands playing its instruments had won three of the last four Belle Vue contests (also citing Wingates).

The number of makers of instruments was also at its highest at the end of the nineteenth century. The largest firms employed considerable workforces.[32] In 1890, Besson & Co. employed 131 hands at its Euston Road workshops, turning out 100 brass instruments per week, and had the addresses of over 10,000 British brass bands on its books. In 1895, Hawkes & Son moved its workshops from Leicester Square to 3,500 square feet of new premises in Denman Street, Piccadilly Circus: the company was then employing nearly 100 men. In 1924 it established the factory at Edgware now operated by Boosey & Hawkes. In 1875, Boosey & Co. closed the former Distin workshops in Great Newport Street and opened a new factory at Stanhope Place, Marble Arch where, in the early 1890s it employed '100 mechanics'. Boosey & Co. appears to have set a limit of 100 hours for a workman to make an instrument.[33] Peter Robinson, the son-in-law of Joseph Higham and proprietor of the firm of J. Higham, was, according to different accounts, employing either 70 or over 90 men in 1892. The Salvation Army made instruments, for its own use, from 1889 to 1972. It established a factory in St Albans in 1901 and turned out around sixteen instruments per week.[34] No British firm, though, was as large as that of Gautrot in France, which employed 560 in the 1880s.

These larger firms produced all the brass band instruments in a range of quality, typically 'Class A', 'Class B' and 'Class C', the cheapest being half the price of the top models. Silverplating was an optional extra, generally available from the 1870s, and elaborate engraving of the bell (occasionally the whole instrument) was extra again. Not surprisingly, most of the instruments surviving from this period are silverplated Class A instruments of quality: we can safely surmise that the large numbers of cheaper and unplated instruments that were sold have long since deteriorated beyond worthwhile repair – cheap 'educational' instruments today hardly last five years.

The widespread used of silverplated instruments gave rise to some brass bands taking the name 'Silver Band'. This little ostentation did not signify any difference at all in instrumentation.

Improvements
The improvements in the instruments themselves were real, if not quite as important as the makers claimed. A clear passage of the windway through the valves was the aim of numerous designs.[35] Distin's 'Equisonant Pistons' and Higham's 'Clear Bore' pistons were typical of the valve designs of the more expensive models.

Lightness of valve action and minimized length of travel were also design objectives. Boosey & Co introduced 'Solbron' (in 1907) and later 'Silbron' valve pistons with special bronze surfaces which (very effectively) reduced friction. From 1922 the same firm produced 'N.V.A.' (New Valve Action) valves for cornets in which depressing the piston extends a spring. Most cornets have top-sprung valves in which the spring is compressed when the valve is operated; most larger instruments are bottom-sprung, also with compression springs. These minor modifications were typical of many with which manufacturers hoped to increase their market share.

At the end of the century, cornets were still supplied with shanks for playing in Bb and A (sometimes also with a crook for Ab). Though most bands were using cornets in Bb, the cornet was widely used orchestrally with the parts frequently written for cornet in A. Rudall Carte's 1903 Patent instrument[36] was one of the first to embody a fixed mouthpipe, the change to A being effected by pulling out an auxiliary tuning slide. Other makers such as Besson provided a 'quick-change' rotary valve. The fixed mouthpipe for brass band cornets surprisingly only became standard after the Second World War.

The first brass bands appear to have used trombones after German models, of medium bore. The tenor in C at Cyfarthfa Castle Museum, Merthyr Tydfil (Plate 14) has a bore of 11.7 mm descending, 11.9 mm ascending; the tenor in C by Wigglesworth at Cliffe Castle Museum, Keighley (probably imported from Germany), has bore of 10.9 mm and 12.6 mm respectively. The G bass in Plate 14 has a bore of 12.0 mm in both inner slide legs and a G bass by John Green of London (*c*.1835) in the Edinburgh University Collection of Historic Musical Instruments has a bore of 12.5 mm. By the 1870s, the narrow-bore French model had become as universally used in brass bands as it was in orchestras. These trombones were often played with a deep funnel-shaped mouthpiece rather than the wider cupped profile now used. The Bb tenor in Plate 10 by G. H. Pace has a bore of 10.3 mm descending, 10.4 mm ascending; the standard instruments of Hawkes and Besson were slightly wider at 11.0 mm. The highly popular Besson Class A bass trombone in G of the 1890s has descending bore 11.4 mm, 11.6 mm ascending. These figures can be compared with the 14.0 mm bore of the Conn 8H Bb tenor model as a present-day point of reference. The effect of this use of narrow-bore trombones, which continued until the 1950s, was to emphasize the contrast between the trombones on one hand, and the baritones and euphoniums on the other, and to exploit the vocal qualities of the instrument in *piano* passages and the crispness of attack of narrow-bore trombones in *forte*. The forceful attack possible on a trombone with half the cross-sectional area of the modern instrument made a

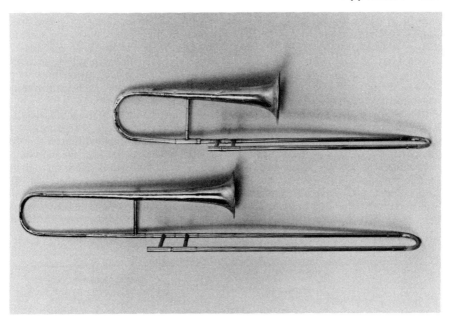

Plate 14 Tenor trombone in C and bass trombone in G (both anonymous, *c*.1845). (*Source: Cyfarthfa Castle Museum and Edinburgh University Collection of Historic Musical Instruments.*)

valued contribution to the sound of a band, particularly in contest playing where percussion was not used.

The most interesting developments in instrument design concerned the euphonium and basses. These developments were the forms of compensation applied to valved instruments by Boosey & Co. and Besson & Co. The need for these arises from the fact that a valve adds a fixed length of tubing to the instrument. Two valves which separately add the correct lengths of tubing will, when operated simultaneously, add a length which falls short of that required to sound in tune. With a large instrument such as an Eb bass, if the first valve allows a Db to be played in tune and the third valve allows a C to be played in tune, the first and third valves together will allow a Bb to be played that is noticeably sharp, and actually needs a further four inches or so of tubing to be added to bring it into tune. On instruments with a fourth valve, the fourth valve will give the Bb in tune, but there are further intonation problems if the fourth valve is used in combination with any of the basic three. The problem is most acute with the euphonium and the basses, since these instruments are frequently used in the lowest parts of their compass which require the valves to be used in combination, and the moving in and out of tuning-slides by the player in the course of performance is not practical.

One solution, offered by Higham and Besson, was to make instruments with five valves, offering the player a choice of fingering for many notes and allowing a reasonably in-tune option for any given note. Although economical, five-valve instruments were not widely used in bands, though a number of professional tubists did use them. The compensating system, however, gives improved intonation without the player having to learn new fingerings. In a three-valve compensating instrument, the tubing brought into play by the third valve is actually led back through the first and second valves; if the first and third valves, say, are operated together, an additional loop of tubing attached to the first valve is brought into play. In the case of the Eb bass, this will give the required four inches. Brass band valved instruments with this system of 'Compensating Pistons' have been made by Boosey & Co. (and, latterly, Boosey & Hawkes) since 1874. Boosey's works manager, David James Blaikley, has been given credit for inventing the system.[37] It was not, however, a new invention, though this was the first commercially successful application. Hawkes & Son and Besson & Co. also made a number of instruments with compensating valves before merging with Boosey & Co. – presumably under licence.

Besson & Co. made numerous brass band instruments with 'Enharmonic Valves', a system which it patented in 1903[38] (see Plate 15) but which, again, was not actually new. It is superior to compensating valves in that the windway is not required to pass through each valve more than once. In a three-valve 'enharmonic' instrument, the mouthpipe leads into the third valve. If the third valve is not operated, the windway leads through the first and second valves, which act in the usual way, back through the third valve to the bell. If the third valve is operated, the windway is led through the first and second valves by a different route including a third valve tuning slide, and in going through different passages

Table 6   Price list for Besson & Co., *c.*1913

	Ordinary	*Enharmonic valves*
Eb Soprano	£4–4–0	
Bb Cornet		
'School' Model	£3–10–0	
'Class A'	£9–9–0	£12–12–0
Echo cornet	£14–14–0	
Flugel Horn 'Class A'	£8–8–0	£11–11–0
Eb Tenor Horn 'Class A'	£9–9–0	£12–12–0
Bb Baritone 'Class A' 3 valves	£11–11–0	£14–14–0
Bb Tenor Trombone 'Class A'	£7–7–0	
G Bass Trombone 'Class A'	£8–8–0	
Bb Euphonion		
3 valves 'Class A'	£12–12–0	£15–15–0
4 valves 'Class A'	£14–14–0	£18–18–0
5 valves 'Class A'	£16–16–0	
Eb Bombardon		
3 valves 'Class A'	£15–15–0	£19–19–0
4 valves 'Class A'	£18–18–0	£24–0–0
Bb Bombardon		
3 valves 'Class A'	£20–0–0	£25–4–0
BBb Bombardon (Monster)		
3 valves 'Class A'	£26–0–0	£31–0–0
Side drum,		
Guards pattern	£3–3–0 to £7–7–0	
Cheese pattern	£2–10–0 to £6–6–0	
Bass drum 32in × 20½in	£7–7–0 to £12–12–0	

Silver-plating extra: cornets £2–2–6, tenor trombones £3–0–0, Monster BBb bombardon £12–10–0 typical.

'Class C' instruments (guaranteed 6 years) priced at half that of 'Class A' (guaranteed 10 years).

Source: author's collection.

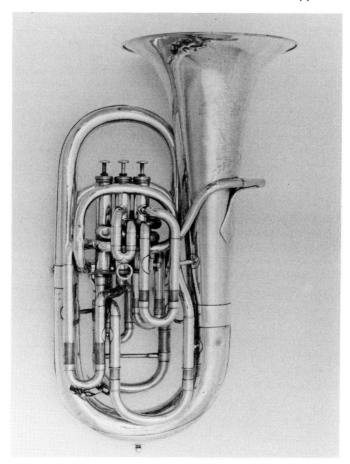

Plate 15 Euphonium with four valves, 'Enharmonic Patent' (Besson & Co.) 1911. (*Source: Edinburgh University Collection of Historic Musical Instruments.*)

in the first and second valves will be directed through separate, longer, loops of tubing if either the first valve or the second valve is operated simultaneously with the third. (This is also the principle of the 'full double' French horn.) The fact that a three-valve instrument with 'enharmonic' valves has two completely different valve loops, each with its own tuning-slide, on the first valve and again on the second, makes for a rather heavy instrument. A four-valve 'enharmonic' instrument is heavier again than a four-valve compensating instrument – this is the only reason that can be put forward to explain why Boosey's compensating valves have continued to be made and Besson's 'enharmonic' valves have not.

Hawkes and Son, their sales of euphoniums probably suffering from the competition, brought out four-valve instruments under the appellation 'The Dictor'. These instruments employ a simplified form of compensation in which the tubing brought into play by the third valves passes through the fourth valve; if the fourth and third valves are operated together, an additional loop of tubing attached to the fourth valve is brought into play.

Boosey's 'Compensating Pistons' and Besson's 'Enharmonic Patent' valves were applied to all the valved instruments except the E♭ soprano cornet. With the cornet and the flugel horn, the extra cost and the added weight led to a limited uptake by bands; with the tenor horn and the baritone, the relative unimportance of the lower tessitura similarly limited adoption. Virtually all the best bands, however, adopted compensating euphoniums and basses. It is probably a tribute to the higher musical standards being attained by British brass bands in the 1870s and later that the subtle refinement in intonation was thought to justify the considerably greater expense of these complicated instruments.

In recent years, cornets and flugels have been equipped with 'triggers' which extend the first and third valve tuning-slides manually. These permit the player to correct the intonation of notes which require the valves to be used in combination without adding significantly to the weight of the instrument.

Mergers

After the First World War, the depression hit the instrument trade, and the smaller makers only survived on repair work. Boosey & Co. and Hawkes & Son merged in 1930 and were joined in 1948 by Besson & Co. and later by Rudall Carte & Co. which, however, had ceased making brass instruments in the 1930s. J Higham was taken over by Messrs Mayers & Harrison in 1930, and ceased manufacturing soon after.

Table 7   Price list for Hawkes & Son, 1927

Cornet in B♭	
'Excelsior' Model	£6–15–0
'Clippertone' Model	£8–12–6
Tenor Saxhorn in E♭	£9–7–6
B♭ Baritone (or Althorn)	
'Excelsior' Sonorous Model	£12–7–6
B♭ Tenor slide trombone	
'Artist's Perfected' Model	£7–17–6
G Bass slide trombone	
'Artist's Perfected' Model	£9–7–6
B♭ Euphonium	
3 valves 'Excelsior' Model	£12–15–0
4 valves 'Excelsior' Model	£15–15–0
4 valves Compensating	£19–13–9
4 valves Dictor Model	£18–15–0
E♭ Bass 'Excelsior' Model	£17–12–6
EE♭ Bass, monster bore	
three valves	£27–0–0
four valves	£32–5–0
BB♭ Bass, monster bore,	
three valves	£33–0–0
Side drum, narrow pattern	£5–5–0 to £8–13–3
Bass drum, 32in diameter	£13–2–6

Silverplating charged extra, ranging from £2–3–2 for a cornet to £13–4–0 for a monster bore BB♭ bass.

Source: author's collection

In the inter-war period, which saw the most important additions to the brass band repertoire, there were no significant developments in instrument design. Mutes, however, were increasingly used. Elgar, in the *Severn Suite*, wrote for muted euphoniums – a request not complied with at the time. Straight or pear-shaped cornet and trombone mutes of fibre or metal were the most commonly used. The modern repertoire requires mutes for all the brass instruments in the band.

More recent changes

The instrumentation of British brass bands has remained remarkably consistent since it crystallized in the late nineteenth century. There was a practice in the 1870s of using up to three flugel horns, so that the second and third cornet parts were doubled by flugels as well as the ripieno (repiano in brass band parlance) cornet part. At the same time there were often four tenor horns.

The Salvation Army bands have never been restricted by contest regulations, though the music published for full band by the Salvation Army (and until very recently not available for use outside the Army) has closely followed the instrumentation of 'outside' bands. Many of the larger Salvation Army bands, however, have been considerably larger than the contesting bands, with much doubling of parts. In these circumstances, the use of more than one flugel horn has been common, and there is often a specially written part for a fourth trombone.[39] The Salvation Army has also regularly published music for a smaller band: the 'Triumph' series is arranged for standard band less repiano and third cornets, flugel and third tenor horn. The 'Unity' series is arranged for first cornet, second cornet (or first horn), second horn (or baritone or trombone) and bass only, with percussion. These arrangements, of course, can also be played by full bands.

There have been frequent suggestions that brass bands should incorporate saxophones, French horns, trumpets, etc. A number of bands (especially in the Salvation Army) in the early years of this century did actually use up to four saxophones.[40] Brass bands, like military bands, have made use of echo cornets, post horns, xylophones, and so on, in a solo capacity.

Low pitch
In the 1960s, brass bands were persuaded to make a change which, in retrospect, could have been made forty years earlier, but even so was accepted reluctantly by many bands. It was announced in April 1964[41] that the instrument makers (that is, Boosey & Hawkes and the Salvation Army) were to cease making high-pitch instruments and that, as a consequence, in time all British brass bands would have to change to low pitch.

As far as we can tell from surviving instruments, the earliest brass bands probably played at a pitch not far from the modern international standard, $A_4 = 440$ Hz. As pitch levels rose in the middle of the nineteenth century, the brass bands apparently kept in line with orchestral and other instrumental practice, which settled at 'Old Philharmonic' pitch, $A_4 = 452.5$ Hz. To reduce strain on operatic and oratorio singers, lower pitch standards were adopted by professional orchestras towards the end of the century, quickly followed by amateur orchestras. British Services military bands changed to low pitch, $A_4 = 439$ Hz, in 1929, leaving British and Commonwealth brass bands as the only sizeable area of musical activity at high pitch. Many bands did not participate in performances alongside orchestras or organs: some which did used alternative tuning slides to bring their instruments down to low pitch. The present standard ($A_4 = 440$ Hz) was agreed internationally in 1939.

By the 1960s, band instrument makers were producing more instruments at international pitch for export than at high pitch for the home market, and put forward reasons of economy to justify their decision to cease making high-pitch instruments. Once it was clear that the change was inevitable, some bands had all their instruments converted by fixed extensions to the tuning slides (damaging both appearance and intonation), some bought new sets of instruments, others used both means in part. One of the first bands to change was York Citadel Salvation Army, which was playing at low pitch by July 1964. The International Staff Band of the Salvation Army was in low pitch by the autumn of the same year. There were complaints from traditionalists that the sound of the brass band would lose brilliance in lowering the pitch. They may have been right – it was the orchestral string players seeking brilliance who had raised the pitch a century previously – but the difference in tone quality due to the change in pitch has been less marked than that due to the adoption of wide bore instruments. By the end of the 1960s, most of the best contesting bands had changed to low pitch, and those bands remaining at high pitch (there are still some) did so out of inertia rather than conviction.

Although the decision of the manufacturers in 1964 to cease production of high-pitch instruments must have resulted in economies in production costs, it made brass bands a marketing target for American and Japanese makers, who were not slow in seizing the opportunity. In November 1964, Barratts of Manchester Ltd ran an advertisement: 'Have you realised that the most exciting advantage of the change to low pitch is that you and your band can now, for the first time, experience the joys of playing a famous Conn instrument?'[42] Before long, medium-wide- and wide-bore American trombones were being used by leading bands. Ever since, cheap instruments have been imported from eastern Europe and China. More recently, Brass Band Instruments Ltd (subsequently Sterling Musical Instruments Ltd) has started making band instruments in England, adding to the keen competition prevailing now, as it was a century ago.

Percussion
Bass drum and side drum have always been used by brass bands on the march, and often cymbals, too. The change from rope-tension bass drums as deep as they were wide to shallow drums with rod tension has been very gradual, starting in the middle of the nineteenth century and only completed in the middle of the twentieth. Bands needed to buy a new bass drum only if the old one was badly damaged, not to help win a contest. Similarly, deep rope-tension 'Guards pattern' side-drums and shallow rod-tension drums were both in use over the same period. For concert work, the band's drummer could until recently make do with little more – but if ambitious he could use a kit including timpani, tambourines, castanets, triangle and more, especially if the band indulged in 'novelty' numbers. There have been no percussion instruments peculiar to brass bands.

For years, composers had written parts for percussion instruments in contest test pieces as well as in 'entertainment' music. *Journey into Freedom* (Eric Ball, 1967) is typical in calling for side drum, bass drum, cymbal, triangle and tambourine with optional timpani: these parts were only played in concert performance, and the music makes sense without them. Similarly, Vaughan Williams included a celeste in *Variations for Brass Band* (1957), knowing that the part would not be heard at all at the National championships for which the work was commissioned. The first major contest to allow percussion was at Belle Vue in 1969. The test piece for this event, Gilbert Vinter's *Spectrum*, is scored for the usual brass instruments plus bongos, claves, wood block, tambourine, triangle, cymbal, side drum and bass drum. Like most subsequent test pieces, it is less than satisfactory if the percussion parts are omitted. The percussion instruments now called for in test pieces for top-section bands include virtually the full complement normally carried by the orchestral percussion section, and occasional imports from dance band drum kits and the Latin American tradition.

Wide-bore instruments
Having followed orchestras down in pitch, bands followed in the adoption of wider-bore instruments in the 1970s. The difference in sound and response to the player is most

striking in the case of the trombone, but noticeable from Eb soprano the BBb bass. During the Second World War, production of instruments ceased as the factories were required for war work. When production of instruments resumed, the export market was given priority, and instruments were only available on the home market from May 1946.[43] From this time, medium-bore trombones were offered (before the war their main use in Britain was in dance bands). The Besson 'Academy' model and the medium-bore Boosey & Hawkes 'Imperial' model were widely adopted by brass bands.

Apart from student models, all the instruments now made for brass bands are wide-bore versions of traditional designs, capable of great power but requiring to be 'well filled' by the players to achieve the richness of sound characteristic of a good brass band.

For a short period in the 1970s, some bands adopted the bass trombone in G with a valve lowering the pitch to D (comparable with the F valve on a Bb trombone) that had been the British orchestral bass trombone of the 1930s and 1940s. By the end of the 1970s, the wide bore Bb and F trombone (sometimes with a second valve giving G, E or D – see Plate 10) had replaced the traditional G bass trombone, which has never evolved into a wide bore version. Medium-wide- and wide-bore Bb + F trombones have also been used for tenor trombone parts in many bands.

It is ironic that brass bands should adopt the instruments originally designed to allow symphony orchestras to fill concert halls seating thousands some fifty to sixty years after the bands could themselves attract audiences of thousands to their concerts.

Acknowledgements

All the photographs in this technical appendix are by Antonia Reeve Photography, Edinburgh.

Notes

1 Jack L. Scott, 'The evolution of the brass band and its repertoire in northern England': PhD thesis, for the University of Sheffield, 1970.
2 Anthony C. Baines, *Bass Instruments*, London, 1976.
3 Trevor Herbert, 'The trombone in Britain before 1800', PhD thesis, Open University, 1984.
4 Reginald Morley-Pegge, *The French Horn* (2nd edn), London, 1971.
5 Philip Bate, *The Trumpet and the Trombone* (2nd edn), London, 1978.
6 Reginald Morley-Pegge and Philip Bate, 'Serpent' in S. Sadie (ed.), *The New Grove Dictionary of Musical Instruments*, London, 1984.
7 Reginald Morley-Pegge and Anthony C. Baines, 'Bass horn' in Sadie, *The New Grove Dictionary of Musical Instruments*.
8 Ralph T. Dudgeon, 'Joseph Haliday, inventor of the keyed bugle', *Journal of the American Musical Instrument Society*, vol. IX (1983), pp. 53–67.
9 French Patent 1849, March 1821, cited in Clifford Bevan, *The Tuba Family*, London, 1978, p. 59.
10 Herbert Heyde, *Das Ventilblasinstrument, seine Entwicklung im deutschsprachigen Raum von den Anfängen bis zur Gegenwart*, Leipzig, 1987.
11 Anthony C. Baines, 'Clavicor' in Sadie, *The New Grove Dictionary of Musical Instruments*.
12 Wessel & Co.'s *Journal for Brass Band* (*c*.1840–5). British Library.
13 Trevor Herbert and Arnold Myers, 'Instruments of the Cyfarthfa Band', *Galpin Society Journal*, vol. XLI (1988), pp. 2–10.
14 John Shaw's first patent for a valve design was no. 5013 of 7 October 1824 for 'Transverse Spring Slides for Trumpets, Trombones, French Horns, Bugles . . .'. His

disk valve patent was no. 7892 of 1 December 1838 for 'Swivel or Pivot Plate' valves.

15 Köhler's 'Patent Lever' instruments are described in *The Crystal Palace and its Contents; an Illustrated Cyclopaedia of the Great Exhibition of 1851*, pp. 285–286.

16 George Robert Samson, 'Improvements in Valves or Cylinders for Wind Instruments', Patent no. 1245 of 29 April 1862.

17 Clifford Bevan, 'Tuba (i)' in Sadie, *The New Grove Dictionary of Musical Instruments*.

18 Wilhelm Wieprecht, 'Die Chromatische Bass-Tuba', Prussian Patent no. 9121 of 12 September 1835. Translated into English in Clifford Bevan, *The Tuba Family*, London, 1978, pp. 201–11.

19 French Patents 15213–15657, 1843, cited in Bevan, *The Tuba Family*.

20 Adam Carse, 'Adolphe Sax and the Distin family', *Music Review*, vol. 6 (1945), pp. 194–201.

21 Enderby Jackson, 'Origin and promotion of brass band contests', *Musical Opinion and Music Trade Review* (1 November 1896), pp. 101–2.

22 Bevan, *The Tuba Family*, pp. 90–100.

23 An example is a german silver cornopean in the Edinburgh University Collection of Historic Musical Instruments, which is inscribed 'Sold by M. Corcoran, Dublin' and also bears the mark of Metzler (London). The design and material of construction, together with the inscriptions of the tuning-slide, shank and crooks (B for Bb, Es for Eb) indicate that the instrument was imported from Germany by Metzler.

24 Lyndesay G. Langwill, *An Index of Musical Wind Instrument Makers* (6th edn), Edinburgh, 1980.

25 Private collection of Raymond Ainscoe, Kirkby Lonsdale, near Lancaster.

26 Arnold Myers, 'A Slide Tuba?', *Galpin Society Journal*, vol. XLII (1989), pp. 127–8.

27 George Metzler and James Waddell, 'Improvements in the Construction and Formation of Valve Musical Instruments' Patent no. 1836 of 12 August 1858.

28 'National Brass Band Championships of Great Britain, Rules' in Allan Littlemore (ed.), *The Rakeway Brass Band Yearbook 1987*, Hollington, 1987, pp. 419–22.

29 Some early recordings of brass bands are preserved in the EMI Music Archives, such as Black Dike Mills Band, *Gems from Sullivan's Operas No 3* of July 1903 (018 238c) and Besses o' th' Barn Band, *Henry VIII Morris Dance (Edward German)* of May 1904 (GC-2-28). The recording methods, however, do not allow a fair assessment of the sound quality of these bands. Clearer impressions of the sound of the brass band playing at high pitch on narrow-bore instruments is given by recordings of the 1930s such as Regal Zonophone MR 2244, Foden's Motor Works Band: *Kenilworth Suite (Arthur Bliss)* of December 1936.

30 Gisborne & Co. Ltd, advertisment, *British Bandsman* 22 July 1905, pp. 338–9.

31 *Besson's Brass Band Budget*, 1907, p. 8.

32 Algernon Rose, *Talks with Bandsmen, a Popular Handbook for Brass Instrumentalists*, London [1895] gives fascinating, if somewhat anecdotal, accounts of the leading makers of brass band instruments and their specialities: Gautrot (p. 82); Silvani & Smith (p. 84); George Potter & Co. (p. 100); Rudall Carte & Co. (p. 102); George Butler (p. 120); Besson & Co. (p. 124); Courtois & Mille (p. 172); Brown of Kennington (p. 188); J. Higham (p. 202); W. D. Cubitt (p. 203); Boosey & Co. (p. 209); William Hillyard (p. 230); Charles Mahillon & Co. (p. 242); and Hawkes & Son (p. 268).

33 The archives of Messrs Boosey & Hawkes, Regent Street, London contain records of instruments made by Distin & Co. and Boosey & Co. at the end of the nineteenth century, giving workmen's names and the hours spent on each instrument (per Lloyd P. Farrar).

34 Brindley Boon, *Play the Music, Play! The Story of Salvation Army Bands* (2nd edn), London, 1978, pp. 172–5.

35 John Webb, 'Designs for brass in the Public Record Office', *Galpin Society Journal*, vol. XXXVIII (1985), pp. 48–54.

36 H. Klussman and others, trading as Rudall Carte & Co., Patent no. 21,295 of 3 October 1903.
37 D. J. Blaikley, Patent no. 4618 of 14 November 1878.
38 Besson & Co., Patent no. 12,849 of 12 May 1904.
39 Many passages in brass band compositions published by the Salvation Army in their 'Festival', 'Triumph' and General series are scored for a quartet of trombones. There is no separate printed part for fourth trombone – the first part is divided and requires two players.
40 Alf Hailstone, *The* British Bandsman *Centenary Book: A Social History of Brass Bands*, Baldock, 1987, cites contemporary reports of short-lived attempts to introduce saxophones into brass bands.
41 Eric Ball, '"Low" Pitch for Brass Bands: definite plans at last', *British Bandsman*, 4 April 1964, p. 1; Dean Goffin, 'Advantages are incalculable', *British Bandsman*, 4 April 1964, p. 2.
42 Barratts of Manchester Ltd, 'Low-down on Low Pitch' (advertisement) *British Bandsman*, 14 November 1964, p. 5.
43 Boosey & Hawkes Ltd advertisment, *British Bandsman*, 4 May 1946, p. 3; Besson advertisement, *British Bandsman*, 25 May 1946, p. 5.

Appendix 2: Calendar of Major Developments of the Brass Band Contest

PREPARED BY CLIFFORD BEVAN

1845	Burton Constable	Band screened from judge
		Draw for position of play
		Drums not allowed
		Maximum of 12 players
		Own choice of piece
1855	British Open	Test piece plus own choice
1856	Hull	Test piece only
1868	British Open	Names of bandsmen submitted one month before contest
1886	British Open	July Contest: a 'grading' system
1889	British Open	No pre-performance of test piece
		Conductors not allowed to play
1893	British Amateur Band Association	Maximum of 24 players
		Approved adjudicators only
		Players registered with only one band
1895	Scottish Amateur Brass Band Championship	Two sections
1900	National Brass Band Championship	Three sections
1902	National Brass Band Championship	Five sections
		Championship section bands in uniform
		Players members of band for three months minimum
1923	National Brass Band Championship	Championship bands play seated
1924	National Brass Band Championship	All bands play seated
1946	National Brass Band Championship	Regional qualifying contests
		National Register of Brass Bandsmen
1973	National Brass Band Championship	Percussion in championship section
1976	National Brass Band Championship	Percussion in all sections

Appendix 3: Winners of the British Open and National Contests, 1853–1989

PREPARED BY CLIFFORD BEVAN

1853   Open. Two own choice selections
1 Mossley Temperance Saxhorn   *William Taylor**
2 Dewsbury Old   *S. Greenwood*
3 Bramley Temperance   *M. Whitley*

1854   Open. Two own choice selections
1 Leeds Railway Foundry   *Richard Smith*
2 Dewsbury Old   *John Peel*
3 Accrington   *T. Bradley*

1855   Open. Own choice and Melling, *Orynthia*
1 Accrington   *Radcliffe Barnes*
2 Leeds Railway Foundry   *Richard Smith*
3 Mossley Temperance Saxhorn   *William Taylor*

1856   Open. Own choice and Flotow, *Stradella*
1 Leeds Railway Foundry   *Richard Smith*
2 Leeds (Smith's)   *Richard Smith*
3 Accrington   *Radcliffe Barnes*

1857   Open. Own choice and Verdi, *Il Trovatore*
1 Leeds (Smith's)   *Richard Smith*
2 Dewsbury Old   *John Peel*
3 Todmorden   *W. Brook*

1858   Open. Haydn, 'On Thee Each Living Soul Awaits' and 'Achieved is the Glorious Work' (*The Creation*)
1 Accrington   *Radcliffe Barnes*
2 Dewsbury Old   *S. Greenwood*
3 Mossley Temperance Saxhorn   *William Taylor*

*Conductor's name given in italics

1859   Open. No contest as only three bands entered

1860   Open. Own choice and Hérold, *Zampa*
1 4th West Yorks Rifle Volunteers (Halifax)   *Isaac Dewhurst*
2 Dewsbury Old   *John Peel*
3 Sherwood Rangers (Newark)   *W. Lilley*

1861   Open. Own choice and Balfe, *Satanella*
1 4th West Yorks Rifle Volunteers (Halifax)   *Isaac Dewhurst*
2 Dewsbury Rifle Corps[1]   *John Peel*
3 Chesterfield   *J. Tallis Trimnell*

1862   Open. Own choice and Auber, 'Muette de Portici' (*Masaniello*)
1 Black Dyke Mills[2]   *Samuel Longbottom*[3]
2 Dewsbury Rifle Corps   *John Peel*
3 Chesterfield   *J. Tallis Trimnell*

1863   Open. Own choice and Gounod, *Faust*
1 Black Dyke Mills   *Samuel Longbottom*
2 4th Lancs Rifle Volunteers (Bacup)   *John Lord*
3 Craven Amateur (Silsden)   *G. O'Brien*

1864   Open. Own choice and *Reminiscences of Auber*
1 4th Lancs Rifle Volunteers (Bacup)   *John Lord*
2 Stalybridge Old   –[4]
3 Leeds Model   *Richard Smith*

1865   Open. Own choice and Verdi, *Un Ballo in Maschera*
1 4th Lancs Rifle Volunteers (Bacup)   *John Lord*
2 Dewsbury Rifle Corps   *John Peel*
3 Matlock Bath   *John Naylor*

1866   Open. Own choice and Meyerbeer (arr. Grosse), *L'Africaine*
1 Dewsbury Old   *John Peel*
2 Matlock Bath   *John Naylor*
3 Healey Hall   *J. Law*

1867   Open. Weber (arr. Winterbottom), *Der Freischütz*
1 3rd Derbyshire Rifle Volunteers (Clay Cross)   *John Naylor*
2 4th Lancs Rifle Volunteers (Bacup)   *John Lord*
3 Compstall Bridge   *Henry Tym[m]*

1868   Open. Meyerbeer, *Robert le Diable*
1 17th Lancashire Rifle Volunteers (Burnley)   *J. Ford*
2 Heckmondwike Albion   *J. Brooke*
3 Black Dyke Mills   *Samuel Longbottom*

1869   Open. Meyerbeer (arr. Winterbottom), *Le Prophète*
1 4th Lancs Rifle Volunteers (Bacup)   *John Lord*
2 Matlock Volunteers[5]   *John Naylor*
3 17th Lancs Rifle Volunteers (Burnley)   *W. Harrison*

1870 Open. Verdi (arr. Winterbottom), *Ernani*
1 Bacup Old[6] *John Lord*
2 Matlock Volunteers *John Naylor*
3 Dewsbury Old *John Lord*

1871 Open. Rossini (arr. Winterbottom), *Il Barbiere*
1 Black Dyke Mills *Samuel Longbottom*
2 Bury Borough *J. Briggs*
3 Bacup Old *John Lord*

1872 Open. (arr. C. Godfrey), *Souvenir de Mozart*
1 Robin Hood Rifles *H. Leverton*
2 Saltaire *John Gladney*
3 Meltham Mills *John Gladney*

1873 Open. Meyerbeer (arr. C. Godfrey), *Dinorah*
1 Meltham Mills *John Gladney*
2 Robin Hood Rifles *H. Leverton*
3 Black Dyke Mills *Samuel Longbottom*

1874 Open. Spohr (arr. C. Godfrey), *Faust*
1 Linthwaite *Edwin Swift*
2 Meltham Mills *John Gladney*
3 Besses o' th' Barn *Tom German*

1875 Open. Balfe (arr. C. Godfrey), *Il Talismano*
1 Kingston Mills *John Gladney*
2 Meltham Mills *John Gladney*
3 Linthwaite *Edwin Swift*

1876 Open. Verdi (arr. C. Godfrey), *Aïda*
1 Meltham Mills *John Gladney*
2 Kingston Mills *John Gladney*
3 Holm Mills *Edwin Swift*

1877 Open. Spohr (arr. C. Godfrey), *Jessonda*
1 Meltham Mills *John Gladney*
2 Black Dyke Mills *Edwin Swift*
3 Holm Mills *Edwin Swift*

1878 Open. Gounod (arr. C. Godfrey), *Romeo e Giulietta*
1 Meltham Mills *John Gladney*
2 Kidsgrove *T. Charlesworth*
3 Denton Original –[7]

1879 Open. Spohr (arr. C. Godfrey), *The Last Judgement*
1 Black Dyke Mills *J. Fawcett*
2 3rd Lancashire RifleVolunteers (Accrington) *John Gladney*
3 37th West Yorkshire Rifle Volunteers (Barnsley) *John Gladney*

1880 Open. Verdi (arr. C. Godfrey), *I Vespri Siciliani*
1 Black Dyke Mills *Alexander Owen*
2 Stalybridge Old *John Gladney*
3 Nelson Old *John Gladney*

1881   Open. Gounod (arr. C. Godfrey), *Cinq Mars*
1 Black Dyke Mills   *Alexander Owen*
2 Meltham Mills   *John Gladney*
3 Stalybridge Old   *John Gladney*

1882   Open. Mozart (arr. C. Godfrey), *Il Seraglio*
1 Clayton-le-Moors   *Alexander Owen*
2 Linthwaite   *Edwin Swift*
3 37th West Yorks Rifle Volunteers (Barnsley)   *John Gladney*

1883   Open. Mercadante (arr. C. Godfrey), *Il Giuramento*
1 Littleborough Public   *Edwin Swift*
2 Burslem   *R. Sowerbutts*
3 Honley   *John Gladney*

1884   Open. Rossini (arr. C. Godfrey), *La Gazza Ladra*
1 Honley   *John Gladney*
2 Oldham Rifles   *Alexander Owen*
3 Black Dyke Mills   *Alexander Owen*

1885   Open. Verdi (arr. C. Godfrey), *Nebucodonesor*
1 Kingston Mills   *John Gladney*
2 Littleborough Public   *Edwin Swift*
3 Besses o' th' Barn   *Alexander Owen*

1886   Open. Donizetti (arr. C. Godfrey), *La Favorita*
1 Kingston Mills   *John Gladney*
2 Heywood Rifles   *John Gladney*
3 Todmorden Old   *Edwin Swift*

1887   Open. Meyerbeer (arr. C. Godfrey), *L'Étoile du Nord*
1 Kingston Mills   *John Gladney*
2 Black Dyke Mills   *Alexander Owen*
3 Besses o' th' Barn   *Alexander Owen*

1888   Open. Wagner (arr. C. Godfrey), *Der Fliegende Holländer*
1 Wyke Temperance   *Edwin Swift*
2 Black Dyke Mills   *John Gladney*
3 Todmorden Old   *Edwin Swift*

1889   Open. Gounod (arr. C. Godfrey), *La Reine de Saba*
1 Wyke Temperance   *Edwin Swift*
2 Kingston Mills   *John Gladney*
3 Leeds Forge   *Edwin Swift*

1890   Open. Weber (arr. C. Godfrey), *Euryanthe*
1 Batley Old   *John Gladney*
2 Leeds Forge   *Alexander Owen*
3 Wyke Temperance   *Edwin Swift*

1891   Open. Kreutzer (arr. C. Godfrey), *Das Nachtlager in Granada*
1 Black Dyke Mills   *John Gladney*
2 Wyke Temperance   *Edwin Swift*
3 Dewsbury Old   *J. Sidney Jones*

1892 Open. Lortzing (arr. C. Godfrey), *Zaar und Zimmerman*
1 Besses o' th' Barn *Alexander Owen*
2 Kingston Mills *John Gladney*
3 Lindley *Edwin Swift*

1893 Open. Bemberg (arr. C. Godfrey), *Elaine*
1 Kingston Mills *John Gladney*
2 Cornholme *Edwin Swift*
3 Rochdale Old *Albert Whipp*

1894 Open. Goring Thomas (arr. C. Godfrey), *The Golden Web*
1 Besses o' th' Barn *Alexander Owen*
2 Kingston Mills *John Gladney*
3 Black Dyke Mills *John Gladney*

1895 Open. Humperdinck (arr. C. Godfrey), *Hänsel und Gretel*
1 Black Dyke Mills *John Gladney*
2 Wyke Temperance *Edwin Swift*
3 Besses o' th' Barn *Alexander Owen*

1896 Open. Pizzi (arr. C. Godfrey), *Gabriella*
1 Black Dyke Mills *John Gladney*
2 Kingston Mills *William Rimmer*
3 Batley Old *J. Wilkinson*

1897 Open. Rossini (arr. C. Godfrey), *Moses in Egypt*
1 Mossley *Alexander Owen*
2 Kingston Mills *William Rimmer*
3 Batley Old *J. Wilkinson*

1898 Open. (arr. C. Godfrey), *Grand Fantasia from the Works of Mendelssohn*
1 Wyke Temperance *Edwin Swift*
2 Hucknall Temperance *John Gladney*
3 Lea Mills *Alexander Owen*

1899 Open. Verdi (arr. C. Godfrey), *Aroldo*
1 Black Dyke Mills *John Gladney*
2 Hucknall Temperance *John Gladney*
3 Lee Mount *William Swingler*

1900 Open. Ponchielli (arr. C. Godfrey), *La Gioconda*
1 Lindley *John Gladney*
2 Black Dyke Mills *John Gladney*
3 Pemberton Old *William Rimmer*
1900 National. J. Ord Hume (arr.), *Gems from Sullivan's Operas No 1*
1 Denton Original *Alexander Owen*
2 Black Dyke Mills *John Gladney*
3 Wingates Temperance *William Rimmer*

1901 Open. Gounod (arr. C. Godfrey), *Mirella*
1 Kingston Mills *Alexander Owen*
2 Lindley *John Gladney*
3 Crooke *P. Fairhurst*

1901   National. J. Ord Hume (arr.), *Gems from Sullivan's Operas No 3*
1 Lee Mount   *William Swingler*
2 Irwell Springs   *William Rimmer*
3 Denton Original   *Alexander Owen*

1902   Open. Appoloni (arr. C. Godfrey), *L'Ebreo*
1 Black Dyke Mills   *John Gladney*
2 Pemberton Old   *John Gladney*
3 Besses o' th' Barn   *Alexander Owen*
1902   National. Coleridge-Taylor (arr. C. Godfrey), *Hiawatha*
1 Black Dyke Mills   *John Gladney*
2 Wyke Temperance   *Edwin Swift*
3 Luton Red Cross Silver   *Angus Holden*

1903   Open. Elgar (arr. C. Godfrey), *Caractacus*
1 Pemberton Old   *John Gladney*
2 Black Dyke Mills   *John Gladney*
3 Irwell Springs   *William Rimmer*
1903   National. Wagner (arr. F. C. Shipley-Douglas), *Die Meistersinger*
1 Besses o' th' Barn   *Alexander Owen*
2 Rushden Temperance   *Alexander Owen*
3 Black Dyke Mills   *John Gladney*

1904   Open. Rossini (arr. C. Godfrey), *Semiramide*
1 Black Dyke Mills   *John Gladney*
2 Pemberton Old   *John Gladney*
3 Lindley   *B. Lodge*
1904   National. C. Godfrey (arr.), *Gems of Mendelssohn*
1 Hebburn Colliery   *A. Holden*
2 Wingates Temperance   *William Rimmer*
3 Irwell Springs   *William Rimmer*

1905   Open. Mozart (arr. C. Godfrey), *Così fan tutte*
1 Irwell Springs   *William Rimmer*
2 Black Dyke Mills   *John Gladney*
3 Lindley   *B. Lodge*
1905   National. Mermet,[8] *Roland à Ronceveaux*
1 Irwell Springs   *William Rimmer*
2 Wingates Temperance   *William Rimmer*
3 Lee Mount   *Alexander Owen*

1906   Open. Meyerbeer (arr. C. Godfrey), *Les Huguenots*
1 Wingates Temperance   *William Rimmer*
2 Goodshaw   *William Halliwell*
3 Rochdale Public   *William Rimmer*
1906   National. W. Short (arr.), *Gems of Chopin*
1 Wingates Temperance   *William Rimmer*
2 Shaw   *William Rimmer*
3 Wyke Temperance   *William Rimmer*

1907   Open. MacFarren (arr. C. Godfrey), *Robin Hood*
1 Wingates Temperance   *William Rimmer*
2 Black Dyke Mills   *John Gladney*
3 Goodshaw   *William Halliwell*

1907   National. W. Short (arr.), *Gems of Schumann*
1 Wingates Temperance   *William Rimmer*
2 Goodshaw   *William Halliwell*
3 King Cross Subscription   *Walter Halstead*

1908   Open. C. Godfrey (arr.), *A Souvenir of Grieg*
1 Black Dyke Mills   *William Rimmer*
2 Rushden Temperance   *John Gladney*
3 Perfection Soap Works   *William Halliwell*
1908   National. Wagner (arr. Cope), *Rienzi*
1 Irwell Springs   *William Rimmer*
2 Perfection Soap Works   *William Halliwell*
3 Wingates Temperance   *William Rimmer*

1909   Open. Marliani (arr. C. Godfrey), *Il Bravo*
1 Fodens Motor Works   *William Rimmer*
2 Black Dyke Mills   *William Rimmer*
3 Perfection Soap Works   *William Halliwell*
1909   National. Wagner (arr. C. Godfrey), *Der Fliegende Holländer*
1 Shaw   *William Rimmer*
2 Fodens Motor Works   *William Rimmer*
3 Perfection Soap Works   *William Halliwell*

1910   Open. Handel (arr. C. Godfrey), *Acis and Galatea*
1 Fodens Motor Works   *William Halliwell*
2 Shaw   *William Halliwell*
3 Perfection Soap Works   *William Halliwell*
1910   National. W. Rimmer (arr.), *Gems of Schubert*
1 Fodens Motor Works   *William Halliwell*
2 Irwell Springs   *Alexander Owen*
3 Spencer's Steel Works   *William Halliwell*

1911   Open. Tchaikovsky (arr. C. Godfrey), *Eugene Onegin*
1 Hebden Bridge   *William Halliwell*
2 Fodens Motor Works   *William Halliwell*
3 Perfection Soap Works   *William Halliwell*
1911   National. Meyerbeer (arr. Rimmer), *Les Huguenots*
1 Perfection Soap Works   *William Halliwell*
2 Fodens Motor Works   *William Halliwell*
3 Wingates Temperance   *Alexander Owen*

1912   Open. Auber (arr. C. Godfrey), *Les Diamants de la Couronne*
1 Fodens Motor Work   *William Halliwell*
2 St Hilda Colliery   *William Halliwell*
3 Shaw   *William Halliwell*
1912   National. Rossini (arr. Rimmer), *William Tell*
1 St Hilda Colliery   *William Halliwell*
2 Irwell Springs   *William Halliwell*
3 Fodens Motor Works   *William Halliwell*

1913   Open. C. Godfrey (arr.), *A Souvenir of Gounod*
1 Fodens Motor Works   *William Halliwell*
2 Shaw   *William Halliwell*
3 Irwell Springs   *William Halliwell*

1913   National. Percy Fletcher, *Labour and Love*
1 Irwell Springs   *William Halliwell*
2 St Hilda Colliery   *William Halliwell*
3 Black Dyke Mills   *John A. Greenwood*

1914   Open. Méhul (arr. C. Godfrey), *Joseph und seine Brüder*
1 Black Dyke Mills   *John A. Greenwood*
2 Wingates Temperance   *John A. Greenwood*
3 Fodens Motor Works   *William Halliwell*
National. No contest

1915   Open. Donizetti (arr. C. Godfrey), *Il Furioso*
1 Fodens Motor Works   *William Halliwell*
2 Horwich Railway Mechanics Institute   *John A. Greenwood*
3 King Cross   *John A. Greenwood*
National. No contest

1916   Open. Verdi (arr. C. Godfrey Jr), *La Traviata*
1 Horwich Railway Mechanics' Institute   *John A. Greenwood*
2 Fodens Motor Works   *William Halliwell*
3 Black Dyke Mills   *John A. Greenwood*
National. No contest

1917   Open. Hérold (arr. C. Godfrey), *Le Pré aux Clercs*
1 Horwich Railway Mechanics' Institute   *John A. Greenwood*
2 Black Dyke Mills   *John A. Greenwood*
3 Woodlands Village   *Alexander Owen*
National. No contest

1918   Open. Marliani (arr. C. Godfrey), *Il Bravo*
1 Wingates Temperance   *William Halliwell*
2 Irwell Springs   *Walter Nuttall*
3 Besses o' th' Barn   *Alexander Owen*
National. No contest

1919   Open. Benedict (arr. C. Godfrey), *The Lily of Killarney*
1 Harton Colliery   *George Hawkins*
2 Wingates Temperance   *William Halliwell*
3 St Hilda Colliery   *William Halliwell*
National. No contest

1920   Open. Verdi (arr. C. Godfrey), *I Lombardi*
1 Besses o' th' Barn   *William Wood*
2 Wingates Temperance   *William Halliwell*
3 Yorkshire Main Colliery   *John A. Greenwood*
1920   National. Cyril Jenkins, *Coriolanus*
1 St Hilda Colliery   *William Halliwell*
2 Lincoln Malleable Iron Works   *William Halliwell*
3 Irwell Springs   *John A. Greenwood*

1921   Open. Wallace (arr. C. Godfrey), *Maritana*
1 Wingates Temperance   *William Halliwell*
2 Barrow Shipyard   *John A. Greenwood*
3 Black Dyke Mills   *John A. Greenwood*

1921   National. Cyril Jenkins, *Life Divine*
1 St Hilda Colliery   *William Halliwell*
2 Foden's Motor Works   *William Halliwell*
3 Wingates Temperance   *William Halliwell*

1922   Open. Wagner (arr. M. Johnstone), *Lohengrin*
1 South Elmshall & Frickley Colliery   *Noel Thorpe*
2 Black Dyke Mills   *William Halliwell*
3 Besses o' th' Barn   *William Wood*
1922   National. Hubert Bath, *Freedom*
1 Horwich Railway Mechanics' Institute   *John A. Greenwood*
2 Luton Red Cross Silver   *William Halliwell*
3 Hebden Bridge   *William Halliwell*

1923   Open. Meyerbeer (arr. C. Godfrey), *Dinorah*
1 Wingates Temperance   *William Halliwell*
2 Creswell Colliery[9]   *John A. Greenwood*
3 Besses o' th' Barn   *Harry Barlow*
1923   National. Henry Geehl, *Oliver Cromwell*
1 Luton Red Cross Silver   *William Halliwell*
2 Black Dyke Mills   *William Halliwell*
3 Fodens Motor Works   *William Halliwell*

1924   Open. T. Keighley (arr.), *Selection from the Works of Liszt*
1 Newcastle Steel Works   *A. H. Baile*
2 Creswell Colliery   *John A. Greenwood*
3 Harton Colliery   *George Hawkins*
1924   National. Henry Geehl, *On the Cornish Coast*
1 St Hilda Colliery   *William Halliwell*
2 Black Dyke Mills   *William Halliwell*
3 Newcastle Steel Works   *A. H. Baile*

1925   Open. Thomas Keighley, *Macbeth*
1 Creswell Colliery   *John A. Greenwood*
2 Nutgrove   *John A. Greenwood*
3 Fodens Motor Works   *William Halliwell*
1925   National. Denis Wright, *Joan of Arc*
1 Marsden Colliery   *John A. Greenwood*
2 Irwell Springs   *William Halliwell*
3 South Moor Colliery   *J. C. Dyson*

1926   Open. Thomas Keighley, *A Midsummer Night's Dream*
1 Fodens Motor Works   *William Halliwell*
2 Wingates Temperance   *William Halliwell*
3 St Hilda Colliery   *William Halliwell*
1926   National. Percy Fletcher, *An Epic Symphony*
1 St Hilda Colliery   *J. Oliver*
2 Carlisle St Stephen's   *William Lowes*
3 Wingates Temperance   *William Halliwell*

1927   Open. Thomas Keighley, *Merry Wives of Windsor*
1 Fodens Motor Works   *William Halliwell*
2 Callender's Cable Works   *Tom Morgan*
3 Milnrow Public   *John A. Greenwood*

1927   National. Denis Wright, *The White Rider*
1 Carlisle St Stephen's   *William Lowes*
2 Callender's Cable Works   *Tom Morgan*
3 Carlton Main Colliery   *Noel Thorpe*

1928   Open. Thomas Keighley, *Lorenzo*
1 Fodens Motor Works   *William Halliwell*
2 Callender's Cable Works   *Tom Morgan*
3 Nutgrove   *William Wood*
1928   National. Gustav Holst, *A Moorside Suite*
1 Black Dyke Mills   *William Halliwell*
2 Harton Colliery   *William Halliwell*
3 Carlisle St Stephens   *William Lowes*

1929   Open. Beethoven (arr. ?), *Pathetic*
1 Brighouse & Rastrick   *Fred Berry*
2 Wingates Temperance   *Harold Moss*
3 Carlisle St Stephens   *William Lowes*
1929   National. Cyril Jenkins, *Victory*
1 Carlisle St Stephens   *William Lowes*
2 Scottish CWS   *John A. Greenwood*
3 Luton Red Cross Silver   *E. S. Carter*

1930   Open. Granville Bantock, *Oriental Rhapsody*
1 Eccles Borough   *J. Dow*
2 Milnrow Public   *John A. Greenwood*
3 Wingates Temperance   *Harold Moss*
1930   National. Edward Elgar, *Severn Suite*
1 Fodens Motor Works   *Fred Mortimer*
2 Black Dyke Mills   *William Halliwell*
3 Irwell Springs   *William Halliwell*

1931   Open. Haydn Morris, *Springtime*
1 Besses o' th' Barn   *William Halliwell*
2 Glazebury   *John A. Greenwood*
3 Milnrow Public   *John A. Greenwood*
1931   National. Hubert Bath, *Honour and Glory*
1 Wingates Temperance   *Harold Moss*
2 Horden Colliery   *J. Foster*
3 Rothwell Temperance   *N. Sidebottom*

1932   Open. Thomas Keighley, *The Crusaders*
1 Brighouse & Rastrick   *William Halliwell*
2 Nelson Old   *William Halliwell*
3 Metropolitan Works   *Harry Heyes*
1932   National. John Ireland, *A Downland Suite*
1 Fodens Motor Works   *Fred Mortimer*
2 Black Dyke Mills   *William Halliwell*
3 Wingates Temperance   *Harold Moss*

1933   Open. Denis Wright, *Princess Nada*
1 Brighouse & Rastrick   *William Halliwell*
2 Baxendale's Works   *John A. Greenwood*
3 Amington   *John A. Greenwood*

1933 National. Granville Bantock, *Prometheus Unbound*
1 Fodens Motor Works *Fred Mortimer*
2 Scottish CWS *George Hawkins*
3 Creswell Colliery *John A. Greenwood*

1934 Open. Herber Howells, *Pageantry*
1 Brighouse & Rastrick *William Halliwell*
2 Black Dyke Mills *William Halliwell*
3 Wingates Temperance *Harold Moss*
1934 National. John Ireland, *A Comedy Overture*
1 Fodens Motor Works *Fred Mortimer*
2 Scottish CWS *George Hawkins*
3 Harton Colliery *William Lowes*

1935 Open. Thomas Keighley, *A Northern Rhapsody*
1 Black Dyke Mills *William Halliwell*
2 Wingates Temperance *Harold Moss*
3 Abram Colliery *William Haydock*
1935 National. Kenneth Wright, *Pride of Race*
1 Munn & Felton's Works *William Halliwell*
2 Creswell Colliery *Joe Farrington*
3 Black Dyke Mills *William Halliwell*

1936 Open. Henry Geehl, *Robin Hood*
1 Brighouse & Rastrick *William Halliwell*
2 Abram Colliery *John A. Greenwood*
3 Luton Red Cross Silver *Harry Mortimer*
1936 National. Arthur Bliss, *Kenilworth*
1 Fodens Motor Works *Fred Mortimer*
2 Black Dyke Mills *William Halliwell*
3 Friary Brewery *John A. Greenwood*

1937 Open. Brahms (arr. D. Wright), *Academic Festival Overture*
1 Besses o' th' Barn *William Wood*
2 Slaithwaite *Noel Thorpe*
3 Black Dyke Mills *William Halliwell*
1937 National. Herbert Howells, *Pageantry*
1 Fodens Motor Works *Fred Mortimer*
2 Munn & Felton's Works *William Halliwell*
3 Black Dyke Mills *William Halliwell*

1938 Open. Maldwyn Price, *Owain Glyndwr*
1 Slaithwate *Noel Thorpe*
2 Black Dyke Mills *William Halliwell*
3 Luton Red Cross Silver *Fred Mortimer*
1938 National. Percy Fletcher, *An Epic Symphony*
1 Fodens Motor Works *Fred Mortimer*
2 Bickershaw Colliery *William Haydock*
3 Black Dyke Mills *William Halliwell*

1939 Open. John Ireland, *A Downland Suite*
1 Wingates Temperance *William Wood*
2 Nelson Old *C. Smith*
3 Brighouse & Rastrick *Noel Thorpe*
National. No contest

1940 Open. Joseph Holbrooke, *Clive of India*
1 Bickershaw Colliery *William Haydock*
2 Creswell Colliery *Harold Moss*
3 Brighouse & Rastrick *Fred Berry*
National. No contest

1941 Open. Brahms (arr. D. Wright), *Academic Festival Overture*; or Geehl, *Robin Hood*; or Keighley, *The Crusaders*
1 Fairey Aviation Works *Harry Mortimer*
2 Carlton Main Frickley Colliery *Albert Badrick*
3 City of Coventry *Harry Heyes*
National. No contest

1942 Open. Keighley, *Lorenzo*; or Howells, *Pageantry*
1 Fairey Aviation Works *Harry Mortimer*
2 Bickershaw Colliery *William Haydock*
3 City of Coventry *Harry Heyes*
National. No contest

1943 Open. Beethoven (arr. D. Wright), *Themes from Symphony No 5*
1 Bickershaw Colliery *William Haydock*
2 Fairey Aviation Works *Harry Mortimer*
3 Creswell Colliery *Harold Moss*
National. No contest

1944 Open. Maurice Johnston, *The Tempest*
1 Fairey Aviation Works *Harry Mortimer*
2 Creswell Colliery *Harold Moss*
3 Bickershaw Colliery *William Haydock*
National. No contest

1945 Open. Kenneth Wright, *Pride of Race*
1 Fairey Aviation Works *Harry Mortimer*
2 Grimethorpe Colliery Institute *George Thompsons*
3 Bickershaw Colliery *Harry Mortimer*
1945 National. Denis Wright, *Overture for an Epic Occasion*
1 Fairey Aviation Works *Harry Mortimer*
2 Horden Colliery *William Lowes*
3 Parc & Dare Workmen's[10] *Haydn Bebb*

1946 Open. Eric Ball, *Salute to Freedom*
1 Bickershaw Colliery *Harry Mortimer*
2 Fairey Aviation Works *Harry Mortimer*
3 Munn & Felton's (Footwear)[11] *Stanley Boddington*
1946 National. Henry Geehl, *Oliver Cromwell*
1 Brighouse & Rastrick *Eric Ball*
2 Fairey Aviation Works *Harry Mortimer*
3 Munn & Felton's (Footwear) *Stanley Boddington*

1947 Open. Maldwyn Price, *Henry V*
1 Fairey Aviation Works *Harry Mortimer*
2 Wingates Temperance *Jack Eckersley*
3 Creswell Colliery *Harold Moss*

1947 National. Hubert Bath, *Freedom*
1 Black Dyke Mills   *Harry Mortimer*
2 Fairey Aviation Works   *Harry Mortimer*
3 Foden's Motor Works   *Fred Mortimer*

1948 Open. Denis Wright, *Music for Brass*
1 CWS (Manchester)   *Eric Ball*
2 Fairey Aviation Works   *Harry Mortimer*
3 Carlton Main Frickley Colliery   *Eric Ball*
1948 National. Henry Geehl, *On the Cornish Coast*
1 Black Dyke Mills   *Harry Mortimer*
2 Cory Workmen's Silver   *Walter Hargreaves*
3 Brighouse & Rastrick   *Eric Ball*

1949 Open. Dean Goffin, *Rhapsody in Brass*
1 Fairey Aviation Works   *Harry Mortimer*
2 Ransome & Marles Works   *Eric Ball*
3 Munn & Felton's (Footwear)   *Stanley Boddington*
1949 National. John Ireland, *A Comedy Overture*
1 Black Dyke Mills   *Harry Mortimer*
2 Fodens Motor Works   *Harry Mortimer*
3 Munn & Felton's (Footwear)   *Stanley Boddington*

1950 Open. Eric Ball, *Resurgam*
1 Fairey Aviation Works   *Harry Mortimer*
2 Cory Workmen's Silver   *Walter Hargreaves*
3 Carlton Main Frickley Colliery   *George Hespe*
1950 National. Herbert Howells, *Pageantry*
1 Fodens Motor Works   *Harry Mortimer*
2 Hanwell Silver   *George Thompson*
3 CWS (Manchester)   *Eric Ball*

1951 Open. Eric Ball, *The Conquerors*
1 Ransome & Marles Works   *Eric Ball*
2 Prescot Cable Works   *J. Capper*
3 CWS (Manchester)   *Eric Ball*
1951 National. Percy Fletcher, *An Epic Symphony*
1 Black Dyke Mills   *Alex Mortimer*
2 Fodens Motor Works   *Harry Mortimer*
3 Brighouse & Rastrick   *Eric Ball*

1952 Open. Henry Geehl, *Scena Sinfonica*
1 CWS (Manchester)   *Eric Ball*
2 Fodens Motor Works   *Harry Mortimer*
3 Munn & Felton's (Footwear)   *Stanley Boddington*
1952 National. Granville Bantock (arr. F. Wright), *The Frogs (of Aristophanes)*
1 Fairey Aviation Works   *Harry Mortimer*
2 Fodens Motor Works   *Harry Mortimer*
3 Black Dyke Mills   *Alex Mortimer*

1953 Open. George Hespe, *The Three Musketeers*
1 National Band of New Zealand   *K. K. L. Smith*
2 Fairey Aviation Works   *Harry Mortimer*
3 Black Dyke Mills   *Alex Mortimer*

1953   National. G. Bailey (arr. F. Wright), *Diadem of Gold*
1 Fodens Motor Works   *Harry Mortimer*
2 CWS (Manchester)   *Jack Atherton*
3 Creswell Colliery   *George Hespe*

1954   Open. Eric Ball, *Tournament for Brass*
1 Munn & Felton's (Footwear)   *Stanley Boddington*
2 Ferodo Works   *George Hespe*
3 John White Footwear   *George Thompson*
1954   National. Jack Beaver (arr. F. Wright), *Sovereign Heritage*
1 Fairey Aviation Works   *Harry Mortimer*
2 CWS (Manchester)   *Alex Mortimer*
3 Fodens Motor Works   *Harry Mortimer*

1955   Open. Eric Leidzén, *Sinfonietta for Brass Band*
1 Ferodo Works   *George Hespe*
2 John White Footwear   *George Thompson*
3 CWS (Manchester)   *Alex Mortimer*
1955   National. Edric Cundell (arr. F. Wright), *Blackfriars*
1 Munn & Felton's (Footwear)   *Harry Mortimer*
2 Ransome & Marles Works   *Eric Ball*
3 CWS (Manchester)   *Alex Mortimer*

1956   Open. Denis Wright, *Tam o' Shanter's Ride*
1 Fairey Aviation Works   *Harry Mortimer*
2 CWS (Manchester)   *Alex Mortimer*
3 Carlton Main Frickley Colliery   *Jack Atherton*
1956   National. Eric Ball, *Festival Music*
1 Fairey Aviation Works   *George Willcocks*
2 CWS (Manchester)   *Alex Mortimer*
3 Munn & Felton's (Footwear)   *Stanley Boddington*

1957   Open. Helen Perkin, *Carnival*
1 Black Dyke Mills   *George Willcocks*
2 Carlton Main Frickley Colliery   *Jack Atherton*
3 Fodens Motor Works   *Rex Mortimer*
1957   National. R. Vaughan Williams, *Variations for Brass Brand*
1 Munn & Felton's (Footwear)   *Stanley Boddington*
2 CWS (Manchester)   *Alex Mortimer*
3 Carlton Main Frickley Colliery   *Jack Atherton*

1958   Open. Eric Ball, *Sunset Rhapsody*
1 Carlton Main Frickley Colliery   *Jack Atherton*
2 Besses o' th' Barn   *William Wood*
3 Black Dyke Mills   *George Willcocks*
1958   National. Edmund Rubbra, *Variations on 'The Shining River'*
1 Fodens Motor Works   *Rex Mortimer*
2 Scottish CWS   *William Crozier*
3 CWS (Manchester)   *Alex Mortimer*

1959   Open. Eric Ball, *The Undaunted*
1 Besses o' th' Barn   *William Wood*
2 Carlton Main Frickley Colliery   *Jack Atherton*
3 Morris Motors   *Stanley Boddington*

1959 National. Lalo (arr. F. Wright), *Le Roi d'Ys*
1 Black Dyke Mills *George Willcocks*
2 Carlton Main Frickley Colliery *Jack Atherton*
3 Fodens Motor Works *Rex Mortimer*

1960 Open. Mozart (arr. Sargent), *Fantasia*
1 CWS (Manchester) *Alex Mortimer*
2 The Fairey Band[12] *Leonard Lamb*
3 Grimethorpe Colliery Institute *George Thompson*
1960 National. Herbert Howells, *Three Figures*
1 Munn & Felton's (Footwear) *Stanley Boddington*
2 Carlton Main Frickley Colliery *Jack Atherton*
3 Black Dyke Mills *George Willcocks*

1961 Open. Eric Ball, *Main Street*
1 The Fairey Band *Leonard Lamb*
2 Wingates Temperance *Hugh Parry*
3 Grimethorpe Colliery Institute *George Thompson*
1961 National. Berlioz (arr. F. Wright), *Les Francs Juges*
1 Black Dyke Mills *George Willcocks*
2 CWS (Manchester) *Alex Mortimer*
3 Crossley's Carpet Works *J. Harrison*

1962 Open. Helen Perkin, *Island Heritage*
1 The Fairey Band *Leonard Lamb*
2 Ransome & Marles Works *George Hespe*
3 Band of Yorkshire Imperial Metals *George Hespe*
1962 National. Verdi (arr. F. Wright), *The Force of Destiny*
1 CWS (Manchester) *Alex Mortimer*
2 Crossley's Carpet Works *J. Harrison*
3 Ransome & Marles Works *George Hespe*

1963 Open. Cyril Jenkins, *Life Divine*
1 The Fairey Band *Leonard Lamb*
2 Grimethorpe Colliery Institute *George Thompson*
3 Black Dyke Mills *Geoffrey Whitham*
1963 National. Arthur Bliss, *The Belmont Variations*
1 CWS (Manchester) *Alex Mortimer*
2 Brighouse & Rastrick *Walter Hargreaves*
3 GUS (Footwear)[13] *Stanley Boddington*

1964 Open. Thomas Keighley, *Lorenzo*
1 Fodens Motor Works *Rex Mortimer*
2 The Lindley Band[14] *Leonard Lamb*
3 BMC (Morris Motors)[15] *Clifford Edmunds*
1964 National. Gilbert Vinter, *Variations on a Ninth*
1 GUS (Footwear) *Stanley Boddington*
2 Black Dyke Mills *Cecil H. Jaeger*
3 CWS (Manchester) *Alex Mortimer*

1965 Open. Cyril Jenkins, *Saga of the North*
1 The Fairey Band *Leonard Lamb*
2 Brighouse & Rastrick *Walter Hargreaves*
3 BMC (Morris Motors) *Clifford Edmunds*

1965   National. Gilbert Vinter, *Triumphant Rhapsody*
1 The Fairey Band   *Leonard Lamb*
2 Cammell Laird's Works   *James Scott*
3 GUS (Footwear)   *Stanley Boddington*

1966   Open. John Ireland, *A Downland Suite*
1 CWS (Manchester)   *Alex Mortimer*
2 Band of Yorkshire Imperial Metals   *Trevor Walmsley*
3 BMC (Morris Motors)   *Clifford Edmunds*
1966   National. Berlioz (arr. F. Wright), *Le Carnaval Romain*
1 GUS (Footwear)   *Stanley Boddington*
2 Black Dyke Mills   *Cecil H. Jaeger*
3 The Fairey Band   *Leonard Lamb*

1967   Open. John Ireland, *A Comedy Overture*
1 Grimethorpe Colliery Institute   *Stanley Boddington*
2 The Fairey Band   *Leonard Lamb*
3 Wingates Temperance   *Hugh Parry*
1967   National. Eric Ball, *Journey into Freedom*
1 John Foster & Son Ltd Black Dyke Mills[16]   *Geoffrey Brand*
2 CWS (Manchester)   *Alex Mortimer*
3 Brighouse & Rastrick   *Walter Hargreaves*

1968   Open. Gilbert Vinter, *John O'Gaunt*
1 John Foster & Son Ltd Black Dyke Mills   *Geoffrey Brand*
2 Wingates Temperance   *Hugh Parry*
3 Grimethorpe Colliery Institute   *George Thompson*
1968   National. Wagner (arr. F. Wright), *The Mastersingers*
1 Brighouse & Rastrick   *Walter Hargreaves*
2 John Foster & Son Ltd Black Dyke Mills   *Geoffrey Brand*
3 GUS (Footwear)   *Stanley Boddington*

1969   Open. Gilbert Vinter, *Spectrum*
1 Grimethorpe Colliery Institute   *George Thompson*
2 Carlton Main Frickley Colliery   *Jack Atherton*
3 The Fairey Band   *Kenneth Dennison*
1969   National. Eric Ball, *High Peak*
1 Brighouse & Rastrick   *Walter Hargreaves*
2 John Foster & Son Ltd Black Dyke Mills   *Geoffrey Brand*
3 CWS (Manchester)   *Alex Mortimer*

1970   Open. Herbert Howells, *Pageantry*
1 Band of Yorkshire Imperial Metals   *Trevor Walmsley*
2 CWS (Manchester)   *Alex Mortimer*
3 Fodens Motor Works   *Rex Mortimer*
1970   National. Gordon Jacob, *Pride of Youth*
1 Grimethorpe Colliery Institute   *George Thompson*
2 Ransome Hoffman Pollard[17]   *Dennis Masters*
3 Hanwell   *Eric Bravington*

1971   Open. Eric Ball, *Festival Music*
1 Band of Yorkshire Imperial Metals   *Trevor Walmsley*
2 John Foster & Son Ltd Black Dyke Mills   *Geoffrey Brand*
3 Grimethorpe Colliery Institute   *George Thompson*

1971 National. Lalo (arr. F. Wright), *Le Roi d'Ys*
1 Wingates Temperance   *Dennis Smith*
2 City of Coventry   *Albert Chappell*
3 The Cory Band[18]   *Arthur Kenney*

1972 Open. Jack Beaver, *Sovereign Heritage*
1 John Foster & Son Ltd Black Dyke Mills   *Geoffrey Brand*
2 Carlton Main Frickley Colliery   *Robert Oughton*
3 The Cory Band   *Arthur Kenney*
1972 National. Eric Ball, *A Kensington Concerto*
1 John Foster & Son Ltd Black Dyke Mills   *Geoffrey Brand*
2 GUS (Footwear)   *Stanley Boddington*
3 Grimethorpe Colliery Institute   *Elgar Howarth*

1973 Open. César Franck (arr. Siebert), *The Accursed Huntsman*
1 John Foster & Son Ltd Black Dyke Mills   *Roy Newsome*
2 Grimethorpe Colliery Institute   *Elgar Howarth*
3 Brighouse & Rastrick   *James Scott*
1973 National. Hubert Bath, *Freedom*
1 Brighouse & Rastrick   *James Scott*
2 CWS (Manchester)   *Derek Garside*
3 John Foster & Son Ltd Black Dyke Mills   *Roy Newsome*

1974 Open. Gilbert Vinter, *James Cook – Circumnavigator*
1 John Foster & Son Ltd Black Dyke Mills   *Roy Newsome*
2 Stanshawe (Bristol)   *Walter Hargreaves*
3 GUS (Footwear)   *Stanley Boddington*
1974 National. Malcolm Arnold, *Fantasy for Brass Band*
1 The Cory Band   *Arthur Kenney*
2 Grimethorpe Colliery Institute   *Elgar Howarth*
3 John Foster & Son Ltd Black Dyke Mills   *Roy Newsome*

1975 Open. Elgar Howarth, *Fireworks*
1 Wingates Temperance   *Richard Evans*
2 The Fairey Band   *Kenneth Dennison*
3 Band of Yorkshire Imperial Metals   *Trevor Walmsley*
1975 National. Robert Farnon, *Un Vie de Matelot*
1 John Foster & Son Ltd Black Dyke Mills   *Peter Parkes*
2 Stanshawe (Bristol)   *Walter Hargreaves*
3 Brighouse & Rastrick   *James Scott*

1976 Open. Percy Fletcher, *An Epic Symphony*
1 John Foster & Son Ltd Black Dyke Mills   *Peter Parkes*
2 Stanshawe (Bristol)   *Walter Hargreaves*
3 Brighouse & Rastrick   *Maurice Handford*
1976 National. Eric Ball, *The Wayfarer*
1 John Foster & Son Ltd Black Dyke Mills   *Peter Parkes*
2 Band of Yorkshire Imperial Metals   *Trevor Walmsley*
3 Wingates Temperance   *Richard Evans*

1977 Open. G. Bailey (arr. F. Wright), *Diadem of Gold*
1 John Foster & Son Ltd Black Dyke Mills   *Peter Parkes*
2 Brighouse & Rastrick   *Derek Broadbent*
3 Fairey Engineering Works[19]   *Richard Evans*

1977 National. Edward Gregson, *Connotations for Brass Band*
1 John Foster & Son Ltd Black Dyke Mills *Peter Parkes*
2 Grimethorpe Colliery Institute *Gerard Schwarz*
3 Band of Yorkshire Imperial Metals *Dennis Carr*

1978 Open. Berlioz (arr. F. Wright), *Le Carnaval Romain*
1 Brighouse & Rastrick *Geoffrey Brand*
2 John Foster & Son Ltd Black Dyke Mills *Peter Parkes*
3 Ransome Hoffman Pollard *Stephen Shimwell*
1978 National. Bliss (arr. Ball), *Four Dances from Checkmate*
1 Band of Yorkshire Imperial Metals *Dennis Carr*
2 Besses o' th' Barn *Roy Newsome*
3 Grimethorpe Colliery Institute *Stanley Boddington*

1979 Open. Berlioz (arr. F. Wright), *Le Carnaval Romain*
1 Fairey Engineering Works *Walter Hargreaves*
2 Desford Colliery *Howard Snell*
3 Grimethorpe Colliery *Elgar Howarth*
1979 National. Robert Simpson, *Volcano*
1 John Foster & Son Ltd Black Dyke Mills *Peter Parkes*
2 The Cory Band *Denzil Stephens*
3 Birmingham School of Music *Roy Curran*

1980 Open. Robert Simpson, *Energy*
1 Band of Yorkshire Imperial Metals *John Price-Jones*
2 GUS (Footwear) *Keith Wilkinson*
3 Desford Colliery *Howard Snell*
1980 National. Dvořák (arr. Brand), *Carnival*
1 Brighouse & Rastrick *Derek Broadbent*
2 John Foster & Son Ltd Black Dyke Mills *Peter Parkes*
3 Fairey Engineering Works *Walter Hargreaves*

1981 Open. Gilbert Vinter, *Variations on a Ninth*
1 City of Coventry *Arthur Kenney*
2 Leyland Vehicles *Richard Evans*
3 Fodens Motor Works *Howard Snell*
1981 National. Elgar (arr. Ball), *Froissart*
1 John Foster & Son Ltd Black Dyke Mills *Peter Parkes*
2 Brighouse & Rastrick *Derek Broadbent*
3 Whitburn Miners' Welfare *Geoffrey Whitham*

1982 Open. Herbert Howells, *Three Figures*
1 Besses o' th' Barn *Roy Newsome*
2 Fairey Engineering Works *Geoffrey Brand*
3 GUS (Footwear) *Keith Wilkinson*
1982 National. John McCabe, *Images*
1 The Cory Band *Arthur Kenney*
2 John Foster & Son Ltd Black Dyke Mills *Peter Parkes*
3 Brodsworth Colliery *David James*

1983 Open. Edward Gregson, *Connotations*
1 John Foster & Son plc Black Dyke Mills[20] *Peter Parkes*
2 Brighouse & Rastrick *James Watson*
3 Grimethorpe Colliery Institute *James Scott*

1983 National. Joseph Horovitz, *Ballet for Band*
1 The Cory Band *Arthur Kenney*
2 John Foster & Son plc Black Dyke Mills *Peter Parkes*
3 GUS (Footwear) *Keith Wilkinson*

1984 Open. John Ireland, *A Comedy Overture*
1 Grimethorpe Colliery Institute *Geoffrey Brand*
2 John Foster & Son plc Black Dyke Mills *Peter Parkes*
3 Fairey Engineering Works *Howard Williams*
1984 National. Edward Gregson, *Dances and Arias*
1 The Cory Band *Arthur Kenney*
2 Sun Life[21] *Christopher Adey*
3 Leyland Vehicles *Richard Evans*

1985 Open. Gilbert Vinter, *Salute to Youth*
1 John Foster & Son plc Black Dyke Mills *Peter Parkes*
2 British Aerospace Wingates[22] *James Scott*
3 Foden OTS[23] *Howard Snell*
1985 National. Stephen Bulla, *Cityscapes*
1 John Foster & Son plc Black Dyke Mills *Peter Parkes*
2 Desford Colliery Dowty[24] *Howard Snell*
3 IMI Yorkshire Imperial[25] *James Scott*

1986 Open. Percy Fletcher, *An Epic Symphony*
1 John Foster & Son plc Black Dyke Mills *Peter Parkes*
2 Fairey Engineering Works *Roy Newsome*
3 GUS (Kettering)[26] *Bramwell Tovey*
1986 National. Derek Bourgeois, *Diversions*
1 Fairey Engineering Works *Roy Newsome*
2 John Foster & Son plc Black Dyke Mills *Peter Parkes*
3 Sun Life *Rob Wiffin*

1987 Open. Hubert Bath, *Freedom*
1 Williams Fairey Engineering[27] *Roy Newsome*
2 Britannia Building Society Foden[28] *Howard Snell*
3 Grimethorpe Colliery Institute *David James*
1987 National. Philip Sparke, *Harmony Music*
1 Desford Colliery Dowty *James Watson*
2 John Foster & Son plc Black Dyke Mills *Peter Parkes*
3 IMI Yorkshire Imperial *James Scott*

1988 Open. Wilfred Heaton, *Contest Music*
1 Rigid Containers Group *Bramwell Tovey*
2 Jaguar Cars (City of Coventry)[29] *Ray Farr*
3 Williams Fairey Engineering *Roy Newsome*
1988 National. Ray Steadman-Allen, *Seascapes*
1 Desford Colliery Dowty *James Watson*
2 Britannia Building Society Foden *Howard Snell*
3 Jaguar Cars (City of Coventry) *Ray Farr*

1989 Open. Derek Bourgeois, *Diversions*
1 Kennedy's Swinton Concert Brass *Gary Cutt*
2 Hammonds Sauce Works *Geoffrey Whitham*
3 Leyland DAF[30] *Richard Evans*

1989   National. Arthur Butterworth, *Odin*
1 Desford Colliery Caterpillar[31]   *James Watson*
2 John Foster & Son plc Black Dyke Mills   *David King*
3 Murray International Whitburn[32]   *James Scott*

Notes and references

1 Change of name from Dewsbury Old.
2 Sometimes appears as Black Dike Mills.
3 Possibly F. Galloway.
4 Following objections to the conductor (?James Melling), players Cooper, Hilton and Robinson directed the band in the contest.
5 Change of name from Matlock Bath.
6 Change of name from 4th Lancs Volunteer Reserve.
7 The conductor may have been Alexander Owen (see also 1900 and 1901).
8 It has not been possible to discover the name of the arranger. Since all the test pieces were published by R. Smith & Co. it could well have been F. C. Shipley-Douglas (see 1903) or William Short who was to arrange the test piece for 1906 and 1907.
9 Sometimes appears as Cresswell Colliery.
10 Sometimes appears as Park & Dare.
11 Change of name from Munn & Felton's Works.
12 Change of name from Fairey Aviation Works.
13 Change of name from Munn & Felton's (Footwear).
14 Change of name from Lindley.
15 Change of name from Morris Motors.
16 Change of name from Black Dyke Mills.
17 Change of name from Ransome & Marles Works.
18 Change of name from Cory Workmen's Silver.
19 Change of name from the Fairey Band.
20 Change of name from John Foster & Son Ltd Black Dyke Mills.
21 Change of name from Stanshawe (Bristol).
22 Change of name from Wingates Temperance.
23 Change of name from Foden's Motor Works.
24 Change of name from Desford Colliery.
25 Change of name from Band of Yorkshire Imperial Metals.
26 Change of name from GUS (Footwear).
27 Change of name from Fairey Engineering Works.
28 Change of name from Foden OTS.
29 Change of name from City of Coventry.
30 Change of name from Leyland Vehicles.
31 Change of name from Desford Colliery Dowty.
32 Change of name from Whitburn Miners Welfare.

Index

St George's Works Brass Band,
Lancaster, 32, 34
St Hilda Colliery Band, 71, 74, 79, 84, 91,
93, 94, 113
St Vincent Boys' Band (Melbourne), 151
Salt, Titus, 24, 42
Saltaire Band, 24
Salvation Army, 47–9, 131, 141, 145, 147,
150, 185, 191
Salvation Army Brass Band Journal, The, 48
Salvation War, 47
Samson, George, 178
Savoy Havana Band, 83
Sax, Adolphe, 8, 16, 18, 20, 41, 113, 175,
178, 179
Scarborough Spa Band, 44
Scoll, A., 21
Scoll's Operatic Band, 21
Scott, J. L., 20, 169
Scottish Amateur Brass Band
Championship, 109
S.E.R. Company, 136
Shaw, George Bernard, 131
Shaw, John, 178
Sheffield Independent, 21
Shields Daily Gazette, 91
Shugg, Harry, 151
Silvani and Smith, 31
Simpson, Robert, 114
Singleton Town Band (New South
Wales), 156
Slater, Richard, 48
Sloan, Major, 29
Smith, Richard, 37, 39, 42, 44, 113, 131
Smith, Richard, & Co. Ltd, 67, 73, 109
Smyth, James, 39, 45
Snell, Howard, 112
Sommer, F., 105, 180
South Street contest (Ballarat), 146, 150,
152, 155
South Yorkshire Railway Company's
Brass Band, 183
Southern, Jimmy, 71, 93
Southowram Band, 72, 85
Souza, John Philip, 5
Spark, Dr William, 117
Spearritt, P., 147
Spohr, 15
Stalybridge Old Band, 21, 42, 104
Stand Band, 34
Stanley Band, 65
Sterling Musical Instruments Ltd, 192
Stölzel, Heinrich, 173, 177, 179

Stourton Memorial Band, 78
Straughan, W. R., 93
Strutt, George and Joseph, 24
Sullivan, Sir Arthur, 109
Sussex Agricultural Express, 132
Sutherland, Captain Thomas, 150
Swanwick, Keith, 135
Swift, Edwin, 8, 44, 114, 115, 131, 135
Swift, George, 84
Sydenham Amateur Band Contest, 107
Sydney Boot Trade Unions, 158
Sydney Professional Musician's Band,
151
Sydney Professional Musician's Union,
159, 160

Taylor, Arthur, 4, 10, 12, 68, 111, 115
Taylor, William, 105
Teddy Joyce's Girl Friends, 65
Temperley, Nicholas, 12
Tester, Scan, 139
Thomason, Raymond, 83
Thompson, Colonel, J. A., 28
Ton Pentre Temperance Band, 47
Tooth's Brewery Band, 148, 152, 154,
155, 156
Tournaire's Circus, 16
Trades Hall Band, 158
Trimnell, Thomas Tallis, 21, 105
'Trombone Billy', 139
Tully's *Tutor for Keyed Bugle*, 18
Tutton, J. R., 45

Valentine, Thomas, 35
Vassies, George, & Co., 110
Vaughan Morris, Edwin, 110
Vaughan Williams, Ralph, 114, 192
Verdi, Guiseppe, 39
Victoria, Queen, 15, 34
Victorian Boot Trade Band, 158
Vinter, Gilbert, 2, 192
Volunteer Corps, 11
Volunteer Service Gazette, 27, 29

Waddell, James, 183
Wadsworth, George, 42
Walker, D., 147
Walker, James, 104
Wallsend Band, 157
Walmsley, Trevor, 74
Walton, William, 167
War Cry, 47
Ward, Cliff, 84